The Evolution of Public Finance and Budgeting:
A Quarter Century of Developments

Edited by

John L. Mikesell

and

Daniel R. Mullins

T0329914

CONTENTS

About the Authors

Roy Bahl is Professor of Economics and Public Administration and Dean of the Andrew Young School of Policy Studies at Georgia State University. He is the author of numerous books and papers on public finance issues, and has served as an advisor to many governments in the US and around the world.

Jean E. Harris is Associate Professor of Accounting at Capital College, the Pennsylvania State University. She holds a Ph.D. in accounting from Virginia Tech and certifications as a CPA and a CGFM. Dr. Harris has published articles about the use by public entities of accounting innovations such as the reporting of tax expenditure, SEA, and infrastructure assets. Currently, she is visiting at INCAE in Costa Rica to investigate the role of external influences on the regulatory structure of accounting, auditing, and corporate governance in several Latin American countries. This work is supported by a sabbatical leave and a Fulbright award.

Philip Joyce is Professor of Public Policy and Public Administration at George Washington University. He has written extensively on budgeting, with his research primarily focusing on the federal budget and the use of performance information in the budget process. Phil has 12 years of public sector work experience, including five years each with the U.S. Congressional Budget Office and the Illinois Bureau of the Budget. He earned a Ph.D. from the Maxwell School at Syracuse University, an M.P.A. from Penn State, and a B.A. from Thiel College. Professor Joyce was recently elected a Fellow of the National Academy of Public Administration.

W. Bartley Hildreth is the Regents Distinguished Professor of Public Finance in the Hugo Wall School of Urban and Public Affairs, a Professor at the W. Frank Barton School of Business, and Director of the Kansas Public Finance Center at Wichita State University. Since 1989, Dr. Hildreth has served as the Editor-in-Chief of the *Municipal Finance Journal*, which is the only academic journal dedicated to the study of the municipal bond market. During Fall 2005, Professor Hildreth held the Fulbright Visiting Research Chair in Public Policy at McGill University in Montreal for his work on comparative infrastructure financing.

Roy T. Meyers is Professor of Political Science at the University of Maryland, Baltimore County; his Ph.D. is in political science from the University of Michigan. He is also Director of the Sondheim Public Affairs Scholars Program, a merit scholarship program for undergraduates who are interested in public service careers. From 1981–1990, Meyers was an analyst at the Congressional Budget Office. Among his publications are *The Handbook of Government Budgeting* (Jossey-Bass, 1999) and *Strategic Budgeting* (University of Michigan Press, 1994), which co-won the Louis Brownlow Book Award from the National Academy of Public Administration in 1996. His current research, consulting, and lecturing activities are on reform of U.S. national budgeting, Maryland budgetary policy and process, performance budgeting, comparative legislative budgeting, and financial management of public sector higher education.

John L. Mikesell is Professor of public and environmental affairs and director of the Master of Public Affairs program at Indiana University. He serves as editor-in-chief of *Public Budgeting & Finance* and has written widely on property and sales taxation and tax administration. He holds a B.A. from Wabash College and an M.A. and Ph.D. in economics from the University of Illinois. He is a member of Phi Beta Kappa and received the 2002 Wildavsky Award for Lifetime Scholarly Achievement in Public Budgeting and Finance from the Association for Budgeting and Financial Management.

Daniel R. Mullins is Associate Professor in the Department of Public Administration and Policy at American University. He has published widely on budgeting and intergovernmental fiscal systems/reform, tax and expenditure limitations, fiscal implications of demographic change, economic development, and metropolitan economic and spatial structure. He has served in advisory capacities at all levels of government domestically and internationally with numerous governments through the World Bank, US-AID, IMF and training organizations. Dr. Mullins' Ph.D. is from the Maxwell School of Citizenship and Public Affairs at Syracuse University. He also has experience in executive-level local government administration and is Managing Editor of *Public Budgeting and Finance*.

Michael A. Pagano is Professor and director of the Graduate Program in Public Administration at the University of Illinois at Chicago, co-editor of *Urban Affairs Review*, and Faculty Fellow of UIC's Great Cities Institute. He has published numerous articles and books on urban finance, capital budgeting, federalism, transportation policy, infrastructure, urban development, and fiscal policy; his latest coauthored book with Ann O'M. Bowman, *Terra Incognita: Vacant Land and Urban Strategies*, was released in 2004 by Georgetown University Press. He has written the annual City Fiscal Conditions report for the National League of Cities since 1991; he writes a regular column for *State Tax Notes*, called "The Third Rail," which examines contemporary local government fiscal issues; and he is the principal investigator for the Pew-supported Government Performance Project responsible for Infrastructure Management.

Irene Rubin is Professor Emerita at Northern Illinois University. Her Ph.D. is from the University of Chicago in sociology. Recent books include, *Balancing the Federal Budget: Eating the Seed Corn or Trimming the Herds?* and *Class, Tax, and Power: Municipal Budgeting in the United States*. The fifth edition of *The Politics of Public Budgeting: Getting, Spending, Borrowing and Balancing*, is forthcoming from CQ Press. Irene was the editor of *Public Budgeting & Finance* from 1994 to 1996, and the Editor of *Public Administration Review* from 1996 to 1999.

Sally Wallace is Associate Professor of Economics and Associate Director of the Fiscal Research program in the Andrew Young School of Policy Studies, Georgia State University. Prior to joining GSU, she was a financial economist at the U.S. Treasury Department, Office of Tax Analysis. Her research interest are in the field of public finance, specifically state, federal, and international taxation and fiscal federalism. She has served on the tax study commissions for the states of Georgia, Ohio, and Nebraska and in Jamaica, Guatemala, Russia, Philippines, Uzbekistan, Ukraine, Kazkhstan, and China. From 1997 to 1999 she served as the Chief of Party in Moscow of GSU's Russia Tax Project, and from 2003 to 2005 she served as the co-director of the Jamaica Comprehensive Tax Reform Project.

C. Kurt Zorn is a Professor in the School of Public and Environmental Affairs at Indiana University, Bloomington and currently serves as Associate Dean for Academic and Fiscal Affairs for SPEA. His research interests focus on state and local public finance, transportation safety, economic development, and gaming. Kurt served as chairperson of Indiana's Citizens' Commission on Taxes and as Chairman of the Indiana State Board of Tax Commissioners in the 1990s. Prior to that he served as Director of State Relations for Indiana University. Kurt received his B.A. in Economics from the State University of New York at Albany in 1976 and his Ph.D. in Economics from Syracuse University in 1981.

Preface

The essays in this volume trace the development of public budgeting and finance over the past quarter of a century. It has been an eventful twenty-five years. Four Presidents, the fall of the Soviet Union, the longest peacetime economic expansion in our history, three recessions, federal deficits as far as the eye can see, federal surpluses as far as the eye can see, a successful attack on the American homeland, a preemptive war, a thriving Internet for communication and commerce, and the list goes on – with each shock adding to the complexities of public budgeting and finance. If nothing else, we should have learned the hazards of predictions and the danger of presuming permanence to political and economic institutions and practices. As the political, economic, social, and technological environment has changed, so too have the concerns of government finances.

The essays in this volume cover the main components of government finance: federal, state, and local budgeting, revenue policy, municipal debt markets, governmental accounting and reporting. Because one of the great changes of the era was the transition to market-oriented democracies of many governments previously under undemocratic, centrally-planned systems, one essay also explores the special circumstances of changing public finance in transition and developing countries. All essays are by important scholars in their field of specialization but they are also individuals who have had an editorial link to *Public Budgeting & Finance*, either as editors, managing editors, associate editors, or members of the editorial board. The essays that follow explore what has happened in these areas over the past twenty-five years.

We intend these essays to capture the developments of the past quarter century amid the political, social, and economic conditions of the period. We hope that students and scholars will find them to be a helpful reflection on how the disciplines have changed over those years and what issues of the future might be. Just as the environment has been eventful, so has the practice of public budgeting and finance.

John L. Mikesell
Indiana University

Daniel R. Mullins
American University

Chapter 1

Alligators in the Swamp: Developments in Local Budgeting and Finance*

DANIEL R. MULLINS and MICHAEL A. PAGANO

This chapter traces developments in budgeting and finance at the local government level over the past 25 years. In doing so, it uses the 290 related articles published in *Public Budgeting & Finance* over this period as its foundation and as a sieve for topic selection. Specific attention is directed to intergovernmental finance, financial management, budgeting and budget reform, alternative service delivery, and capital budgeting. The intent is to sift through important developments in each area, highlight their significance at the time and their importance to the present and future.

INTRODUCTION

Since publication of the inaugural issue of *Public Budgeting & Finance* (PB&F), sweeping changes have occurred at the level of government most responsible for direct public service needs of citizens, namely, the 87,525 units of local government.[1] These changes have largely been a response to and driven by national and local political, demographic, and economic events and conditions, and represent a simultaneous continuation of past trends as well as the emergence of new directions. Change has affected the fiscal, legal, intergovernmental, managerial, and political dimensions of local government and governance. Throughout this period, PB&F has published approximately 290 articles

Daniel R. Mullins is Associate Professor in the Department of Public Administration and Policy, School of Public Affairs, The American University, Washington, DC 20016-8130. He can be reached at *Dmull ins@American.edu*.

Michael A. Pagano is Fellow of the Great Cities Institute and Professor and Director of the Graduate Program in Public Administration, University of Illinois at Chicago, Chicago, IL 60607. He can be reached at *mapagano@uic.edu*.

*This chapter was originally published in *Public Budgeting & Finance*, Vol. 25, Silver Anniversary Edition (2005): 3–45 as Daniel R. Mullins and Michael A. Pagano, "Local Budgeting and Finance: 25 years of Developments."

1. U.S. Bureau of the Census, 2002 Census of Governments: Vol. 1, no. 1, Government Organization *http://www.census.gov/prod/2003pubs/gc021x1.pdf* (accessed 28 August 2005).

directly focused on or related to some dimension of local government budgeting and finance. Among these are at least 45 articles on some aspect of intergovernmental finance, including specific service areas and general dependency; 31 articles on accounting, auditing and financial reporting; 30 related to debt, credit, and leases; 27 related to capital projects, infrastructure, and capital budgets; 19 on local budgetary reform; 18 pertaining to tax and expenditure limitations (TELs); 18 related to financial indicators, financial analysis, and fiscal stress; 17 dealing with general taxation and revenue instruments and forecasting; 13 on alternative service delivery, contracting, and privatization; 12 on general financial management; 11 related to international developments; 10 on contingency reserves and investment pools; 10 pertaining to economic development; and 7 on citizen demand, willingness to pay, and participation.

Using the lens of those articles published in PB&F, we focus on five areas: intergovernmental finance (including TELs), general financial management, general budgeting and budget reform (including performance), alternative service delivery, and capital budgeting. We chose these areas because of both their prominence (and recurrence) in PB&F and the field, and because of our assessment of their salience to local government finance and budgeting over the past quarter century and the foreseeable future. While accounting and debt are prominent in our inventory of articles, separate titles in this special issue deal specifically with developments in these areas and we have, therefore, left detailed treatment to those authors.

We have attempted to sift through the important developments in each area, highlight their significance at the time and their importance to the present and future. The breadth of each topic area is quite expansive and each could form the basis of a stand-alone article. We have, however, attempted to use PB&F as our sieve and focus our analysis of each topic area around coverage provided by the literature appearing in PB&F. As such, our treatment may omit materials considered important and useful in understanding financial management and budgeting at the level of local government. Nevertheless, as the leading journal in the field of public finance and budgeting, we felt it appropriate to review these quarter-century developments from the perspective of manuscripts appearing within its pages. We believe that these pages provide a sufficient depth and breadth of perspective and hope that it is adequately conveyed in this article.

A TRANSFORMING INTERGOVERNMENTAL QUIT: "CRAZY" OR SCHIZOPHRENIC

Intergovernmental relationships, particularly fiscal, have been a recurrent issue over the past 25 years. PB&F was inaugurated in an era of fiscal constraint at all levels of government and intergovernmental dynamics took on added importance.[2] The late 1970s

_____

2. The importance of the fiscal environment was epitomized by the popularity in public administration circles of the title by Charles Levine, *Managing Fiscal Stress: The Crisis in the Public Sector* (Chatham, NJ: Chatham House, 1980).

began a decline and restructuring of federal intergovernmental transfers, ushering in a reshaping (and retrenching) of intergovernmental relationships, which has evolved and continued to the present. Retrenchment occurred, as did a resorting of local, state, and national roles. Reagan's 1981 "New Federalism" initiative, though major elements were not enacted, set the course. Déjà vu accompanied it as either the "newest version of an old and outmoded design or as an exciting means of restoring the venerable outlines of an ancient but heavily overlaid federal structure."[3] It was neither. Similarities to Nixon's version was more in name than substance, as the administration sought to sever direct links between places of need and Washington and trade full federal assumption of Medicaid for subnational responsibility for Aid to Families with Dependent Children (AFDC) and food stamps. At the time, the proposed public assistance trade was seen as inconsistent with tenets of federalism and ultimately failed; however, the federal welfare reforms of the latter 1990s continued down this path.[4]

Table 1 provides a snapshot of the importance of intergovernmental revenue to the local sector in 1980 compared with 2002. The numbers belie what appears to be only a slight aggregate decline in federal transfers to the state and local sector relative to sectoral direct general expenditures or own source general revenue. Rather, there was a 54 percent reduction in federal support as a portion of local direct general expenditures and over a 65 percent reduction to municipalities and counties. The trough in the federal fiscal role occurred during the late 1980s; however, the reemerged fiscal relationship into the 1990s through present was vastly altered.

In 1980, approximately 65 percent of federal intergovernmental transfers were directed to support general services and projects of state and local governments; by 2004, 65 percent supported direct payments for services to individuals and nearly 47 percent went for health care alone (Table 2).[5] Over the period, the portion of aid directed to health nearly tripled, while the portion directed to general government declined by 77 percent, natural resources and environment by 75 percent, agriculture by 71 percent, community development by 56 percent, education training and social services by 44 percent, and transportation by 28 percent. Income security saw a slight increase (5 percent) and justice increased by 160 percent. While between 1980 and 2002 the actual real-dollar magnitude of federal transfers to the state and local sector grew by 95 percent, population grew by 27 percent and state/local direct expenditures grew by 119 percent, with own source revenue growing by 128 percent. Real increases in heath-care transfers

---

3. George F. Break, "Changes in Intergovernmental Fiscal Patterns," *Public Budgeting & Finance* 2, no. 4 (1982): 42–57.

4. The 1997 elimination and replacement of AFDC with block grant funding for Temporary Assistance for Needy Families (TANF) works to increasingly shift redistributive spending to the subnational level, without an offsetting federal assumption of Medicaid.

5. See *Analytic Perspectives, Budget of the United States Government, Fiscal Year 2006* (Washington, DC: U.S. Government Printing Office, 2006), Table 8-3. or *Historical Tables, Budget of the United States Government, Fiscal Year 2006* (Washington, DC: U.S. Government Printing Office, 2006), Tables 12.1–12.3.

TABLE 1

Intergovernmental Revenue (IGR) as Percent of Local Direct General Expenditures and Own-Source General Revenue, Total, from Federal and from State, 1980 and 2002 ($ 000,000)

Type of Local Government	Direct General Expenditures	Own-Source General Revenue[1]	Total Inter-governmental Revenue	IGR Directly from Federal	IGR from State	Intergovernmental Revenue as Percentage of Direct General Expenditures			Intergovernmental Revenue as Percentage of Own-Source General Revenue		
						Total	Federal Direct	State Direct	Total	Federal Direct	State
1980											
State/local sector	367,339	269,596	85,462	85,462		23.3	23.3	NA	31.7	31.7	NA
All local[2]	223,621	129,980	102,425	21,136	81,289	45.8	9.5	36.4	78.8	16.3	62.5
Municipalities	70,426	47,753	28,270	10,872	15,939	40.1	15.4	22.6	59.2	22.8	33.4
Counties	51,383	29,814	24,746	4,948	18,968	48.2	9.6	36.9	83.0	16.6	63.6
School districts	80,681	35,834	45,976	1,198	43,679	57.0	1.5	54.1	128.3	3.3	121.9
2002											
State/local sector	1,730,809	1,324,241	360,534	360,534	NA	20.8	20.8	NA	27.2	27.2	NA
All local[2]	986,371	597,359	398,497	42,953	355,544	40.4	4.4	36.0	66.7	7.2	59.5
Municipalities	279,753	200,431	85,114	15,201	62,405	30.4	5.4	22.3	42.5	7.6	31.1
Counties	243,290	158,036	98,648	7,539	86,759	40.5	3.1	35.7	62.4	4.8	54.9
School districts	360,474	151,249	199,544	3,632	191,145	55.4	1.0	53.0	131.9	2.4	126.4

[1]Figures for 1980 estimated based on intergovernmental revenue as a percent of own-source general published in Table 39, ACIR, *Significant Features of Fiscal Federalism, 1980–81 Edition* (Washington, DC: U.S. Government Printing Office, 1981); figures for 2002 are from U.S. Census Bureau, *Local Government Finances*, Table 2 Local Government Finances by Type of Government and State: 2001–2002, and Table 1 State and Local Government Finances by Level of Government and by State: 2001–2002, electronically accessed http://www.census.gov/govs/estimate/0200ussl_2.html.
[2]Includes townships and special districts.

TABLE 2

Functional Distribution of Federal Aid to State and Local Governments as a Percent of Total Federal Aid 1980, 1990, and 2004

Function	Percent of Total 1980	Percent of Total 1990	Percent of Total 2004
Natural resources and environment	5.9	2.7	1.5
Agriculture	0.7	1.0	0.2
Transportation	14.2	14.2	10.2
Community and regional development	7.1	3.7	3.1
Education, training, employment, and social services	23.9	16.1	13.3
Health	17.3	32.4	46.7
Income security	20.2	27.2	21.2
Administration of justice	0.5	0.4	1.3
General government	9.4	1.7	2.2
Other	0.8	0.6	0.3
Total	100.0	100.0	100.0

Sources: Budget of the United States Government, Fiscal Year 2006, Analytic Perspectives (Washington, DC: U.S. Government Printing Office, 2005), Table 8-3, p. 131; and *Budget of the United States Government, Historical Tables* (Washington, DC: U.S. Government Printing Office, 2005), Table 12.2, p. 227.

(primarily to individuals) of 366 percent accounted for 83 percent of total real federal increases to the sector.[6] The only other functions to see real increases were income security (doubling in real terms) and transportation, increasing by 46 percent.[7] The federal role in financing general services has declined dramatically.

Direct federal transfers to local jurisdictions actually declined in real terms by 6 percent (see Table 3). Transfers to all local jurisdiction from states increased by 103 percent, more than doubling for counties and school districts and increasing by 82 percent for municipalities.[8] As a proportion of local jurisdiction revenue and expenditures, total transfers (of the national and state governments) and transfers from states to local jurisdictions have declined across all categories of local governments, except for state transfers as a ratio to school district own source revenue (Table 1).

In chronicling these changes over the course of the past quarter century, PB&F has provided exposure to a variety of intergovernmental fiscal issues.

---

6. Through federal fiscal year 2000, health accounted for 95 percent of the total real increase since 1980.

7. Education, training, employment, and social services nearly held constant through to 2002 and saw a very slight real gain by 2004 (not considering changes in the student population).

8. However, in response to the 2001 recession, states reduced aid to cities by 2.1 percent in FY 2003 and 9.2 percent for FY 2004. See Christopher Hoene and Michael Pagano, "States Decrease Their Aid to Cities," *The American City and County* 118, no. 11 (2003): 6–8.

Centralization/decentralization/dependency? With a backdrop of *fiscal stress,* PB&F's second issue included "fiscal dependency" as a feature topic. To Astrid Merget (1981) the periods "irrational" and "convoluted" federalism better reflected a Jackson Pollock painting than the traditional "marble cake" or "picket fence." The fiscal autonomy of U.S. cities was supplanted by a "precarious" level of dependency:[9] a consequence of increased federal and state aid. Lauded for the potential to reduce disparities, previous aid-induced increases in public services were feared would push "some cities over the brink into bankruptcy,"[10] as state and national governments withdrew fiscal support.

Contrary to expectations about economic development and decentralization, the 1957–1986 trend was toward revenue centralization within the states (and expenditure centralization in the North/East), as states accounted for an increasing portion of total state/local revenue.[11] Table 1 shows this trend has continued. During the 1980s, the federal/state/local shares of spending across functions appeared relatively stable, though in slight decline as national centralizing trends subsided.[12] Growing subnational government reliance on transfers was an international phenomena;[13] however, the degree of *true* "centralization" depends on the transfer systems design.[14]

Equalization is an objective of many transfer systems. Cross-national comparison revealed an international tendency to target funds to lower-income regions to reduce fiscal disparities. The exception was the United States "where the nature of the grant system fails to discriminate ... in favor of low income areas."[15] Variations in intergovernmental transfers in the United States were driven by "variations in government structure" and service responsibilities. "[V]irtually, all jurisdictions were receiving similar shares of local

---

9. Astrid E. Merget, "The Fiscal Dependency of American Cities," *Public Budgeting & Finance* 1, no. 2 (1981): 20–30.

10. While fears of bankruptcy were possibly overstated, recent evidence demonstrates that changes in federal grant forms and levels do affect the level and composition of state debt issued. The effect differs for guaranteed versus nonguaranteed debt. Grants stimulate the issuance of full-faith and credit debt. Reductions in grants stimulate the use of nonguaranteed debt. See Christine R. Martell and Bridget M. Smith, "Grant Levels and Debt Issuance: Is There a Relationship? Is There Symmetry?", *Public Budgeting & Finance* 24, no. 3 (2004): 65–81.

11. Jeffrey M. Stonecash, "Fiscal Centralization in the American States: Findings from Another Perspective," *Public Budgeting & Finance* 8, no. 4 (1988): 81–89.

12. Lawrence W. Hush, "The Federal, and the State and Local Roles in Government Expenditures," *Public Budgeting & Finance* 13, no. 2 (1993): 38–55.

13. Roy Bahl, "The Design of Intergovernmental Transfers in Industrialized Countries," *Public Budgeting & Finance* 6, no. 4 (1986): 3–18.

14. See Ibid., and George M. Palumbo, "The Report on Federal-State-Local Fiscal Relations: A Review," *Public Budgeting & Finance* 7, no. 3 (1987): 26–34.

15. Harold Wolman and Edward Page, "The Impact of Intergovernmental Grants on Subnational Resource Disparities: A Cross-National Comparison," *Public Budgeting & Finance* 7, no. 3 (1987): 82–98, 95.

TABLE 3
Intergovernmental Revenue (IGR) to Local Governments in Constant Dollars, Total, from Federal and from State, 1980 and 2002 (Base Year 2002, $ Millions)[1]

Type of Local Government	Total Intergovernmental Revenue		IGR Directly from Federal		IGR from State	
	1980	2002	1980	2002	1980	2002
State and local sector	NA	NA	184,206	360,534	NA	NA
All local[2]	220,769	398,497	45,557	42,953	175,212	355,544
Municipalities	60,934	85,114	23,434	15,201	34,355	62,405
Counties	53,338	98,648	10,665	7,539	40,884	86,759
School districts	99,097	199,544	2,582	3,632	94,146	191,145

[1]Implicit price deflator for state and local government purchases of goods and services. Bureau of Economic Analysis, 2000 base year values of 48.862 (1980) and 105.318 (2002) converted to 2002 base (48.862/105.318).

resources from intergovernmental transfer regardless of their size, location, demographic performance, or relative incidence of distress."[16]

By international standards, subnational jurisdictions in the United States show lower levels of fiscal dependency and higher spending shares,[17] within transfer structures that are less centralizing,[18] resulting in relatively high levels of decentralization. Lower levels of dependency and more effective subnational accountability purports enhanced efficiency; however, issues of intergovernmental coordination (and equity) remain.

National/Local Issues

Issues of fair share Expansion of the direct national–local fiscal linkage of the 1960s and 1970s made federal aid distribution a contentious issue. An article in the introductory volume of PB&F concluded that nonmetropolitan communities were "shortchanged."[19] The boom in direct federal aid focused on urban problems, contained eligibility provisions favoring larger jurisdictions (or excluding smaller jurisdictions), was not adapted to rural environments and required sophisticated grant-seeking capacity. The proliferation of categorical aid was seen as nonresponsive to nonmetropolitan applications and beyond local administrative capacity to secure. Suggested remedies included more flexible and adaptable block grants, altered distribution formulas and alternative program

16. Richard L. Florida, "The Distribution of Transfers to Various Types of Cities," *Public Budgeting & Finance* 6, no. 3 (1986): 81–91.

17. Luiz R. De Mello Jr., "Intergovernmental Fiscal Relations: Coordination Failures and Fiscal Outcomes," *Public Budgeting & Finance* 19, no. 1 (1999): 3–25.

18. Bahl, 3–18.

19. Mark W. Huddelston and Marian Lief Palley, "Shortchanging Nonmetropolitan America: Small Communities and Federal Aid," *Public Budgeting & Finance* 1, no. 3 (1981): 36–45.

options for nonmetropolitan areas. Existing aid was also seen to distort decision making and democratic processes in small communities and to confer sometimes devastating and unforeseen operating costs via capital projects.

Some later attention was given to determining optimal allocations of federal aid between cities. Descriptive assessments of allocation distributions and the political process for them were seen to be inadequate. PB&F included a proposed allocation mechanism based on maximizing the relative marginal rate of return for the expenditure of federal funds across places or one based on multiattribute utility theory, depending on the number of dimensions to and measurability of the federal objective.[20] While more flexibility did emerge via grant consolidation, to a great degree these issues subsided with the general retrenchment in direct federal aid to general purpose governments. Elimination of general revenue sharing and adoption of a greater role for state pass through in managing federal aid programs meant targeting of remaining federal aid became more responsive to individual state priorities.

Federal retrenchment In 1981, Congress enacted "the largest cuts in peacetime federal domestic spending"; reducing domestic spending outlays by 7.8 percent and budget authority by 11.6 percent. Among those hardest hit were welfare programs funded through grants to states and localities (seeing a 25.4 percent decline in budget authority and a 7.4 percent decline in outlays), and direct grants to state and local governments (with outlay/authority declines of 31.6 and 16.6 percent).[21] The 1981 Reagan reductions reflected a sweeping continuation of aid reduction begun under Carter. Carter's reductions focused on the "elimination of counter cyclical spending programs and General Revenue Sharing payments to state governments"; Reagan's reductions were much broader.[22]

While the rather monumental changes of 1981 were cushioned over time, the two Reagan presidential terms (1981–1988) saw federal aid to state and local governments decline by nearly 20 percent compared with pre-1981 baseline policy.[23] Much of the initial effect occurred through a consolidation of 57 categorical grant programs into nine block grants in 1981 and two additional block grants in 1982.[24] Funding was typically reduced by 20–25 percent, but retrenchment was not equally distributed across functions. Highway spending

20. Stuart S. Nagel, "Optimally Allocating Federal Money to Cities," *Public Budgeting & Finance* 5, no. 4 (1985): 39–50.

21. John W. Ellwood, "Congress Cuts the Budget: The Omnibus Reconciliation Act of 1981," *Public Budgeting & Finance* 2, no. 1 (1982): 50–64.

22. These reductions included eliminating General Revenue Sharing transfers to local jurisdiction September 30, 1986. Enacted in 1972, the general revenue sharing program provided $84.2 billion in transfers to state and local governments over its 15-year life. It provided $5.1 billion in revenue to local governments during the last year of disbursements. One study of the effect of its elimination on Ohio communities shows the absence of a resulting fiscal crisis. This was the case even though these funds were frequently programmed for operating purposes and was because of the prior notice provided to local jurisdictions, cuts in spending, revenue enhancement, and increased borrowing. See Paul R. Dommel and Keith P. Rasey, "Coping with the Loss of General Revenue Sharing in Ohio," *Public Budgeting & Finance* 9, no. 3 (1989): 43–51.

23. Andrew F. Haughwout and Charles J. Richardson, "Federal Grants to State and Local Governments in the 1980s," *Public Budgeting & Finance* 7, no. 4 (1987): 12–23.

24. These block grants were established in health care, community service, community development, social services, energy assistance, mass transit, and job training.

followed a roller-coaster track to an actual increase of 50 percent; grants for wastewater treatment, mass transit, community development, employment training, and subsidized housing saw declines of between 25 and 60 percent, and elementary and secondary education funding saw a nearly offsetting reversal of initial cuts by the end of the period.[25] Stability was in short supply.

Mandates as a substitute By 1989 focus shifted to federal attempts to impose policy prescriptions through mandates rather than financial enticements. Greater state/local flexibility via block grants was far more than countered by the elimination of general revenue sharing and an increase in crosscutting requirements, crosscutting sanctions, direct orders, and partial preemption. This led to calls for reimbursement of state and local governments for costs imposed by federal law or regulation and legislation attempting to, at minimum, assure that the costs of *new* mandates were considered in congressional proceedings. Several states had enacted legislation requiring that localities be reimbursed for mandates imposed by their state government; a similar set of safeguard was being sought nationally.

Spirited debate ensued about the propriety of enacting national policy by compelling state and local expenditures. Some saw this as a basic shift in the tenor of federalism, driven by relative fiscal sacristy and deficit crisis at the national level and more robust state/local revenue and institutional systems. The intergovernmental dynamic was "competitive federalism" in a "fend-for-yourself" environment.[26] Focus shifted to the questioned legitimacy of federal mandates and the implicit failure in accountability associated with divorcing policy determination from fiscal responsibility, along with the desirability and feasibility of various mechanisms of reimbursement.[27] Procedural rules limiting (or prohibiting) unfunded mandates, requirements for cost reimbursement and general compensating grants were suggested to alleviate the burden of federal policy on state and local governments. Distinctions were made between legitimate mandates dealing with constitutional and individual rights (legitimately unfunded), and those dealing with domestic policy or a legislative enhancement of individual rights.

The debate culminated with Public Law 104–4 Unfunded Mandates Reform Act of 1995. It required estimates of the qualitative (and if possible quantitative) impact of legislation imposing mandates on the state/local sector and that *consideration* be given to compensating subnational jurisdictions for corresponding costs. Failure to do so can result in a point-of-order vote in either the House or Senate. Enacted in response to questions of the propriety of unfunded mandates, this legislation has done relatively little to require funding. Significant exceptions to its provisions exist, such as mandates to enforce the constitutional rights of individuals, prohibit discrimination, require financial accounting compliance, provide emergency assistance, promote national security, or based on a presidential/congressional emergency designation. Even when these conditions do not apply,

25. The greatest magnitude of reductions occurred in education, training and employment, followed by general-purpose fiscal assistance, income security, community and regional development, and natural resources and the environment. See also Richard P. Nathan and John R. Lago, "Intergovernmental Relations in the Reagan Era," *Public Budgeting & Finance* 8, no. 3 (1988): 15–29.

26. John Shannon and James Edwin Kee, "The Rise of Competitive Federalism," *Public Budgeting & Finance* 9, no. 4 (1989): 5–20.

27. See Ray D. Whitman and Roger H. Bezdek, "Federal Reimbursement for Mandates on State and Local Governments," *Public Budgeting & Finance* 9, no. 1 (1989): 47–62.

reimbursement remains unrequired. It should be noted that states, school districts, and the National Education Association (NEA) are presently suing for full funding of the Bush administration's No Child Left Behind program requirements;[28] prospects for success are limited.

State/Local Issues and Local Fiscal Constraints

Limiting fiscal autonomy Reduction in federal funding resulted in a call for a state response to aid local jurisdictions. However, local fiscal difficulties were actually magnified in the 1980s by institutional limitations on local jurisdictions' ability to raise revenue from traditional sources.[29] In response to the "tax limitation movement," typified by California's 1978 adoption of Proposition 13 and Massachusetts proposition 2 1/2 in 1980, 46 states have adopted some form of statewide limitation on the ability of local jurisdictions to generate revenue or make expenditures. Seventeen states did so between 1970 and 1976; approximately half were adopted after 1977.[30] Not a fleeting occurrence of the 1970s and 1980s, the 1990s saw the enactment of the most severe restrictions since Proposition 13, with new provisions being voted on to the present. These are broad-brush constraints, imposed by constituencies or governments at the state level on local fiscal options, and acerbated local fiscal conditions. This is particularly the case in central cities where lagging income growth, suburbanization, and poverty concentration have magnified fiscal difficulties. States stepped up during the later 1980s to target-needed aid, but state-level fiscal difficulties and the general increased role of states in domestic affairs (in response to federal retrenchment) mitigated their ability and/or desire to do so.[31]

Limitations also mitigated the ability of the local sector to adjust to federal aid retrenchment and were argued to have promoted a neglect of capital needs by introducing a bias against capital expenditures, particularly "pay-as-you-go" financing. Debt service exemptions promoted debt finance.[32] Nationwide analyses of these limitations have shown a significant effect on local fiscal structure. There has been an erosion of reliance on property and other broad-based tax sources, increased use of fees and charges, and increased state aid. The relative state/local role has also shifted, with greater reliance on state revenues and increased state authority for sectoral expenditures (except for welfare and particularly for education). This has adversely affected local autonomy and has promoted a more

28. See "Connecticut to Sue over NCLB," *UPI*, April 6, 2005; Savana Tikotsy, "No Child Left Behind Act Challenged by States," *Daily Forty-Niner*, May 11, 2005; Korey Clark, "States Rebel against No Child Left Behind," *State Net Capitol Journal*, June 13, 2005; "School District Challenges Funding for No Child Left Behind Act,"*Municipal Litigation Reporter*, May 15, 2005; and "3 States, NEA Lead Charge against NCLB," *Your School and the Law*, May 4, 2005.

29. John Yinger, "States to the Rescue? Aid to Central Cities under the New Federalism," *Public Budgeting & Finance* 10, no. 2 (1990): 27–44.

30. Daniel R. Mullins and Bruce A. Wallin, "Tax and Expenditure Limitations: Introduction and Overview," *Public Budgeting & Finance* 24, no. 4 (2004): 2–15.

31. Yinger, 27–44, and Richard P. Nathan and John R. Lago, "Intergovernmental Relations in the Reagan Era," *Public Budgeting & Finance* 8, no. 3 (1988): 15–29.

32. Henry J. Raimondo, "State Limitations on Local Taxing and Spending: Theory and Practice," *Public Budgeting & Finance* 3, no. 3 (1983): 33–42.

state-centered sector.[33] Some of the most severe restrictions on local governments have occurred in the west, producing heightened concerns of fiscal centralization and diminished local autonomy.[34] Autonomy has been most constrained in the fiscally weakest jurisdictions. The ability of jurisdictions serving the most disadvantaged populations has been reduced, promoting increased disparities in services delivered by both general-purpose governments and school districts.[35]

Devolving fiscal stress State policies have affected local revenue options, levels of fiscal assistance, service delivery responsibilities, and have conveyed mandates.[36] States often force added retrenchment and fiscal stress at the local level when faced with their own fiscal difficulties. In 1990, Oregon enacted new property tax limitations and New Jersey tightened existing limitations. Local fiscal assistance was reduced in absolute terms in Massachusetts and increases were cut in California, Connecticut, Maine, New York, North Carolina, and Virginia. Recessions induced fiscal distress in 1991 and soaring Medicaid spending led to numerous additional shifts resulting in "fend-for-yourself federalism."[37] Illinois eliminated $156 million in aid to cities and counties, Maine cut aid by $18 million, Maryland by more than $180 million, Massachusetts by 10 percent (or $238 million), and New York by over $600 million. Aid was reduced in, at minimum, 15 states.[38] The situation for cities and counties was often the reverse of that of school districts, where school aid rose on an average of 8.9 percent for FY 1992.[39,40]

---

33. Daniel R. Mullins and Philip G. Joyce, "Tax and Expenditure Limitations and State and Local Fiscal Structure: An Empirical Assessment," *Public Budgeting & Finance* 16, no. 1 (1996): 75–101.

34. See Alvin D. Sokolow, "The Changing Property Tax in the West: State Centralization of Local Finances," *Public Budgeting & Finance* 20, no. 2 (2000): 85–104.

35. Daniel R. Mullins, "Tax and Expenditure Limitations and the Fiscal Response of Local Government: Asymmetric Intra-Local Fiscal Effects," *Public Budgeting & Finance* 24, no. 4 (2004): 111–147.

36. Steven D. Gold and Sarah Ritchie, "State Policies Affecting Cities and Counties: Important Developments in 1990," *Public Budgeting & Finance* 11, no. 2 (1991): 33–46.

37. California realigned spending responsibilities by shifting mental and indigent health and social services to counties in exchange for a share of state sales tax revenue and vehicle license fees. To balance the state budget, Arizona required a contribution from counties for health. New Hampshire assigned responsibility to counties for Medicaid audits. See Steven D. Gold and Sarah Ritchie, "State Policies Affecting Cities and Counties in 1991: Shifting Federalism," *Public Budgeting & Finance* 12, no. 1 (1992): 23–46.

38. Michigan froze tax assessments for one year and Minnesota froze tax increases. New Jersey tightened limitations and Illinois limited property tax increases to 5 percent or inflation in urban Chicago counties. See Gold and Ritchie, 23–46.

39. State actions were also taken to improve local fiscal conditions. In 1990, Wisconsin increased local assistance. Responsibility for several social assistance programs previously financed by counties was assumed by the state in New Jersey. Arizona and South Carolina added revenue diversification by providing counties the authority to levy sales taxes. California relaxed local expenditure limitations. In 1991, Idaho assumed indigent health-care responsibility from counties. Local revenue enhancements were enacted in 16 states; however, most were quite minor. Local property tax limitations were liberalized in five states and tightened in four others. Idaho removed a 5 percent limit and replaced it with a "truth in taxation" provision. Minnesota established a local government trust, funded by 2 cents of the sales tax. Pennsylvania increased aid to programs for children and mass transit.

40. Mandates also appeared. Montana mandated local juvenile detention facilities, and Oregon, solid waste recycling and improvements in local pensions. South Dakota mandated improved treatment for the

Similar patterns of aid reductions, some revenue enhancements and shifts in expenditure responsibilities continued with the fiscal stress of 1992, along with more provisions attempting to limit state imposition of unfunded mandates.[41] The result was described as "a period of de facto federalism" with the system "evolving through an accumulation of many small decisions that result in increased decentralization."[42] While not documented in PB&F, similar measures shifted burdens to local jurisdictions during the aftermath of the 2001 recession. Aid reductions to school districts and local governments totaled billions of dollars. FY 2004 proposals in California, Massachusetts, New York, Minnesota, and Texas alone included $5 billion in reductions to school districts and nearly $4 billion in reductions to general-purpose local governments. Reductions continued for 2005, including California's proposed school funding reduction of $2 billion, $180 million reduction in Georgia, and New York's $500 million shortfall. FY 2005 reductions to general-purpose governments included a $1.3 billion shift of property taxes from cities, counties, and special districts to school districts in California to offset the need for state aid to school districts, and reductions of $40 million in Connecticut and $185 million in Michigan.[43] A study by the National League of Cities showed a national aggregate 9.2 percent reduction in state aid to cities for FY 2004. Combined 2003–2004 reductions reached 100 percent in Kansas, 59.7 percent in California, 47.4 percent in Texas, and 39.1 percent in West Virginia.[44]

Developments by Function

Capital grants—roads to anywhere? Capital project grants were significant in the 1970s buildup of national assistance to local governments. By 1980, this aid provided 36 percent of total state and local capital spending.[45] New York financed 44 percent of its capital spending with federal aid and Cincinnati 39 percent. Federal capital assistance was seen as instrumental in preventing more rapid infrastructure deterioration in older urban areas. The largest capital programs were highway construction, wastewater treatment, and community development. During the 1980s, conditions changed. After decades of growth,

---

(footnote Continued)
mentally ill. Tennessee adopted new requirements for solid waste and the certification of building and fire inspectors. In 1990, Florida adopted a constitutional provision allowing unfunded state mandates to be ignored by local governments.

41. Steven D. Gold and Sarah Ritchie, "State Policies Affecting Cities and Counties in 1992," *Public Budgeting & Finance* 13, no. 1 (1993): 3–18.

42. Steven D. Gold and Sarah Ritchie, "State Actions Affecting Cities and Counties, 1991–1993: De Facto Federalism," *Public Budgeting & Finance* 14, no. 2 (1994): 26–53.

43. See Andrew Reschovsky, "The Implications of State Fiscal Stress for Local Governments," presented at State Fiscal Crises: Causes, Consequences & Solutions, April 3, 2003, The Urban Institute; and Elizabeth McNichol and Makeda Harris, "Many States Cut Budgets as Fiscal Squeeze Continues," Washington, DC: Center for Budget and Policy Priorities; April 26, 2004.

44. Hoene and Pagano, 6–8.

45. Raymond A. Rosenfeld, "Federal Grants and Local Capital Improvements: The Impact of Reagan Budgets," *Public Budgeting & Finance* 9, no. 1 (1989): 74–84.

capital grants declined in both constant and current dollar terms.[46] Federal retrenchment has been linked to major degradation in urban infrastructure during the 1980s and a reshaping of the federal infrastructure role. The emphasis of federal programs shifted from redevelopment to development, resulting in significant relative losses of funding for the nation's older urban areas and relative gains for newer (more recently urbanized) areas. Older areas experienced greater difficulties maintaining infrastructure spending without these federal funds. In 1980, highway construction funds accounted for 36 percent of capital grants, and by 1986 it was 67 percent; redevelopment funding saw a precipitous decline.[47] Transportation-related capital funding surged in 1991, with the adoption of the Intermodal Surface Transportation Efficiency Act (ISTEA), providing $155 billion in funding over six years. Reauthorization in 1998 as The Transportation Equity Act for the 21st Century (TEA 21) provided an additional six years at $217.78 billion, and the Safe, Accountable, Flexible, Efficient Transportation Equity Act, signed August 10, 2005, provides a historic $286 billion over five years. Development-related capital projects are again in vogue as a conveyor of "political capital."

Housing—the new model The National Affordable Housing Act of 1990 was the most comprehensive housing legislation since 1974. It established fiscal parameters for the HOME investment partnership (for new construction, rehabilitation, unit acquisition, and tenant-based rental assistance), HOPE grants (to convert public housing to private ownership), along with shelter, elderly, and self-sufficiency programs. It established a new intergovernmental relationship and reflected national government attempts to promote state/local consistency with national policies in a period of fiscally limited national government. Matching became a "fundamental part of housing programs"[48] via a complex mix of rates differing between and within subelements of different federal objectives. To limit substitution, program requirements attempted to constrain the ability of local jurisdictions to match federal funds in housing programs with other federally provided resources and sought to channel program resources to redistributive rather than development expenditures. In addition to stimulating local spending, the variable matching requirements were intended to (i) impose federal standards, (ii) increase efficiency and control costs, (iii) require state/local assumption of political responsibility, and (iv) promote resource coordination for social programs. This shift in housing policy in a period of "competitive federalism" reflected a national attempt to channel both federal and state/local resources

---

46. The current dollar decline between 1981 and 1982 was 16.2 percent; however, a rebound occurred with expansion of highway funding. Between 1980 and 1986 funding (in constant 1980 dollars) declined from $22.18 billion to $15.95 billion, suggesting a 28 percent real decline. These figures, however, assume that 70 percent of general revenue sharing (GRS) funds were devoted to capital improvements and, thus, the elimination of GRS for 1986 significantly affects these totals. GRS funds were unrestricted in their usage and assignment as capital project grants is problematic. Without this assumption, 1980 grant-funded capital spending was $18.99 billion, resulting in a 16 percent real decline and an 11.8 percent nominal increase.

47. The level of the increase reported in this research may be, again, overstated, because of the assumption that 70 percent of 1980 GRS funds were devoted to capital improvements.

48. Jill Khadduri, "New Matching Requirements for Housing Programs: Intergovernmental Conflict and the National Affordable Housing Act of 1990," *Public Budgeting & Finance* 12, no. 4 (1992): 3–18.

toward national priorities, by increasing implicit federal control over the use of local (and previously more flexible federal) resources.

Welfare reform—federalism redefined The comprehensiveness of housing reform was far exceeded by Welfare Reform in 1996 and took quite a different trajectory. The Personal Responsibility and Work Opportunity Reconciliation Act substituted 60 years of entitlement-based, categorical federal matching assistance (via AFDC) with block grant funding for TANF. While the most direct fiscal effects exist for state governments, it conveyed locally significant potential shifts in responsibility for meeting the needs of dependent populations. A shift to work requirements and in-kind (work supporting) service-based assistance suggests a heightened local administrative role in program implementation, and enforcement of time limits for receipt of public assistance suggests a need for local (and private) services to fill what might become growing gaps in program eligibility. "By eliminating the federal entitlement to welfare and leaving states largely on their own to provide assistance to poor children and their families as they see fit, the act brought about the most thoroughgoing reconfiguration of the national—state relationship in sixty years."[49] Such change is not possible without significant ramifications for local governments.

Block grant funding was set at nominally fixed dollar amounts based on 1994 case loads. Between January 1993 and December 2002, program reform and economic growth induced a case load reduction of 59 percent. This allowed a surplus of unspent TANF funds to accumulate equal to 11 percent of the total program funding by the first half of FY 2001 and the onset of the 2001 recession.[50] By FY 2003, closing the gap in state budgets required a combined $50 billion in revenue enhancements or expenditure reductions; lagging economic performance still resulted in a $25 billion aggregate state-level deficit by year-end. Projections for 2004 anticipated a gap of 85 billion or more, with deficits in 25 individual states to exceed 10 percent of spending. Lagging resources, unemployment and growing population needs severely taxed state budgets. TANF balances were down to approximately 1.4 percent through FY 2004.[51] TANF block grant funding means that states bear 100 percent of the additional costs of administering the program during a recession.[52] Incentives exist for states to limit the recipient base by creating tighter barriers to public assistance eligibility and cushioning the state fiscal impact through past unspent TANF

49. Robert C. Lieberman and Greg M. Shaw, "Looking Inward, Looking Outward: The Politics of State Welfare Innovation under Devolution," *Political Research Quarterly* 53, no. 2 (2000): 215–240.

50. Howard Chernick and Andrew Reschovsky, "State Fiscal Responses to Welfare Reform during Recessions: Lessons for the Future," *Public Budgeting & Finance* 23, no. 3 (2003): 3–21.

51. U.S. Department of Health and Human Services, Administration for Child and Families, *FY2004 TANF Financial Data*, Table G—Combined Federal Awards, Transfers and Expenditures for All FY Years through FY 2004. *http://www.acf.hhs.gov/programs/ofs/data/2004/tableG_2004.html*

52. There is a TANF contingency fund which provides "needy states" matching funds in periods of "unfavorable economic conditions." These funds require that a state spend an amount equivalent to 100 percent of the amount spent on AFDC-related program in 1994 and provide a federal match for amounts beyond this based on the federal medical assistance percentage matching rate. See U.S. Government, *Catalogue of Federal Domestic Assistance 93.558 Temporary Assistance for Needy Families,* 1995. However no state received contingency funds during the October 2001–August 2003 period. Center on Budget and Policy Priorities, "The Senate Finance Committees Reauthorization Bill," Revised May 12, 2004, *http://www.cbpp.org/9-9-03tanf.htm*

funds. However, this cushion erodes annually with price and administrative cost increases. In any event, barriers to state assistance programs and an inability to maintain state funding to meet the needs of low-income populations implicitly shifts the burden to local governments and the nonprofit community.

The implications of this reform for local government are still emerging and vary by state. Some see devolved welfare policy as responsive to competitive theories of federalism, which suggest that, even in the absence of national control, states will follow national policies because of pressures of conformity, particularly pronounced in redistributive policies. If this is the case, emerging state policies are not likely to address local conditions or meet local needs and demands in the manner that the decentralizing model of federalism might predict.[53] This leaves the task open for local governments. With a reduced federal commitment and state responsive to the competitive environment, local capacity to fill assistance gaps is likely to be critical. Nongovernmental community service organizations are quite variable in their ability to fill these gaps across communities, putting significant pressures on local government housing, health care, and general social support structures. Community nonprofit agencies are not a replacement for the role of local government and, in fact, tend to work in tandem. Communities with local government(s) committed to meeting the needs of the poor also tend toward a more comprehensive nongovernmental social safety net.[54] "Second-order devolution" is occurring as components of public assistance responsibilities are shifted to local governments.

Education—put up or shut up! At 34 percent of direct general expenditures, education is the single most important function of the state and local public sector. It has also witnessed substantial intergovernmental shifts, leaving education finance as one of the most transformed areas of state/local finance since 1970.[55] This transformation is characterized by a shift in responsibility from local jurisdictions to states, and has recently seen the encroachment of the national government, albeit without a corresponding increase in federal fiscal responsibility.[56] Table 4 shows a declining relative local fiscal role in education and an increasing state role since 1970; state regulatory intervention is even more pronounced. Relative federal support over this period remained unchanged, even with the enactment of No Child Left Behind (NCLB).[57]

The shift in education finance emanated largely from concerns for equity in educational opportunity across school districts. It has most often been either compelled by the courts or

53. Lieberman and Shaw, 215–240.

54. Katherine V. Byers and Maureen A. Pirog, "Local Governments Fiscal Response to Welfare Reform," *Public Budgeting & Finance* 23, no. 4 (2003): 86–107.

55. Steven D. Gold, "State Aid for Local Schools: Trends and Prospects," *Public Budgeting & Finance* 4, no. 4 (1984): 30–67.

56. The origins of this most recent national foray into education (as a whipping boy) can be traced to the Reagan administration and the release of the report *A Nation at Risk: The Imperative for Education Reform*, National Commission of Excellence in Education, April 1983.

57. In fact, figures from the National Conference of State Legislatures indicate only modest relative increases in the total federal education fiscal role since passage of the No Child Left Behind Act in 2001 and only a 0.4 percent increase between 2003 and 2004 and a .1 percent increase between 2004 and 2005. See National Conference of State Legislatures, *Task Force on No Child Left Behind: Final Report* (Washington, DC: NCSL, February 2005), Table 4.

TABLE 4

Public Elementary and Secondary Education Revenue Shares : Local, State, and National Selected Years, 2003 Dollars in Billions

Year	Local $	Local %	State $	State %	Federal $	Federal %
2003	187.96	42.7	215.55	49.0	36.81	8.4
1992	147.53	46.2	151.12	47.3	20.51	6.4
1980	96.83	43.5	104.12	46.7	21.88	9.8
1970	103.85	53.1	75.63	38.6	16.21	8.3

Sources: Bureau of the Census, Governmental Finance Series: Public Elementary and Secondary Education Finance Data 2002–2003 (Washington, DC: U.S. Government Printing Office, 2005); Bureau of the Census, Governmental Finance Series: Public Elementary and Secondary Education Finance Data 1991–1992 (Washington, DC: U.S. Government Printing Office, 2005); Bureau of the Census, Statistical Abstract of the United States: 1995, education section (Washington, DC: U.S. Government Printing Office, 1995); Bureau of Economic Analysis, "Table 3.15.4 Price Indexes for Government Consumption and Gross Investment by Function," http://www.bea.doc.gov/bea/dn/nipaweb/.

has occurred in an attempt to ward off court intervention. In some cases, equity in finance has been sought to placate efforts toward equity in outcomes. From 1970 to 1995, education finance systems were court challenged in at least 43 states[58] and reforms were instituted in many. Education equity in a traditional sense (1970s and 1980s) had been defined relative to disparities in fiscal resources available to students across districts. More recently, it has evolved to a pursuit of adequacy, implying a minimum threshold of student funding and/or threshold levels of student achievement. "[A]dequacy-based legal challenges are more likely to focus on whether educational resources are sufficient to provide students the opportunity to meet state standards or more general educational goals."[59] Estimates based on 1997 funding levels suggest that between $15.6 billion and $18.5 billion (precisely targeted) would be needed to bring funding to a level of "adequacy" across all school districts in the United States. States with the greatest per pupil deficiencies include California, Louisiana, Mississippi, Arizona, and Utah.[60] Increasingly, equity is defined relative to outcomes rather than opportunity, as for NCLB.

Prominent fiscal reforms have included those enacted in Michigan and Vermont. Michigan's 1994 education finance reform placed a strict limit on local property taxes, combined with a two percentage point increase in the state general retail sales tax and increased tobacco taxes devoted to education. To promote "equity" (defined as reducing the variation in per student education spending), lower-spending districts were leveled up to a per student spending floor and strict caps were erected to limit spending in higher-spending

---

58. Steven M. Sheffrin, "The Future of the Property Tax: A Political Economy Perspective," in *The Future of State Taxation*, ed. David Brunori (Washington, DC: The Urban Institute, 1998), chapter 8, 131.

59. Ross Rubenstein, "Providing Adequate Educational Funding: A State-by-State Analysis of Expenditure Needs," *Public Budgeting & Finance* 22, no. 4 (2002): 73–98.

60. See Rubenstein, 73–98.

jurisdictions, even if they were willing to pay for it through local taxes.[61] The result was "radical" regarding the "drastically increased role" of the state government in funding and determining Michigan public school education. It transformed Michigan's K–12 education system "from one dominated by individual districts to one … dominated by state government."[62] Michigan's previous guaranteed tax base (power equalization) system of education finance was restructured as a foundation guarantee. The likely results are less-than-desired spending in previously higher-spending districts, greater-than-desired spending in lower-spending districts, a questionable ability of the state to maintain funding levels and public support, and likely lower overall education spending.

Vermont's 1997 Act 60 education reform was motivated by a State Supreme Court ruling. It combined a flat per pupil grant, funded by a uniform state property tax levy, with a guaranteed tax base system. Property taxes generated from a local jurisdiction above a specified threshold are partially credited to a state pool for distribution across school systems. Some jurisdictions' contribution is as much 70 cents per dollar. Local jurisdictions are free to raise taxes to fund education, but reap only part of the benefit of the revenue generated.[63]

In both cases, the state government was attempting to limit *its* outlays to reach *its* education objectives. Michigan did so by limiting the range of variation it would presumably need to offset via sales taxes. Vermont did so by pooling what had previously been local resources for state purposes. In each case, local populations responded creatively to attempts to constrict local choice. In Michigan, off-budget foundations were established by residents in many of the state's high education service districts to allow continued spending above the caps.[64] In Vermont, community pressure was brought to bear on resident and particularly business taxpayers to make voluntary contributions to fund education in lieu of a tax increase.[65] Taxpayers were given the choice of appearing noncommunity oriented and risking higher "official" tax increases (because of high proportionate diversions to the state pool) or paying the informal assessment.[66] In both cases, a rather complicated structure (with relatively high coordinating and transaction costs) was established to circumvent restriction on the use of local resources.[67]

61. Matthew J. Knittel and Mark P. Haas, "Michigan's Proposal A: A Retrospective," *State Tax Notes,* October 26, 1998, 1061–1083.

62. Robert W. Wassmer and Ronald C. Fisher, "An Evaluation of the Recent Move to Centralize the Finance of Public Schools in Michigan," *Public Budgeting & Finance* 16, no. 3 (1996): 90–112.

63. See Daniel G. Swaine and Lynn E. Browne, "Can Guaranteed Tax Base Formulas Achieve Either Wealth Neutrality or Spending Equality Part 2?", *New England Fiscal Facts*, Spring/Summer (1999) (21). David Brunoir, "Did Tax Base Sharing Fall Prey to the Suburban Sharks?", *State Tax Notes,* February 8, 1999, 401–402.

64. Mark Hornbeck, "Schools Build Private Reserves," *The Detroit News*, December 24, 2001.

65. See Associated Press, "School Fund Nears Goal," Dorset, VT, April 27, 2001; and Associated Press, "Manchester Raises Enough Money to Avoid Act 60 Sharing Pool for Two Years," Manchester, VT, May 5, 1999.

66. In protest of the new education finance system, numerous communities across the state withheld their payments to the "shark pool." Some also withheld their payment of the state property tax levy.

67. An attempt to implement school finance "reform" in New Jersey between 1990 and 1996 also illustrates its responsiveness to state political and economic pressures. In 1990, the State Supreme Court

FINANCIAL MANAGEMENT PRACTICE

Like beauty, the meaning of "financial management" is in the eye of the beholder. Studies that might be subsumed under the rubric of public financial management often assume the aura of good-government accounting, or improving decision processes, or measuring financial condition, or managing (cash) resources. To make government's operations and decisions more transparent (and legal) and to accurately assess the financial condition of local governments were certainly key motivators for studying and evaluating financial management practices in the early years of PB&F. Indeed, public financial management has evolved to encompass these, and other, dimensions of what might have been lumped together at one time under public budgeting practices.

Revenue Adequacy and Fiscal Instability

The lead article in the first issue of PB&F, published in the spring of 1981, centered on the financial management problems of revenue adequacy and fiscal instability. Naomi Caiden noted that traditional revenue sources and approaches to budget balancing needed to be revisited during the economic recession that ravished the nation in the late 1970s and early 1980s with both hyperinflation and growing unemployment.[68] The theme was picked up in the next volume by Caiden and coauthor Jeffrey Chapman, this time with a focus on California in an article in which they traced the disappearance of the state's fiscal surplus after the Proposition 13 drawdown and examined the impact of the economic recession on California's fiscal position.[69] In the same issue, the fiscal crises of key states were also examined, including Massachusetts,[70] Michigan,[71] and

---

(footnote Continued)

ruled (in *Abbott v. Burke*) per pupil education expenditures too low in 28 urban school districts and ordered legislative revision to state education funding to assure spending in those districts be brought to a level consistent with wealthy suburban districts. Governor Jim Florio attempted to used income and sales tax increases to reduce variations by reducing aid to wealthy and increasing funds to poorer jurisdictions. Political opposition to aid reductions and tax in cases generated intense legislative efforts to minimize redistribution and roll back increases to a degree that a heightened state education finance role was not sustainable. Opposition to local property taxes led to a reprogramming of resources away from education aid and toward general municipal aid. Efforts to level down higher-spending jurisdictions were "stymied" and efforts to level up lower-spending jurisdictions were "circumscribed" by political opposition. See Robert A. Peters, "School Finance Reform's Impact on New Jersey's State Spending Priorities," *Public Budgeting & Finance* 16, no. 3 (1996): 74–89.

68. Naomi Caiden, "Public Budgeting amidst Uncertainty and Instability," *Public Budgeting and Finance* 11, no. 1 (1981): 6–19.

69. Naomi Caiden and Jeffrey I. Chapman, "Constraint and Uncertainty: Budgeting in California," *Public Budgeting & Finance* 2, no. 4 (1982): 111–129.

70. Jerome Rothenberg and Paul Smoke, "Early Impacts of Proposition 2 1/2 on Massachusetts State-Local Public Sector," *Public Budgeting & Finance* 2, no. 4 (1982): 90–110.

71. Harvey E. Brazer, "Anatomy of Fiscal Crisis: The Michigan Case," *Public Budgeting & Finance* 2, no. 4 (1982): 130–142.

Texas.[72] Moreover, Roy Bahl provided a synthesis of the state and local government sector, exploring the large and growing variation in revenue structures.[73]

If the 1970s was the decade of the taxpayer revolt, the subsequent decade witnessed the federal government's retreat from providing aid to local governments. Local governments became increasingly more independent of federal aid.[74] A 1988 article examined the fiscal surplus position of the state and local sector, concluding that "Rather than relying on the federal government to finance its growing expenditures, it [the state and local government sector] has become increasingly self-reliant,"[75] a commentary that summed up the decade-long decline in federal aid. By 1989, large cities were scrambling to enhance budgeting processes and procedures, especially in light of the demise of federal funding in the form of GRS.[76] As local governments abandoned the prospects of a federal bailout, studies and reports intensified on enhancing financial management. Just how, then, could we tell a well-managed local government from a not-so-well-managed government?

Assessing Relative Fiscal Performance

Revenue/expenditure imbalance was identified as the principal variable in measuring fiscal performance.[77] Important questions were also raised about the need for "performance measures" in a study of why local governments could not answer a simple question of what federal cutbacks would mean to them.[78] And an assessment of the information needs of investors in municipal bonds found that "environmental and demographical information along with financial information" were important.[79]

One of the more daunting tasks in a federal republic is to compare governments' fiscal positions. On the one hand, each general-purpose local government is unique in its spending authority, revenue-raising capacity, taxing authority, political will to adjust

72. Glen Hahn Cope and W. Norton Grubb, "Restraint in a Land of Plenty: Revenue and Expenditure Limitations in Texas," *Public Budgeting & Finance* 2, no. 4 (1982): 143–156.

73. Roy Bahl, "The Fiscal Health of State and Local Governments: 1982 and Beyond," *Public Budgeting & Finance* 2, no. 4 (1982): 5–21. Bahl's article is derived from his outstanding book on state and local fiscal issues in the 1980s. See Roy Bahl, *Financing State and Local Finances in the 1980s* (New York: Oxford University Press, 1984).

74. For an analysis of increasing reliance on federal aid in the 1970s, see Astrid Merget, 20–30.

75. John T. Carnevale, "Recent Trends in the Finances of the State and Local Sector," *Public Budgeting & Finance* 8, no. 2 (1988): 47. See also Bruce Wallin, *From Revenue Sharing to Deficit Sharing* (Washington, DC: Georgetown University Press, 1997); Dommel and Rasey, 43–51.

76. Stanley Botner, "Trends and Developments in Budgeting and Financial Management in Large Cities of the United States," *Public Budgeting & Finance* 9, no. 3 (1989): 37–42. For a discussion of the political climate surrounding GRS, see Bruce Wallin.

77. Earl R. Wilson, "Fiscal Performance and Municipal Bond Borrowing Costs," *Public Budgeting & Finance* 3, no. 4 (1983): 28–41.

78. Susan A. MacManus, "Coping with Retrenchment: Why Local Governments Need to Restructure Their Budget Document Formats," *Public Budgeting & Finance* 4, no. 3 (1984): 58–66.

79. Thomas P. Howard and Douglas A. Johnson, "Municipal Financial Reports for the 1980s," *Public Budgeting & Finance* 1, no. 4 (1981): 80–84.

revenue and expenditure patterns, and political culture. Yet, on the other hand, local governments compete with one another in the efficient and effective provision of public services at a competitive tax price.[80] Local governments, then, not only pride themselves in their "uniqueness," they simultaneously compare their operations with others. As contradictory as these two assessments appear, one of the more active areas in research in financial management is along the dimension of comparative spending and taxing.

Revenue capacity The representative tax system (RTS) was created by the Advisory Commission on Intergovernmental Relations (ACIR) as a mechanism for measuring the revenue-generating capacity of disparate governments with differential revenue-generating authority.[81] The RTS defines tax capacity as the amount of revenue the local governments would raise if the national average was applied to the taxable base. Tannenwald has updated RTS in recent years, as ACIR was defunded by Congress in 1996. Ladd and Yinger created measures, again based on national averages, for both revenues and expenditures and incorporated an element of tax structure that is crucial to cities' fiscal well-being, namely, their capacity to export some of the cost of city services to nonresidents. Tax exporting is particularly important in understanding tax burden on residents of central cities (or employment centers) with a significant commuting population in which the city has the constitutional authority and political will to impose a commuter tax (e.g., nearly all Ohio municipalities). Results of the study could be interpreted as demonstrating that, indeed, cities are unique or that cities' revenue-generating capacity was so constrained by state control that their fiscal problems were unlikely to be resolved by their own devices, but rather with financial (state aid) or legal support (state granting taxing authority, such as the commuter tax, to cities). The upshot, among others, is to encourage a diversification to the revenue mix of local governments. A recent study of revenue diversification found that greater revenue diversification was more likely in cities that were younger, experiencing growth, less reliant on the property tax and more reliant on the sales tax, and had home rule.[82]

Financial management indicators The International City/County Management Association (ICMA) and the Government Finance Officers Association (GFOA) have been in the forefront of encouraging and assisting local governments in employing financial management techniques and measures. ICMA's well-known *evaluating financial condition* was designed to provide "managers of local governments with a method for monitoring their government's financial condition";[83] GFOA created financial management indicators for local governments.[84] Others also provided advice on how to monitor and manage their

---

80. Charles Tiebout, "A Pure Theory of Local Expenditures," *Journal of Political Economy* 64 (1956): 416–424.

81. U.S. Advisory Commission on Intergovernmental Relations, *State Fiscal Capacity and Effort 1991* (Washington, DC, 1993).

82. Rebecca Hendrick, "Revenue Diversification: Fiscal Illusion or Flexible Financial Management," *Public Budgeting & Finance* 22, no. 4 (2002): 52–72.

83. Sanford M. Groves and Maureen Godsey Valente, revised by Karl Nollenberger, *Evaluating Financial Condition,* 4th ed. (Washington, DC: International City Management Association, 2003), 1.

84. Jesse W. Hughes and Raymond Laverdiere, "Comparative Local Government Financial Analyses," *Public Budgeting & Finance* 6, no. 4 (1986): 23–33.

local governments' finances.[85] ICMA's financial trend monitoring system identified 36 indicators for the purpose of understanding and assessing a local government's fiscal position.[86] In many ways, then, these indicators of financial condition were measures of performance as well. By the 1990s, performance budgeting and performance measures were staging an important resurgence in the field.

Tax expenditures A 1988 PB&F article strongly argued that financial management indicators on performance, needs and resources be supplemented with an assessment of tax expenditures. These were defined as "(1) exclusions, exemptions, and deductions, which reduce taxable income; (2) preferential tax rates, which reduce taxes by applying lower rates to part or all of a taxpayer's income; (3) credits, which are subtracted from taxes as ordinarily computed; and (4) deferrals of tax, which result from delayed recognition of income or accelerated recognition of deductions."[87] Although the federal government reports tax expenditures, local governments are not required to estimate or report the full range of tax expenditures, an oversight which results in under- or nonreporting of these (hidden) spending programs and removes programs from public scrutiny in violation of the transparency principle. The exhortation from nearly two decades ago still resonates today as local governments continue to provide tax expenditures often with little oversight, outcome indicators or performance measures.

Cash management Often considered part of a system of performance management, cash management requires careful analysis. Students of cash management may recall the mnemonic device safety, liquidity, yield (SLY), which refers to objectives of sound investment strategies. The North Carolina Local Government Commission's (LGC) cash management requirements, in place since the Great Depression, were reviewed in PB&F.[88] Local governments' performance was measured according to the five "investment norms" established by the LGC and variations were found in practices across types of government (e.g., public authorities) and within governments (e.g., cities). Not surprisingly, cities with a population over 10,000 and larger counties performed better on the "investment norms" than did public authorities.

The "S" in SLY can also be thought of in risk terms. Local governments have attempted to reduce managerial risk and potential liabilities by pooling their resources (and risk) in the last 20 years or so. A 1989 article examined the structure of risk management pools and explained their proliferation as resulting from the abandonment of private insurers of municipalities in the 1970s.[89] The motivation behind creating, and belonging to, insurance

85. See, inter alia, George Peterson et al., *Urban Fiscal Monitoring* (Washington, DC: The Urban Institute, 1978); Philip Dearborn, *Elements of Municipal Financial Analysis* (Boston: The First Boston Corporation, 1977); Terry Clark et al., *How Many New Yorks?* (Chicago: University of Chicago Press, 1976).

86. Sanford M. Groves, W. Maureen Godsey, and Martha A. Shulman, "Financial Indicators for Local Government," *Public Budgeting & Finance* 1, no. 2 (1981): 5–19.

87. Jesse W. Hughes and Janne Motekat, "Tax Expenditures for Local Governments," *Public Budgeting & Finance* 8, no. 4 (1988): 68.

88. Charles K. Coe, "The Effects of Cash Management Assistance by States to Local Governments," *Public Budgeting & Finance* 8, no. 2 (1988): 80–90.

89. Peter C. Young, "Local Government Risk Financing and Risk Control Pools: Understanding Their Forms, Functions, and Purposes," *Public Budgeting & Finance* 9, no. 4 (1989): 40–53.

pools is to expand capacity and reduce uncertainty. Today, risk management is an essential function of most local governments and is integral in understanding local government financial management.

Adequacy in the Present Context

Local government financial managers are challenged to design revenue structures that support desired levels of services, withstand the vagaries of the business cycle and anticipate future shocks. Revenue elasticities are critical to revenue adequacy and financial managers are encouraged to design systems that are stable through business cycles. The property tax, the traditional foundation of local finance, is not responsive to economic cycles, while income and corporate profits taxes have the highest cyclical swings, and sales taxes show "relatively high cyclical swings."[90] The property tax is, therefore, cyclically stable; however, its longer-term secular trend is generally inelastic. Adequacy, then, is reflective of both the revenue mix and economic environment. Reinforcing the importance of the economic environment is the sharp decline in sales tax revenues associated with the latest recession (2001). Sales tax receipts actually fell in 2002 and 2003, while property tax revenues continue to reflect a robust housing market.[91]

The financial difficulties confronting local governments in the past few years are reminiscent of themes from a symposium issue which assessed "major recent changes in America's economic and political climate."[92] In that issue, the concerns were that the economic recession was taking a toll, that California's 1978 Proposition 13 and the property tax revolt in general were reshaping the revenue profiles of local governments, that the New York City fiscal crisis of 1975 still reverberated throughout the credit markets, and that a new conservative mood following the election of Ronald Reagan was sweeping the nation's local governments. All of these events required financial managers to be even more vigilant, a challenge to their practices that are echoed today.

The economic recession, although officially ended in 2001, continues to linger as the effects of the "jobless recovery" and low consumer confidence prevent the expected fiscal rebound. Buffalo, Pittsburgh, San Diego, among others, are facing challenges not unlike the fiscal imbalances of the 1970s and 1980s. The Taxpayer Bill of Rights (TABOR), which imposes revenue-generating limitations on state and local governments, and other TELs have resulted in hamstringing governments (Colorado is currently reconsidering the wisdom of the statewide TABOR), which in turn pushes user fees to a position of fiscal importance comparable with the property tax (especially for municipalities).

---

90. See John L. Mikesell, "The Cyclical Sensitivity of State and Local Taxes," *Public Budgeting & Finance* 4, no. 1 (1984): 32–39.

91. Michael A. Pagano, "City Fiscal Conditions in 2004," *State Tax Notes* 34, no. 10 (2004): 665–690.

92. Jay H. Abrams was symposium editor of "Local Government Finance, Redirections," *Public Budgeting & Finance* 2, no. 1 (1982): 3. See his "Local Government Finance: Realities and Directions," *Public Budgeting & Finance* 2, no. 1 (1982): 3–8.

Enterprise funds and user fees are also on the rise. Between 1989 and 1999, a study of 124 cities showed an aggregate increase in the number of enterprise funds of 12 percent (from 491 to 551).[93] This increase in enterprise fund usage might be attributable to the greater feasibility of raising fee rates than tax rates, or to an increased interest in privatization, or to federal mandates (especially in the environmental arena). The average annual growth rate in a city's enterprise fund revenues exceeded (usually by a substantial margin) the growth rate in a city's general fund revenues. Local governments also significantly increased their reliance on user charge revenue from 1962 to 1989.[94] Municipal user fees now constitute nearly the same proportion of own-source revenues as property taxes.

Even as these salient changes continue to reverberate in local government financial circles, whether these represent a philosophical shift to the right in the current era may be more difficult to discern compared with a quarter century ago, at least at the local government level.

The heightened emphasis on financial management practices today, then, is as important to local governments' financial well-being as it was during the economic and fiscal crisis era of the early 1980s. The threats to local governments' fiscal well-being in the early years of this journal, namely, TELs, tax revolts, and federal aid declines, have been supplanted by other, longer-term issues, which might be more deleterious to the fiscal health of local governments. If the tax revolt of the 1970s spurred the movement for government efficiency, competitiveness, and responsiveness, and triggered the adoption of more transparent performance measures, underfunded pension obligations and unfunded health obligations might become the next "shot heard round the world" in financial management circles.

CONTROL, MANAGEMENT, PLANNING: RECURRENT ISSUES IN LOCAL GOVERNMENT BUDGETING

Budgets and the term *budgeting* are as common in the daily parlance of public finance as is sunshine on a summer afternoon. It was not always so. "In 1900 governmental budgeting was virtually unknown in the United States."[95] Municipal governance in the United States was seen as the "most corrupt in Christendom."[96] "Scientific method" was advocated to purge graft and corruption. Systems of accounting and control were needed; without them "good government" would not be possible. Comprehensive budgeting was an essential component.

---

93. Beverly Bunch, "Changes in the Usage of Enterprise Funds by Large City Governments," *Public Budgeting & Finance* 20, no. 2 (2000): 20.

94. Dick Netzer, "Differences in Reliance on User Charges by American State and Local Governments," *Public Finance Quarterly* 20, no. 4 (1992): 499–511.

95. Richard K. Fleischman and R. Penny Marquette, "The Origins of Public Budgeting: Municipal Reformers during the Progressive Era," *Public Budgeting & Finance* 6, no. 1 (1986): 71–77.

96. Ibid.

Municipal budget movement–control The U.S. budget movement was first initiated at the municipal level. In 1899, the National Municipal League advocated uniform accounting methods and, by 1904, uniform accounts had been adopted by 80 cities. In 1902, Ohio mandated adoption and within ten years Illinois, Massachusetts, New York, Wisconsin, Michigan, New Jersey, Indiana, Iowa, California, Utah, and Nevada followed.[97] The budget movement included a "gospel of efficiency" and open discourse and disclosure, cost accounting, uniformity of methods, centralization, accrual accounting, unit costs, output measurement, work process studies, intercity cost comparisons, and assessments of program effectiveness. By the 1920s, however, with the establishment of uniform account classification and comprehensive budgetary systems, the fervent interest in municipal reform had waned. "These accomplishments largely obviated the need for additional guarantees of honest and efficient city government. . . . the outcome was '. . . one of almost total victory. . . .'"[98]

Control was firmly established through these early systems. Managerial efficiency and effectiveness has been a continuing objective. In the early life of PB&F, the importance of integrating "budgeting, accounting, reporting and performance measurement" was recognized and emphasized.[99] However, control has not (nor should it have) relinquished its prominence. Still, its pursuit in budgeting can overwhelm other important objectives. The value of a broader informational perspective often presents itself in a period when introducing augmented systems is least achievable. There are frequent references to the need for systems to make more rational decisions in the presence of fiscal stress. Approaches based on across-the-board cuts, narrow efficiency determinations, vanquishing the programmatically vulnerable, and short-sighted service pricing and contracting strategies are nearly universally rejected in concept in favor of more programmatically oriented approaches based on an assessment of priorities, goals and objectives.[100] However, in practice, the prior are nearly universally implemented. The onset of fiscal difficulties is most successfully mitigated (from the control perspective) by quick response. Political salability and the absence of prior establishment of more rational mechanisms reinforces this reliance.

Alligators in the fiscal swamp "[W]hen you are up to your . . . [ass] in alligators, its hard to remember that your original objective was to drain the swamp."[101] This analogy was used to portray nonmetropolitan county budgeting in New York State during the late 1970s to early 1980s (a time of "insidious fiscal constraint," which included federal aid reductions, recessions, and tax revolts).[102] A control orientation (detailed line itemization and focus on travel restrictions, personnel controls, and transfer controls) detracted from

97. Ibid.

98. Ibid, 77.

99. MacManus, 58–66.

100. Jeremy F. Plant and Louise G. White, "The Politics of Cutback Budgeting: An Alliance Building Perspective," *Public Budgeting & Finance* 2, no. 1 (1982): 65–71.

101. Jane Massey and Jeffrey D. Straussman, "Budget Control Is Alive and Well: Case Study of a County Government," *Public Budgeting & Finance* 1, no. 4 (1981): 3–11.

102. MacManus refers to these as the three "R's," reduction, recessions, and revolt, see 58–66.

focus on priorities in service delivery, because of emphasis on the alligators of fiscal constraint. Necessities of quick cost cutting, and a lack of financial and political resources, often squeeze out focus on service objectives and reinforce a continued control emphasis. Control was reinforced by internal strides toward "professionalism" and external pressure for expenditure growth, driven by state and federal mandates in areas of mental and public health, social services, and jail staffing and facilities.[103] Some of the budgetary progress over the course of the past 25 years must be registered as the imposition of improved management and planning elements in recognition of their current utility and anticipation of future need, rather than as a crisis response.

Recovery from the 1990–1991 recession coincided with new interest in output and outcome orientations of budget decision making.[104] Widespread interest emerged for governmental efficiency and effectiveness and in restructuring reporting and accountability structures to more visibly accommodate these desires. This appeared at the local level absent fiscal crisis as a motivation and evolved (into the mid-1990s) in an era of relative prosperity, when resources to accommodate a broader perspective were available. To be sure, interest was driven by a coalescence of political and popular sentiments, partially because of the absence of fiscal balance and national budgetary fiscal stress; however, locally, fiscal crisis was not the prevalent factor. The still-evolving call for increased performance reflected a reopening of the book of budget reform. In large, there was little difference in this call for reform beyond that recognized by the New York Bureau of Municipal Research during the first two decades of the last century, and extended by performance budgeting of the late 1940s through 1950s, program budgeting of the 1960s, and management by objectives and zero-based budgeting of the 1970s. The environment was, however, altered and computer-enhanced information processing and analytic capabilities promised improved capacity for realizing the presumed benefits of a performance focus. Interest, however, did appear to wane with the unprecedented economic expansion of the mid- to late 1990s. With the 2001 recession, while the potential for performance-based decision making may have been increased, the budgetary alligators returned in force with severe fiscal restraint at the state and local level. What, then, has been the "progress" in local budgeting?

The Right Stuff?

Proper budgeting pronouncements The elements of a "proper" budget system can presumably be inferred from the GFOA's criteria for designating jurisdictions as distinguished in their budgetary presentation. The award program, begun in 1984, rates budget presentation through a review of the formal budget document and is, therefore, incomplete as an assessment of system quality. Still, its emphasis is illustrative of the presumed standard for the field. The GFOA evaluates a budget based on its effectiveness as a (i) "policy document," (ii) "financial plan," (iii) "operations guide," and (iv) "communications

---

103. Massey and Straussman, 3–11.

104. See David Osborne and T. Gaebler, *Reinventing Government* (Reading, MA: Addison Wesley, 1992); and Al Gore, *From Red Tape to Results: Creating a Government that Works Better and Costs Less,* *Report of the National Performance Review* (New York: Times Books/Random House, 1993).

device."[105,106] Edward Lehan criticizes the GFOA approach because of a lack of emphasis on underlying systems that support the budget process, preparation, and execution, and emphasizes a "key requirement that budget allocations be related to output and/or outcome indicators." Accordingly, elements of appraisal should include the following: (i) comprehensiveness of scope, integrity and accuracy of estimates, consistency of accounting, and accounting controls; (ii) significance of cost centers, linkage to measurable outputs, and accountability of management; (iii) existence of a multiyear perspective, formulation process/content, and source documentation; (iv) employment of allocation criteria such as unit measures, investment returns, and weighting and scoring; (v) quality and accuracy of revenue and expenditure estimation, and appropriate balance between current obligations and resources; and (vi) sufficiency of control via allotment, reserves, and execution reviews and reporting. Actual budget developments at the local level over the course of the past quarter century, if not systematic in their progress, have incrementally moved toward greater responsiveness to these concerns.

State of the art The actual "state of the art" often leaves substantial room for improvement. A review of 155 Texas city and county budgets for assorted fiscal years between 1980 and 1989 gives an indication of the range and status of local budget presentations. Using the GFOA's criteria and its five-point rating scale,[107] the average overall score for cities was "acceptable," while for counties it was "weak." Approximately 30 percent of city and 96 percent of county budgets were considered unacceptable. County budgets scored lowest on the policy and operations dimensions and reached acceptable levels on none. City budgets scored lowest as a communication device, but acceptable on policy, financial planning and operations. Populations size appeared to be somewhat of a factor, with larger jurisdictions (particularly larger counties) scoring better. Earlier budgets (i.e., those closer to 1980) also scored lower, implying a trend toward improved budgeting practice. Still, improved presentation is not synonymous with improved decision making.[108]

A budget requirement also appears insufficient as a vehicle for improved practice. Most municipalities in Illinois do not adopt a budget per se. Illinois requires appropriations ordinances; budgets are optional. Municipalities can choose to follow either law from the 1800s specifying an appropriations ordinance, classified by department and object of expenditure, or a 1967 law requiring an annual operating budget and budget system. In 1988,

105. See Edward A. Lehan, "Budget Appraisal—The Next Step in the Quest for Better Budgeting," *Public Budgeting & Finance* 16, no. 4 (1996): 3–20; Joseph T. Kelley, "The GFOA Budget Awards Criteria and Lehan's 'Budget Appraisal,'" *Public Budgeting & Finance* 16, no. 4 (1996): 26–30; and Robert C. Rickards, "City and County Budget Presentations in Texas: The Current State of the Art," *Public Budgeting & Finance* 10, no. 2 (1990): 72–87.

106. Policy criteria addresses "what the government is trying to achieve." Financial plan focus is on "balance" and "comprehensiveness." Operations guide relates to "work plan" and "tasks to be accomplished." Communications relates to information summaries and relevance to various audiences. See Kelley, 26–30.

107. On this scale 1 is very weak, 2 is marginal, 3 is acceptable, 4 is distinctive, and 5 is exemplary.

108. A 1994 study of state budgeting concluded that "Including performance measure information in the budget does not appear to change the way budget decisions are made." See Cheryl A. Broom, "Performance-Based Government Models: Building a Track Record," *Public Budgeting & Finance* 15, no. 4 (1995): 3–17, 14.

91 percent (1,150) of municipalities functioned under the appropriations law. There are significant conceptual and operational differences between the two, with budgeting being "more formalized, rational, and routinized set of activities." The appropriations act allows little within-year modification, producing a tendency to authorize expenditures significantly beyond expected. The budget system requires a budget officer, enactment of a budget, and appropriation prior to the start of the fiscal year, and allows for a capital improvement fund. However, a review of practice in Illinois suggests that distinctions in application are less significant.[109]

Illinois municipalities that budget pay more attention to planning; however, little evidence suggest that it results in improved program or service management. Municipalities operating under appropriations requirements appear to have adopted similar supporting systems, supporting Lehan's need to look significantly beyond the document. In fact, 70 percent of these responding cities indicate that they do prepare an operating budget. Administratively the systems differ in process, information content, and central authority. However, differences in emphasis of control and management elements appeared absent and differences in planning were not significant. The conclusion was that "a budget system makes little or no difference in attention to either the management or control functions of fiscal decision making. Fiscal officers of budget cities appear to see no more relationship between their fiscal processes and efficient management or financial control than do their counter parts in appropriations cities."[110] The budget document itself is simply the most visible element of the financial management iceberg. Sights should be set below the surface to meaningfully evaluate the adequacy of practice and need for reform.

The implications and determinants of a local budgeting control orientation have also been assessed in Virginia school districts.[111] Virginia districts are dependent units of city or county governments. Budgets are approved by the superior jurisdiction. However, at the superior jurisdiction's discretion, approval is either lump sum or categorical. Each reflect different levels of control. Lump-sum approvals do not specify allocations to particular purposes or categories of expenditure. Categorical allocations specify 12 separate spending categories, conferring a higher level of control. Districts allocated funds on a lump-sum basis showed higher levels of accuracy in total budget execution, suggesting a possibly unexpected conclusion that budget flexibility promotes execution adjustments across categories that maintains overall budgetary parameters. An alternative explanation is that districts which budget under categorical allocations do so because of an a priori perception of a need for exante controls. Fiscal stress is positively (but statistically insignificantly) related to the use of categorical allocations. Interestingly, more homogenous jurisdictions were more likely to use lump-sum allocations, suggesting that diversity of objectives may promote a reliance on greater budgetary control.

A 1988 assessment of trends in budgeting and financial management in large U.S. cities revealed an interesting interaction between environmental conditions and budgeting. Rev-

---

109. Osbin L. Ervin, "Appropriating vs. Budgeting: A Comparison of Municipal Fiscal Processes," *Public Budgeting & Finance* 8, no. 4 (1988): 45–53.

110. Ibid., 50.

111. Catherine L. Staple and Marc A. Rubin, "Budget Control in Virginia Public School Districts," *Public Budgeting & Finance* 17, no. 1 (1997): 74–88.

enue constraint (the alligator in the swamp) not only forced a shift toward "alternative" revenue sources and user fees, but it also significantly increased the emphasis placed on accountability and operational efficiency and the focus on object of expenditure (line-item) budget classification.[112] While moves toward "program budgeting" were frequently identified as trends, 54 percent of respondents indicated an accentuated role for object classification. This occurred simultaneously to increased concentration on efficiency and performance monitoring. In fact, within this emphasis on control, the shorter-term trend (since 1982) also revealed:

> an increase in . . . program budgeting . . . , a decrease in zero-based budgeting . . . and management by objectives . . . , a sharp increase in . . . management information systems, and an increase in performance monitoring.[113]

The expanded use of computers increased the availability of "analysis and evaluation" by freeing analysts from routine work. Seventy-eight percent indicated that increased electronic data processing resulted in both centralization and decentralization in decision making, with the central budget office gaining greater "insight" *across* decision areas and department staff receiving heightened discretion *within* them. Revenue constraints also heightened the importance of multiyear revenue and expenditure projections (if not multiyear budgeting) and the role of strategic planning. More attention was placed on capital budgeting and "creative financing" of capital projects, with 73 percent of respondents reporting the use of a separate capital budget.

For smaller cities, trends in budget innovation are muted. Smaller jurisdictions' adoption of "improved" practices appears related to educational level of local officials.[114] Greater homogeneity in policy preferences and reduced range of programmatic activity may both reduce the need for and benefit of budget innovation.

Performance measurement More recent evidence suggests that use of output and outcome measurement is increasing. A 1998 survey of U.S. counties with a population above 50,000 found that two-thirds use performance measurement at some stage of their budget process.[115] Northeastern counties use them more heavily and averaged more than four years experience doing so. Of these two-thirds, the greatest usage occurs in "budget execution and evaluation" and "executive preparation." Seventy-eight percent indicate use in preparation of departmental requests and 79.7 and 75.3 percent (respectively) use them in monitoring efficiency/effectiveness and results.

Performance measures are less frequently used for legislative review and consideration and resource allocation, but still more than 50 percent indicate doing so. There is some

---

112. Stanley B. Botner, "Trends and Developments in Budgeting and Financial Management in Large Cities of the United States," *Public Budgeting & Finance* 9, no. 3 (1989): 37–41.

113. Ibid., 38.

114. See Carl D. Ekstrom, "Budgetary Practice in Smaller Units of Government," *Public Budgeting & Finance* 9, no. 2 (1989): 76–82.

115. Xiaohu Wang, "Performance Measurement in Budgeting: A Study of County Governments," *Public Budgeting & Finance* 20, no. 3 (2000): 102–118.

political resistance by county legislative bodies because of a perception that performance information strengthens the executive's relative influence and shifts power. Still, in counties employing performance measurement, most indicate general executive, departmental, and legislative support. Not surprisingly, greater support leads to greater breadth and depth of use. Responsibility for performance measurement most often rests with the county manager or budget/finance offices. A heightened central management (county manager) role increases the breadth and depth of usage. Technical obstacles to goal identification, measurement, and analysis appear to be declining; however, departmental and staff capacity issues remain, and capacity is also associated with the breadth and depth of use. Significant majorities of respondents indicate that determination of service efficiency and effectiveness, and accountability is improved via the measurement system. However, systematic studies of actual use during the 2001 recession and subsequent fiscal difficulties of cities and counties are lacking.

The most recent treatment of performance/outcome-oriented budgeting at the local level attempts to assess the extent of application by reviewing the content of budget documents of 30 of the nation's largest cities for FY 2001 or 2002.[116] Twenty-one include performance measures in their budget.[117] Measures are reported quite pervasively; however, a comparative context (i.e., across years and to previous targets) is often lacking. The greatest application occurs in the community and neighborhood development function, followed by police, parks and recreation, and fire and emergency medical services. Output measures (volume of activity measures, such as tons of trash collected or lane miles of roads striped) are far more frequent than outcome measures.[118] Still, confirming the existence of measures does little to identify the extent and effectiveness of their use in budgetary decision making. In fact, opinion regarding the efficacy of such measures is not universally positive. It appears that a useful line of inquiry would be assessing their actual decision value. Do they provide information sufficiently nuanced to actually inform budgetary decisions in a manner not provided by previous management systems, or are they reflective of the most recent faddish budgetary application in the march of the Duke of York's 10,000 men?

GASB to the rescue? The Governmental Accounting Standards Board (GASB) has heightened interest in performance measurement over the past two decades. At least since 1987, it has flirted with the introduction of a performance reporting standard as a requirement in general-purpose external financial reporting (GPEFR).[119] In defining the

---

116. See Alfred Ho and Ann Ni, "Have Cities Shifted to Outcome-Oriented Performance Reporting?: A Content Analysis of City Budgets," *Public Budgeting & Finance* 25, no. 2 (2005): 61–83.

117. Five of the nine cities without performance measures included in their budget document do have some form of separate performance reporting document. Nonetheless, they were excluded from analysis. It should be noted that inclusion in the budget document should not be considered, a priori, reflective of a superior system, and exclusion of these cities from an assessment of the extent of performance reporting is problematic.

118. Outcome measures constituted 11 percent. Outcome measures were more pervasive for police functions, constituting 21 percent of measures for this function.

119. See Governmental Accounting Standards Board (GASB), *Concepts Statement No. 1, Objectives of Financial Reporting* (Norwalk, CT: GASB, 1987); and Governmental Accounting Standards Board (GASB), *Concepts Statement No. 2, Service Efforts and Accomplishments Reporting* (Norwalk, CT: GASB, 1994). Reporting would be via the comprehensive annual financial report (CAFR) or general-purpose financial statements (GPFS).

objectives of financial reporting in *Concept Statement 1*, GASB indicated that "financial reporting should provide information to assist users in assessing the service efforts, costs, and accomplishments of the governmental entity." Inquiry was begun into performance measurement under a "service efforts and accomplishments" (SEA) initiative. In 1994, GASB issued *Concepts Statement 2, Service Efforts and Accomplishments Reporting*, and requested comments from interested parties about the introduction of performance reporting standards. GASB concluded that performance reporting was essential to accountability and suggested the incorporation of both financial and nonfinancial performance indicators into GPEFR.

The response was less than fully supportive, and critical assessments of the viability of such a requirement emerged.[120] Before the release of *Concept Statement 2*, GFOA took a strong position that GASB refrain from requiring incorporation of SEA standards. GFOA reasoned that such standards were both beyond the expertise and purview of GASB and that, essentially, GASB should limit itself to accounting and financial reporting. In 2002, while indicating support for performance measurement through its own initiatives and that of the International City/County Management Association (ICMA), the GFOA again went on record "opposing in the strongest possible terms the efforts of the GASB to play a role in the development of performance measurement in the public sector."[121] GFOA further states that "GASB's involvement with SEA (Service Efforts and Accomplishments) is fundamentally incompatible with the [GFOA's] understanding of performance measurement . . ." and that:

- Performance measures are inherently budgetary and managerial in character and clearly fall outside the purview of accounting and financial reporting. . . . The GFOA emphatically rejects GASB's attempt to assert its own self-imposed and ill-defined concept of "accountability.". . .
- [G]oals and objectives are the concrete realization and reflection of public policy. . . . [I]t is the unique prerogative of elected and appointed officials to set public policy. . . . GASB . . . would effectively be usurping this prerogative.
- There is no such thing as a "neutral" performance measure. The selection of what to measure will inevitably drive performance. Therefore, it is unrealistic to believe that performance measures mandated by GASB would remain purely informational and somehow not have an effect on how governments manage their programs. . . .

---

120. See Jean Harris, "Service Efforts and Accomplishments Standards: Fundamental Questions of an Emerging Concept," *Public Budgeting & Finance* 15, no. 4 (1995): 18–37; and Richard E. Brown and James B. Pyers, "Service Efforts and Accomplishments Reporting: Has Its Time Really Come?", *Public Budgeting & Finance* 18, no. 4 (1998): 101–113.

121. Government Finance Officers Association, policy statement, "Service Efforts and Accomplishments Reporting," June 23, 1992; and Government Finance Officers Association, policy statement, "Performance Measurement and the Governmental Accounting Standards Board," June 18, 2002. *http://www.gfoa.org/services/policy/gfoapp1.shtml#plact6*

One-half of all responses to *Statement 2* were critical or nonsupportive of SEA standards. Criticisms included questions regarding historical antecedents[122] and caution in movement beyond the traditional limits of financial accounting. Specific concerns were (i) compliance costs, (ii) possibility for measurement manipulation, (iii) lack of credible measurement-based decision models, and (iv) lack of demand. These were coupled with general concerns about the quality of measurement, the ability to interpret measures, and the dubious value of standardized measures across governments with different environmental and demographic characteristics and service desires. Concerns also exist about the value of measures for internal management versus external reporting. Measures appropriate for the former are likely to be quite detailed (and numerous); those appropriate for the latter must be broader.

The greatest utility of performance measurement appears to be for internal oversight. Measures appropriate for this may not aid external accountability. The use of these measures for external reporting also appears inconsistent with existing models of political and managerial accountability. Focus on standardized measures fails to recognize the existence of many alternative sources of performance reporting available to budgetary actors. Insistence on standardization might also impair and distort information for financial decision making, while at the same time imply the need for potentially very costly auditing processes. "The costs of SEA reporting may include a diversion of resources from other goals and the creation of adversarial tension, distortion of decisions, and weakening of the power to impose accountability in a bureaucratic environment."[123] Actual reviews of responses to *Statement 2* conclude that "it is apparent that proposals for SEA standards are not motivated by the demands of potential users,"[124] but are motivated more by desires for internal oversight and, therefore, provide little justification for external reporting. Opponents suggest that arguments for SEA imply a desire for an "empirical" assessment of performance; however, the value of standardized measurement lacks an empirical demonstration of its own viability and utility.

Strong caution has emerged regarding the differences between financial reporting and performance reporting and against the application of performance reporting standards. Subsequent to the *Statement 2* comment period, GASB concluded that there existed a need for additional study and experimentation.[125] While during 1998 some suggested that the time had come for adoption of SEA standards, GASB's Sloan Foundation-funded research continues today. The modified view still suggests the potential value of situationally appropriate performance measures, but appears to recognize the serious limitations of reporting standards. In its study, GASB may have effectively relearned the lesson of the turn of the last century.

---

122. Early accounting literature on the topic dates to the first decade of the 20th century.
123. Harris, 28.
124. Ibid., 2.
125. To some, this has been more of a "cooling-off period," Brown and Pyer, 105.

ALTERNATIVE SERVICE DELIVERY: FASTER, BETTER, CHEAPER?

Reduced intergovernmental transfers, sagging revenue because of the 1980 and the 1981–1982 recessions, tax revolt, escalating public service costs, and federal tax reform (reducing marginal tax rates and increasing the after-tax cost of state and local services to itemizing taxpayers) coalesced to motivate a drive for cost cutting and "efficiency" in local public service delivery. The early 1980s were replete with examples and studies of mechanisms to reduce service expenditures through expanded use of the private sector in public service delivery. While not a new phoneme for local governments, the term "privatization" took on a new (if technically improper) meaning as it was used to represent an array of approaches ranging from shedding service delivery and facility ownership to the private sector, to franchising, to private sector service contracting, to vouchers, to voluntarism, to self-service and service coproduction.

Faster, Better, Cheaper?

Anything but government! Much literature was produced during the 1980s related to these alternatives as a means of economizing on local spending. Much debate also emerged over *actual* implications of various methods for cost saving, service quality and equity, the importance of contract specification, the need for vigilance in monitoring contract compliance and maintenance of competition, and the potential difficulties associated with contracting services with broader social and public objectives. The 1980s' motivations were predominantly fiscal, suggesting the use of the private sector as an efficiency/economizing strategy; by the late 1990s, there had been a shift toward improved service performance. The fourth issue in the first volume of PB&F highlighted alternative delivery modes for their potential to enhance efficiency and reduce spending in the face of "[r]ecurring financial crises in American cities" and presented a framework analyzing public services and modes of delivery.[126] The now-common provision versus production distinction was reflected in differentiating between roles of "service consumer," "service producer," and "service arranger." A typology of service delivery modes was defined ranging from "government service" to "self-service." Satisfaction was assumed to "be greatest when the consumer is also the arranger," efficiency greatest when the consumer directly pays the producer for the service, and cost lowest when government is not the producer.

Research over the course of the past two decades has shown these assumptions to be more nuanced and less than universally supported. Arrangement by individual consumers for the production of "public goods" is fraught with difficulties, not the least of which is the classic potential for underproduction and free ridership. Efficiency and responsiveness is not assured by direct consumer payments to producers, particularly under conditions of a sole supplier, public or private. Notorious evidence of this is cable television franchises and the widespread charges of inflated prices and poor service subsequent to the enactment of the Cable Com-

---

126. E. S. Savas, "Alternative Institutional Modes for the Delivery of Public Services," *Public Budgeting & Finance* 1, no. 4 (1981): 12–20. It should be noted that desires for improved performance were also stated; however, the primary concern was cost savings.

munications Policy Act of 1984 limiting local jurisdictions' ability to regulate prices on behalf of the "arranging" and "paying" consumer.[127] Finally, many examples of local government workforces outperforming private contractors on cost effectiveness exist. This, coupled with the need for contract monitoring, difficulties of service specification and outcome measurement, the existence of external effects, importance of accountability to public objectives, and somewhat incompatibility between scale economies and market competition, has moderated the expected and claimed gains from "privatization."[128]

Ebbs, flows, and divestiture. In fact, "privatization" has been moderated in practice. Table 5 shows the use of alternative service delivery arrangements of cities and counties in the United States for 1982, 1992, and 2002 and identifies the percent using an entirely public workforce for functions within a service category, those using mixed public/private production modes, and those using totally private production.[129] While because of sampling and response rate differences these survey results are not precisely comparable, they do provide interesting context and epilogue to the "privatization movement." Two prominent conclusions emerge from a review of this table. First, the use of the private sector was already widespread at the beginning of the privatization movement. As such, it was more a realization of existing practice than a paradigm shift in service delivery. Second, since 1982, the aggregate use of the private sector for public service delivery has not markedly increased. To be sure, significant improvements in service delivery were frequently made, and often in very visible jurisdiction which had been slower to adopt alternative practices. In fact, the 1992–2002 trend is toward a reintegration of previously contracted service into the public workforce. This may be a confirmation (in miniature) of the lessons learned by cities across the country during the last decades of the 19th and first decades of the 20th centuries. During this period, city leadership was struggling to overcome the excesses, inefficiencies, unresponsiveness, and ineffectiveness of private spatial monopolies over transportation (traction and plank roads companies), unregulated gas and power companies, telephone service, and even bread bakeries.[130] According to local government respondents in 2002, restoring services to in-house production was a function of problems with service quality, unfulfilled expectations for cost savings, improved internal capacity, and difficulties in performance monitoring and contract specification.[131]

Missing from Table 5 is a third, possibly most important, trend toward divestiture of public responsibility; city and county governments are shedding services ("privatizing" in the technical meaning of the word). While the trend is to more in-house production by those local governments providing services, of 67 services studied by the ICMA, the percentage of local governments providing them dropped for all but three. Areas

---

127. Cable Communications Policy Act of 1984, P. L. 98–549.

128. See, Daniel R. Mullins and C. Kurt Zorn, "Is Activity-Based Costing Up to the Challenge When It Comes to Privatization of Local Government Services?", *Public Budgeting & Finance* 19, no. 2 (1999): 37–58.

129. Private production modes include contracting, franchises, nonprofit organizations, and volunteers.

130. Melvin G. Holli, *Reform in Detroit: Hazen S. Pingree and Urban Politics* (Oxford, UK: Oxford University Press, 1973).

131. Mildred Warner and Amir Hefetz, "Pragmatism over Politics: Alternative Service Delivery in Local Government, 1992–2002," in *Municipal Year Book 2004* (Washington, DC: International City/County Management Association, 2004), chapter 2, Table 2/6.

TABLE 5
Use of Alternative Service Delivery, 1982–2002

Cross-Category Service Averages	Entirely Public Employee Produced				Mixed Production				Totally Private Production			
	% 1982	% 1992	% 2002	% Δ 1982–2002	% 1982	% 1992	% 2002	% Δ 1982–2002	% 1982	% 1992	% 2002	% Δ 1982–2002
Public works/transportation	54.53	50.49	51.95	0.01	21	20.71	25.03	0.24	24.47	28.8	23.03	0.16
Public utilities (meter reading only)	64	65.4	77.6	21.25	23	9.8	9.4	-59.13	13	24.8	13	0
Public safety	54.86	56.97	59.97	0.14	17.57	10.84	15.91	-0.04	27.57	32.19	24.11	0.07
Health and human services	27.73	23.57	33.34	0.41	25	16.4	28.1	0.22	47.27	60.03	38.56	-0.17
Parks and recreation	67.33	68.5	63.67	-3.88	23.33	17.67	24.83	16.64	9.33	13.83	11.5	15.97
Cultural and arts programs	26.67	28.2	34.8	50	30.33	20.17	29.4	-7.98	43	51.63	35.8	-16.27
Support functions	69.86	66.11	65.54	-0.07	20	18.69	24.12	0.23	10.14	15.19	10.34	0.1
Average across all common categories	52.43	49.94	52.89	0.12	21.8	17.63	24.18	0.16	25.78	32.44	22.93	0.04

Source: Calculated from Rowan Miranda and Karlyn Andersen, "Alternative Service Delivery in Local Government, 1982–1992," in *Municipal Year Book 1994* (Washington, DC: International City/County Management Association, 1994), chapter 3, Table 3/2; and Mildred Warner and Amir Hefetz, "Pragmatism over Politics: Alternative Service Delivery in Local Government, 1992–2002," in *Municipal Year Book 2004* (Washington, DC: International City/County Management Association, 2004), chapter 2, Table 2/2.

The Evolution of Public Finance and Budgeting

experiencing the largest reduction in local government provision were health and human services, support functions (such as tax collection and assessing and title records), public safety (in the form of ambulance service and vehicle towing), and public works (sludge and solid waste). To be sure, services are also added. However, the most significant legacy of the previous two decades in service delivery may be retrenchment in the service range of the local public sector; an outcome which was an underlying objective for traditional privatization advocates.

Cautionary tales With noted exceptions, the pages of PB&F have been relatively quiet regarding contracting and privatization, even given the oft-stated fiscal motivations for changes in-service delivery. Given Table 5, this may have been appropriate. Treatment in PB&F has been largely cautionary. Focus has included cost/benefit considerations and a stipulated need for systematic assessment and "comprehensive statement of service goals which facilitates the measurement of outcomes."[132] Fully considering direct, indirect, and social costs (including equity, accountability, and participation), issues of sovereignty and managerial control have been emphasized to guard against exaggerated claims of cost savings of faulty decisions. The lack of output homogeneity has been stressed along with the difficulty it poses for evaluating the "public mandate."

Concerns over contract specification in wastewater treatment provide an example of the importance of preserving proper economic motivations. Privatization of wastewater treatment was encouraged by changes in law of the early 1980s. "Bilateral monopolies" created by privatization agreements may be nontrivially unfavorable to municipalities. "[T]he cost to the municipality of efficient private sector production under an unfavorable privatization agreement could exceed the cost of inefficiently producing the service by itself."[133] A review of contracts revealed that, in most, production costs are passed on to municipalities, reducing or eliminating incentives of the private firm to economize. Without cost-reduction incentives (generated by allowing private firms to both benefit from efficient operations and experience the cost of inefficiencies), fiscally beneficial results would not be expected. "[T]he theoretical advantages that privatization advocates see have been largely eliminated by the design of the contract. . . ."[134] This may be a function of bargaining position and information advantage. In fact, empirical comparison of the cost of privatized versus municipally operated facilities showed that on average privatized facilities were the more costly alternative. A case study of Indianapolis' contracted operation of its award-winning wastewater treatment facilities exposed similar concerns regarding savings. These included the potential problematic ramifications of political motivations for showing savings, problematic attribution of capital conversion costs corresponding to contracting and a change in treatment processes, inability to compare costs because of changed outputs, questions regarding cost attribution and service quality, difficulties in compliance monitoring, and problematic competition and cost incentives.[135]

132. Stanley C. Wisniewski, "Analyzing the Contracting-Out of Government Services: Relevant Cost–Benefit Considerations," *Public Budgeting & Finance* 11, no. 2 (1991): 95–107.

133. Randall G. Holcombe, "Privatization of Municipal Wastewater Treatment," *Public Budgeting & Finance* 11, no. 3 (1991): 28–42.

134. Ibid., 37.

135. Mullins and Zorn, 37–58.

PB&F's cautionary perspective continued in the area of education, where the link between theoretical underpinnings of vouchers and the reality of their achievement have been questioned. With conceptual origins back to Adam Smith and John Stuart Mill, vouchers for education are not a recent intellectual innovation. A review of experiments in "quasi-vouchers" in schools systems in eight cities suggested problematic effects including increased inequality (via creaming), administrative, cultural and financial barriers to choice, active recruitment of the academically talented, and failure to accommodate special-needs children.[136] Poorer-performing students were more concentrated in "underfunded" and demoralized public schools. Those households exiting the public school system were those most capable of voice and those most likely to stimulate improvement in existing institutions, decreasing the likelihood of generally increased adequacy of education in the "public schools." Potential threats to education equity and adequacy exist as (with the desires of powerful and vocal majorities fulfilled through voucher-based school choice), the political impetus for fiscal support for and improvement in public schools wanes and is replaced by desires to withdraw public support, leaving those behind with inferior educational prospects. An increasingly fragmented educational system may develop, reducing the role of education in establishing a core common community value structure, as achievement toward equity of the public schools is undone and curriculums reflect factionalized interests.

Performance—"Back to the Future." Much of the debate on alternative service delivery is really a debate on performance. However, this is often a politically and philosophically charged exchange and preconceptions have been found to drive analysis. As evidenced in the previous section of this paper, performance measurement is often at issue. Thus, the privatization issue is in essence a government performance issue and is interlaced with the budgetary issues described above. The construction of valid performance measures is a technically demanding task and must vary based on desired usage. Two primary variations in usage relate to the use of measures to hold organizations accountable for promised or expected/desired levels of achievement, and for relative levels of achievement. The first, while difficult, relates to comparisons of an organization's performance to itself over time and is much more tractable (and is more frequently found in budget measures). The second is comparison of an organization or unit to other similar organizations or units in a form of benchmarking: a much more difficult undertaking.

Because of the susceptibility of public service outcomes to environmental (both physical and social) conditions, relative comparisons (in raw form) are likely to be more a reflection of these differentials than of any differences in the effectiveness of a public workforce or administration.[137] To be useful, adjustment must be made for these environmental factors. While this is certainly possible, it requires significant analytic capability.[138] A component of this second usage is also for cost comparison and "privatization." While this comparison

---

136. Jim Waring, "Educational Vouchers: The Case for Public Choice Reconsidered," *Public Budgeting & Finance* 16, no. 3 (1996): 63–73.

137. This also explains the zeal with which jurisdictions fortunate enough to possess favorable physical and social environments seek to be benchmarked. A successful (favorable) comparison is virtually assured.

138. See Leanna Stiefel, Ross Rubenstein, and Amy Ellen Schwartz, "Using Adjusted Performance Measures for Evaluating Resource Use," *Public Budgeting & Finance* 19, no. 3 (1999): 67–87.

presumably holds constant environmental characteristics, it has been shown to be fraught with complexities. Difficulties in establishing accurate comparisons for privatization of more "public" local services are suggestive of the difficult row to hoe in making general performance comparisons between places. Still, the call for "privatization" has matured over the past two and one-half decades. Analytic propositions and techniques have improved, as has contract specification and monitoring, and services provided are more effective because of the competition. Also matured is an understanding of the realistic contribution of "privatization" to the performance of public functions. It is (or can be) an aid to efficiently and effectively satisfy the desires of the public (a position consistent with the beginning of the period); maturation is reflected in a "back to the future" understanding that it is not a universal panacea.

CAPITAL BUDGETING AND FINANCE

"America in Ruins"—The Crisis of Infrastructure

The first issue of PB&F was published the same year that the popular press reported on the impending "infrastructure crisis." *Time, Newsweek, U.S. News & World Report,* and others repeated the "America in Ruins" theme, popularized by a short tract that summarized several reports that had been released in the late 1970s.[139] Social science academicians, for the most part, tended to ignore capital budgets and capital finance in their research, writing, and teaching. Any scholarship and reports that did examine the capital side of local government budgeting and finance were more concerned with debt finance, underwriters, and insurers than the process of capital budgeting, project selection and prioritization, funding projects from nondebt sources, or maintaining fixed assets, which is typically an operating budget concern. Research, professional training, and studies on local government-owned infrastructure, as a public management concern, were often conceded to engineers (construction), MBA finance professionals (bond market analysis), the planning profession (location), and lawyers (covenants and official statements). Indeed, it is curious that while the capital budget was understudied, most states and local governments employed dual budgeting systems in which both an operating budget and a capital budget existed in uneasy harmony.

The literature on public budgeting almost invariably ignored the capital side, while becoming obsessed about how operating budgets were decided (with much scholarly output examining approaches to the operating budget or the federal budget exclusively). Gradually, however, the capital budget received serious coverage as an accepted area of study a few years after the publication of Peterson's plea to not ignore the sunk public capital costs of infrastructure in the nation's older cities.[140]

---

139. Patrick Choate and Susan Walter, *America in Ruins* (Washington, DC: Council of State Planning Agencies, 1981).

140. George Peterson, "Capital Spending and Capital Obsolescence: The Outlook for Cities," in *The Fiscal Outlook for Cities*, ed. Roy Bahl, (Syracuse, NY: Syracuse University Press, 1978), 49–74. See also

Rationalized Capital Planning/Budgeting/Reporting?

In the late 1970s and early 1980s, several large-scale research projects examined the capacity of local and state governments' capital budgeting systems.[141] The projects found inadequate information or data on project selection criteria, spotty information on current infrastructure condition assessment, no cross-walks between projects funded through the capital budgets and maintenance/repair activities funded through the operating budget, and poorly designed capital planning processes with inadequate public participation. The National Council on Public Works Improvement (NCPWI), which was created by Congress in response to reports on "crumbling infrastructure," proclaimed that capital planning documents often contained projects that were little more than "wish lists" and not rationally designed to meet the demographic, economic, and financial needs of the public today, or in the future,[142] and that capital budgeting should become a process that rationally allocates resources based on economic, financial, service, and other criteria with the long-term implications of those investments firmly implanted.[143] The emphasis on "rational" budgeting motivated Lisle Bozeman to conclude that capital budgeting "ties together the major components needed for a rational budget."[144]

A major Urban Institute project on "setting priorities for capital investment," which identified critical performance and evaluative criteria that local governments should establish, was summarized in PB&F.[145] Echoing the NCPWI report, the article concluded that the "literature on capital budgeting does not really help local government officials select among diverse and competing capital projects"[146] and continued to suggest a list of selection criteria (ranging from operating and maintenance estimation, health and safety impacts, funding availability, conformance to long-range plans, to a host of other usual suspects). But, looming ominously, was the "political task reflecting the jurisdiction's values and priorities."[147] That is to say, the "political" side was not accounted for in these studies.

(footnote Continued)

Nazir G. Dossani and Wilbur A. Steger, "Trends in U.S. Public Works Investment," *National Tax Journal* 33, no. 2 (1980): 123–148.

141. John Kamensky, "Budgeting of State and Local Infrastructure: Developing a Strategy," *Public Budgeting & Finance* 4, no. 3 (1984): 3–17.

142. National Council on Public Works Improvement, *Fragile Foundations: A Report on America's Public Works* (Washington, DC: U.S. Government Printing Office, 1988).

143. Bradley Doss Jr., "The Use of Capital Budgeting Procedures in U.S. Cities," *Public Budgeting & Finance* 7, no. 3 (1987): 57–69.

144. J. Lisle Bozeman, "The Capital Budget: History and Future Directions," *Public Budgeting & Finance* 4, no. 3 (1984): 18–30.

145. Annie Millar, "Selecting Capital Investment Projects for Local Governments," *Public Budgeting & Finance* 8, no. 3 (1988): 63–77.

146. Ibid., 64.

147. Ibid., 73.

The arcane world of capital budgeting, which seemed to evoke visions of men in smoke-filled rooms deciding who would be rewarded with new sidewalks and resurfaced streets, was to be opened to scrutiny and analysis under GASB guidelines. If local governments had to inventory their assets or had to estimate the depreciated value of their assets, elected officials and the public ought to have a better understanding of the financial value of assets. When commentators, a few decades ago, spoke of the sunk value that public infrastructure represented, they could only assume that the infrastructure had any value. Governments did not depreciate their assets as a rule and one was hard pressed to convincingly assess the value of a fixed asset. But to expense an asset means that government leaders now have to think about replacing it, rather than moving on to the next ribbon-cutting ceremony. And possibly, the new documentation required by GASB would encourage more careful and deliberative public investment decisions.[148] This newly required activity of governments led to a symposium issue in fall 2001.[149] In it, the authors described the new reporting model, its rationale, audit issues, and its implications for public budgeting. A new, revolutionary reporting model would now raise the capital budget and fixed assets to a position of importance to all stakeholders in local governments.

The earlier studies on capital budgeting emphasized the need for tools and techniques that were designed to bring rationality to the decision process. As the "mechanism for executing long-term capital plans to facilities economic growth," capital budgeting was often discussed as a rational decision-making effort.[150] A study of capital investment decisions in Fort Worth, Texas, demonstrated the complex interactions between private and public investment.[151] A descriptive narrative on Cleveland's infrastructure investments demonstrated that a "supportive political environment" is key in rationalizing capital spending plans.[152] Those plans, in turn, are tied up with the city's private investment behavior.

---

148. Beverly Bunch, "Current Practice and Issues in Capital Budgeting and Reporting," *Public Budgeting & Finance* 16, no. 2 (1996): 7–25.

149. William R. Voorhees and Robert S. Kravchuk, "The New Governmental Financial Reporting Model under GASB Statement No. 34: An Emphasis on Accountability," *Public Budgeting & Finance* 21, no. 3 (2001): 1–30; Terry K. Patton and David R. Bean, "The Why and How of the New Capital Asset Reporting Requirements," *Public Budgeting & Finance* 21, no. 3 (2001): 31–46; Earl R. Wilson and Susan C. Kattelus, "Implications of GASB's New Reporting Model for Municipal Bond Analysts and Managers," *Public Budgeting & Finance* 21, no. 3 (2001): 47–62; John H. Engstrom and Donald E. Tidrick, "Audit Issues Related to GASB Statement No. 3," *Public Budgeting & Finance* 21, no. 3 (2001): 63–78; James L. Chan, "The Implications of GASB Statement No. 34 for Public Budgeting," *Public Budgeting & Finance* 21, no. 3 (2001): 79–87.

150. See, e.g., J. Lisle Bozeman, "The Capital Budget: History and Future Directions," *Public Budgeting & Finance* 4, no. 3 (1984): 18–30.

151. Samuel Nunn, "Public Capital Investment and Economic Growth in Fort Worth: The Implications for Public Budgeting and Infrastructure Management," *Public Budgeting & Finance* 11, no. 2 (1991): 62–94.

152. Susan Hoffmann, Norman Krumholz, and Kevin O'Brien, "How Capital Budgeting Helped a Sick City: Thirty Years of Capital Improvement Planning in Cleveland," *Public Budgeting & Finance* 20, no. 1 (2000): 24–37.

Yet, as a fundamentally political decision, recognition of the political nature of the capital budget cannot be discounted. *GASB 34* might encourage more transparent decisions, but other factors are important as well. How, then, does a local government choose to include a capital project in the capital budget? What decision rules are employed and what analytical techniques? Capital budgeting techniques can be grouped based on five criteria.[153] While generally regarded (at least conceptually) as a superior decision criteria, pitfalls and limitations of discounted cash-flow analysis (importantly, that it often ignores nonquantifiable goals such as health and safety) often work to seriously impair its application. This may occur to such a degree that the "analytical hierarchy process" might in reality prove to be an adequate decision-making tool for municipal capital budgets. It involves the assignment of values to qualitative goals of capital projects as well as a financial impact and asset replacement measure. This decision-making approach has the advantage of addressing multiattribute problems associated with capital project selection.

The politics of infrastructure has also been brought front and center in that it has been linked firmly to growth management initiatives.[154] Incumbents faced electoral defeat when infrastructure issues, negatively viewed, were highly visible items. This brings us full circle: To the extent that infrastructure was given much attention in the past, it was because of its linkage to the "politics of pork." Today, infrastructure condition and demand command our, and the electorate's, attention because of its visible linkage to voters' quality of life.

Maintenance, No Longer the Stepchild?

At about the same time as the Urban Institute was undertaking its "Guides to Managing Urban Capital Series," an influential study by Leonard examined the institutional and political biases against maintaining public fixed assets and in favor of new construction with the requisite media-covered ribbon-cutting ceremonies.[155] It would not be an exaggeration to conclude that local governments' capital budgeting processes at that time were not transparent to the public or to elected officials. Another study of Cleveland, for example, documented the distribution of capital projects along political dimensions.[156] Pork and new projects were accepted practices of demonstrating political strength and a sure-fire way to be reelected. Yet, in the absence of publicly available information about infrastructure conditions, needs, depreciation, and use, one's choice of a project might be just as good as anyone else's.

153. Yee-Ching Lilian Chan, "Use of Capital Budgeting Techniques and an Analytic Approach to Capital Investment Decisions in Canadian Municipal Governments," *Public Budgeting & Finance* 24, no. 2 (2004): 40–58.

154. Susan A. MacManus, "'Brick and Mortar' Politics: How Infrastructure Decisions Defeat Incumbents," *Public Budgeting & Finance* 24, no. 1 (2004): 96–112.

155. Herman B. Leonard, *Checks Unbalanced: The Quiet Side of Public Spending* (New York: Basic Books, 1986).

156. Heywood Sanders, "Politics and Urban Public Facilities," in *Perspectives on Urban Infrastructure*, ed. Royce Hanson (Washington, DC: National Academy Press, 1984), 143–177.

Even with the studies on best infrastructure-management practices, it was not until *GASB 34* that transparency in the capital budgeting and selection process started to become important to a broader community. *GASB 34's* legacy of "shining a bright light" on the capital side of local government budgeting might be most noteworthy in the area of infrastructure maintenance. GASB requires governments to present information on infrastructure condition and infrastructure depreciation. Maintenance of public facilities, long a neglected area of study for academics or a concern of elected officials, now is at center stage. Although the expectation for *GASB 34* was to require governments to prepare accurate statements on fixed assets, it does not require cross-linking capital budgets with long-term maintenance outlays. Closer coordination between the capital and operating budgets is an important step in addressing the problem of underfunded maintenance.[157] Because maintenance and repair activities tend to be funded from the operating budget and because these are asset-related activities, a crosswalk between capital projects funded through the capital budget and longer-term maintenance and repair activities funded through the operating budget would more fairly present the true costs of building a fixed asset over its lifetime.

Over the last 30 years, then, the capital budgeting and finance literature has evolved from an academic arena of unknowns, except to accountants, engineers, and bond analysts, to one with extensive efforts toward developing quantitative measures of infrastructure performance, financial return on investment, asset management, and the like.

QUESTIONS, ISSUES, THE FUTURE

The last 25 years have seen a shakeout of intergovernmental fiscal relationships. The national government has reduced substantially its fiscal support for subnational general services and, because of demographic factors, has shifted from a policy of fiscal transfers to places to transfers for direct services to individuals, primarily health care, support for infrastructure (primarily transportation) and security, and pursuit of national policy through regulation and mandates. The national government's fiscal condition and its longer-term prospects (given war, health-care costs, and resource needs of social insurance programs) suggest the prospects for a larger federal fiscal role are dim. State governments are similarly saddled with growing Medicaid costs and potentially escalating public assistance responsibilities, and state actions of the recent past have as frequently as not constrained local jurisdiction's fiscal abilities. While the prospect is for a continuation of "fend-for-yourself" finance, local autonomy is likely to be further constrained by competition for policy direction from above, particularly in areas of education and public safety. Local governments will likely find themselves continuing

---

157. Michael A. Pagano, "Notes on Capital Budgeting," *Public Budgeting & Finance* 4, no. 3 (1984): 31–40; Robert Bland and Samuel Nunn, "The Impact of Capital Spending on Municipal Operating Budgets," *Public Budgeting & Finance* 12, no. 2 (1992): 32–47.

what has become a virtual perpetual search for revenue (and service delivery models) in an attempt to match capacity to population service expectations, in ways that fragment revenue structures and accountability.

The focus on "performance" is also likely to continue, at least as a stated policy/ managerial directive. However, the degree to which actual public gains are engendered by requirements for performance measurement, budgeting, and reporting reforms is less certain. What is certain is that the alligators of fiscal stringency will remain and at times thrive, reinforcing a budgetary orientation toward fiscal control. The simultaneous search for efficiency and effectiveness in public service provision and production will also foster continued experimentation as the pendulum likely swings between the predominance of one or the other, and as political and economic environments allow or require.

Infrastructure and capital budgeting and financing will remain a salient issue. Irrespective of requirements for reporting and analysis, the political environment will continue to determine allocations and, at least periodically, maintenance will be deferred and fall victim to more immediately visible operating concerns. Rational decision making will likely advance the effectiveness of both operating and capital budget decisions, as information management and support systems improve. However, V. O. Key's basic budgetary problem will remain technically unresolvable even at the local level.[158]

Although it is impossible to accurately predict the challenges facing local government financial management in the next 25 years, we hazard a few observations about the short-term challenges, one on stagnant fiscal systems and the other on easy political decisions.

First: The "shifting" economic and fiscal systems will surely challenge financial managers in nearly all local governments. Although local governments have become more sophisticated in budgeting and financial management, these tools of modern government will become less relevant to service delivery if their economic bases continue to slide out from under their taxing authority. Current tax structures for most local governments reflect an economic base that has gradually eroded the efficiency of those systems. The modern economy has moved from a manufacturing and tangible-goods base to one that increasingly emphasizes knowledge production and service consumption. The taxation of local governments' economic bases, assuming a fair tax burden, should be imposed on all wealth-generating aspects of the economy, and reconsidered. In 1960, according to Tannenwald's study,[159] only 40 percent of national consumption was for services, while 60 percent was for tangible goods. The percentages have reversed in 2000. Local tax systems have not adjusted to this shift. Making such adjustments will be a critical requirement for local fiscal adequacy.

Second: One of the easiest "solutions" to financial management problems is to "punt" the problem to the next generation. Underfunding infrastructure maintenance is a good illustration. The political consequences of this practice tend to be postponed until after a

---

158. This is the case irrespective of Tiebout's model of local government efficiency.

159. Robert Tannenwald, *Are State and Local Revenue Systems Becoming Obsolete?* (Washington, DC: National League of Cities, 2004).

The Evolution of Public Finance and Budgeting

new administration has assumed office. But another, possibly more catastrophic, event for the fiscal health of local governments looms on the very near horizon. Exhortations by good-government organizations to make governments fully transparent may not be nearly as influential as GASB's directives. *GASB 34* made governments fully measure the value of fixed assets, hoping to inform capital planning decisions. Another long-term liability of governments has not been measured and made available to elected leaders and the public. Unfunded nonpension liabilities or what GASB calls "Accounting for Termination Benefits" are lurking. *GASB Statement No. 45, Accounting and Financial Reporting by Employers for Postemployment Benefits Other than Pensions,* is effective for larger governments, December 15, 2006, and will be phased in over three years. It will require fair appraisals of—and disclosure notes to the financial statements on—termination benefits including early-retirement incentives, severance benefits, and other termination-related benefits, such as health care. These reflect unrecognized cost for local governments across the nation and an impending fiscal bubble.

GASB's requirement is a recognition of the potential significance of this bubble and the clear and present need for it to be addressed. The political expediency of generational cost shifting tends to assure a recurrent formation of such bubbles. The "infrastructure crisis" was, and still is, one of those bubbles; health-care liabilities are today's. A present and future challenge of financial management is to uncover and "prick" these bubbles while the financial implications are manageable.

Chapter 2

The State of State Budget Research*

IRENE RUBIN

This essay examines the research on state budgeting that has appeared in *Public Budgeting & Finance* since its founding, with a view to summarizing the key themes and outlining what we have yet to learn. It also offers some suggestions for future research strategies, how to pick topics and cases, and theorize about the findings. The goal is not to utilize theories from other fields which may or may not be relevant to budgeting, but to theorize about what we know and get to a deeper level of understanding.

WHAT HAVE WE STUDIED?

Research on budgeting at the state level that has appeared in *Public Budgeting & Finance* (PB&F) can be loosely grouped into two categories. One set of studies focuses on those elements of state budgeting that are different from the national-level government, while the second set pays more attention to issues that are similar to those at the national level.[1] These two groups overlap a bit at the margins.

The states play a much smaller role in controlling or moderating the swings of the economy through spending or taxing policies than does the federal government, and, unlike the federal government, the states have to balance their budgets every year or

Irene Rubin is Professor Emerita at Northern Illinois University. Her Ph.D is from the University of Chicago in Sociology. Recent books include *Balancing the Federal Budget: Eating the Seed Corn or Trimming the Herds?* and *Class, Tax, and Power: Municipal Budgeting in the United States.* The fifth edition of *The Politics of Public Budgeting: Getting, Spending, Borrowing, and Balancing,* is available from CQ Press. Irene was the editor of *Public Budgeting & Finance* from 1994 to 1996, and the editor of *Public Administration Review* from 1996 to 1999. She can be reached at *irubin@niu.edu.*

*This chapter was originally published in *Public Budgeting & Finance*, Vol. 25, Silver Anniversary Edition (2005): 46–67.

1. Understanding the differences between states and the federal government can be helpful when reforms or processes developed in the states are proposed for the federal government. In this essay I make a first-pass effort to draw the distinction, but further refinement would be useful from a policy perspective.

44   **The Evolution of Public Finance and Budgeting**

biennium, regardless of economic conditions.[2] They are not allowed to "deficit spend" in order to stimulate the economy. Further, unlike the federal government, many of the states have tax and expenditure limitations (TELs) some of which have been initiated by citizens or passed in public referenda. Finally, the states generally maintain a separate capital budget while the national government blurs capital and operating into a single budget.

Despite these differences, states resemble the federal government in key ways. Structurally, both levels of government rely on separation of powers between the executive and legislative branches. They both struggle to fund entitlement programs that make unpredictable claims on the budget. States, like the national government, have to accommodate partisan politics. Divided government, when it occurs (the executive and legislative branches in different hands) presents the same kind of problems at the state level as it does at the national level. Like the federal government, most states have executive budget processes. And like the federal government, states grant citizens and companies tax breaks, or tax expenditures. The states experience the same kinds of problems making executive branch agencies accountable to executive policy direction and efficiency requirements that the national government encounters and both deal with similar problems of public accountability.

Understanding the political or budgetary dynamics at one level can often help explain what is going on at the other level of government. Because of the variation between states and their relatively smaller size and simpler functions, it is often easier to see how institutions function at the state level and then apply that understanding at the national level. For example, one article in PB&F by Lindsay Pjerrous-Desrochers examines the relative importance of the budgetary roles of the executive and legislative branches (advocates and guardians) on the one hand and partisanship on the other. The article examines how budgetary roles and partisanship operate to control or increase spending and how they interact.[3] The answer at the state level is not likely to be identical to the answer for the national government, but may have implications for the national level, at the least in terms of creating testable hypotheses.

Features of State Budgeting that Differ from the National Level

A substantial chunk of state budgeting research reported in PB&F has been on those issues that differentiate states from the federal government. The states have to balance their budgets annually or biennially, which the national government does not have to do. While the federal government sometimes engages in countercyclical spending, the actions that states take during recessions, including spending reductions and tax increases, may actually exacerbate rather than moderate economic downswings. Much of the literature on

---

2. Vermont is often cited as an exception to this rule, but Vermont also has a requirement for a balanced budget; it just does not require the budget to balance immediately but allows a deficit to lag briefly into the following year.

3. Lindsay Pjerrous-Desrochers, "Fiscal Roles and Partisanship in California," *Public Budgeting & Finance* 1, no. 3 (1981): 3–15.

state-level budgeting follows the states' adaptation to and responses to cycles of boom and bust in the economy, including prevention (building up reserve funds that can be used in times of recession), temporizing (using delaying tactics to tide the state over until the economy improves), and balancing (increasing revenue and/or decreasing spending). It is not that the federal government does not have to adapt to recessions; it is that the tools available to the federal government that enable it to adapt are different, it has more time to rebalance the budget, and there is less need to temporize or build buffer funds.

Adapting to boom and bust. The combination of declining or slow-growing revenues, rising expenditures, and balanced budget requirements has generated problems for the states when the economy slows down.[4] Because the problems reoccur with each new recession, articles in PB&F have addressed the topic many times, to the point that authors add to the end of titles the words "revisited" or "again." The recurrence of business cycles and the literature that springs up to describe them has given this portion of the budget literature some historical depth and an ability to build on past research.

This long time perspective has allowed researchers to examine what it is that legislators or executive branch officials learn from recessions. When recessions are particularly severe, they result in painful cuts and/ or tax increases, which may, in turn, create a determination not to get caught again unprepared when the next recession arrives. This resolution may lead to the creation or strengthening of rainy-day funds, or the funding of them more adequately during the period of recovery. A recent pair of studies comparing Georgia's and Wisconsin's experiences dealing with the most recent cyclical downturn suggests that states that manage one recession without much stress or difficulty are less prepared for the next one.[5]

The ability to compare periods of boom and bust as states adapt to the economy has also focused attention on the differences between cyclical downturns of the economy that depress revenues and structural gaps between revenues and expenditures, resulting from policy decisions that result in expenditures growing more rapidly than revenues.[6] Fiscal stress that results from cyclical changes in the economy can often be handled by temporizing strategies, delaying expenses, borrowing for capital or from internal funds until the economy improves and the debts can be paid off. Fiscal stress that results from structural gaps cannot be solved or addressed by delaying tactics. These structural gaps result from increased spending programs and/or tax reductions when the budget is flush during the upswing in the economy. These policy changes during growth make the states more vulnerable to recessions.

Research not only documents the differences between cyclical and structural problems but also suggests why some states have created the structural problems during the boom

---

4. The reduction in the number of people on welfare after welfare reform may have attenuated the increase in expenditures during a recession, but the shift of some states toward a higher proportion of revenue sources that are highly elastic with respect to the economy may exaggerate revenue declines during downswings of the economy.

5. Thomas P. Lauth, "Budgeting during a Recession Phase of the Business Cycle: The Georgia Experience," *Public Budgeting & Finance* 23, no. 2 (2003): 26–38; James Conant, "Dealing with the Bust Phase of Boom and Bust, Again," *Public Budgeting & Finance* 23, no. 2 (2003): 5–25.

6. Russell Gould, "Surviving a Revenue Collapse: Shortfall and Recovery in California," *Public Budgeting & Finance* 10, no. 2 (1990): 62–71; Lauth, 2003; Conant, 2003.

years that come home to roost during the downswing of the economic cycle. One model argues that intense and bitter partisan competition—called fiscal brinksmanship—can pressure the executive to increase program spending and tax cuts[7]; a second suggests the dominance of a conservative political strategy to reduce revenues, produce deficits, and then cut spending to rebalance the budget in order to reduce the size of government.[8]

The articles in PB&F that deal with reactions to boom and bust take a comparative look at how states have responded to budget gaps when they occur. One conclusion from this research is that states that used to use both revenue increases and spending decreases to close gaps have in recent years ruled out tax increases, leading nearly exclusively to spending reductions.[9] Second, looking across the states, even with some expenditures mandated by federal entitlements, states differ in what they protect and what they cut. Why was Wisconsin's state university system able to fend off budget cuts and Colorado's unable to do so?[10]

The literature in PB&F on boom and bust separates out the cyclical revenue changes because of openness of budgeting to the economy from the impact of policy changes, including taxing and spending changes but it generally does not include the effects of TELs of various sorts. This latter theme has developed separately, over time, as researchers respond to each successive wave of tax limits or spending caps.

Tax and expenditure limits and caps. A second difference between the states and the national government is that many of them have passed formal and sometimes rigid tax and/or expenditure limitations or caps.[11] Some of these limits are constitutional and hence long lasting and difficult to reverse or modify. Many of the states grant citizens rights to initiate or approve or disapprove proposals, including constitutional amendments, in referenda. Citizens, taxpayers' associations, and other lobbying groups have often used initiatives and referenda to limit taxes and spending. Even the states without formal tax or expenditure limits often adopt informal limits as a way of staving off pressure for stringent and inflexible constitutional amendments. The nature of these taxing and spending limits, how and why they are passed, and their consequences over time are questions that have attracted considerable research attention in PB&F.

The recent literature on Colorado and the Taxpayer Bill of Rights (TABOR) amendment, a tax limit adopted by referendum, illustrates that tax limits and caps should be considered among the reasons for structural deficits—they can exaggerate the effects of recessions and make recovery more difficult. The Colorado version of TABOR has wording in it that limits future growth in taxation to population and inflation increases, based on the prior year's actual collection, not the amount permitted under the formula. If actual

---

7. Conant, ibid.

8. Harvey Brazer, "Anatomy of a Fiscal Crisis: The Case of Michigan," *Public Budgeting & Finance* 2, no. 4 (1982): 130–142.

9. Brazer, ibid.

10. Conant, 5–25; Franklin James and Allan Wallis, "Tax and Spending Limits in Colorado," *Public Budgeting & Finance* 24, no. 4 (2004): 16–33.

11. There were spending caps associated with the federal budget enforcement act of 1990, now expired, but they were legislatively determined, not based on formulas or absolute limits as they typically are in the states. These caps applied only to the discretionary portion of the budget; the entitlements were not capped, though there has been considerable discussion about doing that.

revenues drop below that permitted by the formula because of a recession, the next year's increase is added to the new, lower base, which is now substantially behind inflation and population growth. Each succeeding year of recession will push the state further behind. Under the constitution, as amended by TABOR, the state will not be able to catch up.[12]

Colorado's TABOR amendment is an example of adopting a policy of tax reduction when the state was flush with growth and revenues, then suffering through a recession with an unusual degree of fiscal stress. Because of a second policy that requires any extra revenue collected to be returned to the taxpayers, it has been impossible even to set aside money for rainy-day funds that would help buffer against recessions. The Colorado case suggests the two sets of research themes in PB&F, the TELs and spending caps[13] on one side and the adaptations to economic shifts between boom and bust on the other, are beginning to merge.

Because of the historical reach of the articles on TELs and spending caps, and because there have been so many studies over time, researchers have been able to compare states over time, looking at a reasonable set of comparative questions, including the reasons for the adoption of the tax or spending limit, the degree of its severity and rigidity (constitutional, statutory, voluntary, what kinds of override provisions there are, and coverage—general fund, other), and reactions to it over time, such as increased state centralization and shift from property taxes to more reliance on user fees.[14] One recent article in PB&F looked at the campaigns for adoption of these TELs, examining the organizations that support them, finding that most are not in fact grassroots organizations, but organizations led by policy entrepreneurs, funded by wealthy individuals and/or corporations, using marketing research to find the phrasing that will appeal to the largest number of individual beneficiaries.[15]

The articles on TELs in PB&F are intriguing, because their comparative focus reveals that it is not always the states with high taxes that opt for rigid TELs. For example, Colorado's tax burden was low when the TEL was put in place.[16] The structural predisposing factor that is most important is the ease of putting a measure on the ballot; it is also

---

12. James and Wallis, 2004.

13. TELs are tax and expenditure limitations. They limit the amount of taxes that can raised, for example, limiting tax rates to 1 percent of assessed value of property. Spending caps are less often phrased in absolute terms and more often based on limits linked to a formula or percentage growth of population in the state or to inflation, or a combination of both. Or the linkage may be to growth in per capita income. The idea is either to freeze the size of government as a proportion of the economy or to limit tax growth to what people can afford, not increasing the share of their income that goes to taxation. Spending caps should be more flexible than TELs, but they can sometimes be too tight, as TABOR has proven to be in Colorado. One problem is the rate of inflation used is often the CPI, or some other measure of inflation than government costs, which rise more quickly than inflation in the economy as a whole. See David Lowry, "The Hidden Impact of Fiscal Caps: Hidden Implications of the Beck Phenomenon," *Public Budgeting & Finance* 3, no. 3 (1983): 19–32.

14. Daniel Mullins and Philip Joyce, "Tax and Expenditure Limitations and State and Local Fiscal Structure: An Empirical Assessment," *Public Budgeting & Finance* 16, no. 1 (1996): 75–101.

15. Daniel A. Smith, "Peeling Away the Populist Rhetoric: Toward a Taxonomy of Antitax Ballot Initiatives," *Public Budgeting & Finance* 24, no. 4 (2004): 88–110.

16. James and Wallis, 2004.

important whether only a single issue can be raised or whether multiple issues can be placed on the same ballot. Putting multiple issues on the same ballot facilitates passage, in the same way that legislation can gain supporters by putting on additional clauses sought by different legislators. In Colorado, multiple issues were put on the same ballot measure, helping to gain support for it, and then the ability to put multiple measures on the same ballot was withdrawn, making it more difficult to pass another referendum moderating or withdrawing the TABOR structure. Articles in PB&F also note that many states without formal TELs have adopted them informally,[17] warning us perhaps to be cautious in our cross-sectional research looking for differences between states based on whether or not they have formal, legislative, or constitutional adoptions of TELs. These articles also suggest the importance of studying informal procedures more generally.

A further issue raised by the articles in PB&F on TELs is the ability of states to act, or in some cases overact, and then deal with the consequences, intended and unintended, over time.[18] Some TELs are stickier than others, some can deal with the constraints by overrides, supermajorities, or exceptions, where appropriate and within the spirit of the law, while others are too rigid to allow for adaptation. Colorado's inability for years to put money into a rainy-day fund may be a good example of a set of laws so rigid that adaptation to its negative impacts is difficult if not impossible. Other states besides Colorado also have automatic provisions to return to the taxpayers any money collected above the revenue limits, making it difficult or impossible to save for a rainy day.[19]

These essays on TELs underscore the need to look at budgeting issues over time, as when they were first passed, many of them were not particularly stringent, did not seem to have much impact, and hence seemed unimportant. As time has passed and boom gave way to bust, the intended and unintended consequences have become much clearer. Budget researchers are in position to monitor the set of proposals for new TABORs across the country, with a set of questions in mind as they watch. The questions are shifting from why would a state tie its head in such a tight noose, to how and why TABORs pass, when do they fail to pass, and what policy options are open to making them less destructive of the capacity to budget.

Some TELs and caps are initiated by citizens or approved by referendum. Often sold as representing an uprising of the public who cannot take it any more, one article indicates the process can be hijacked by a few determined wealthy companies or interest groups, and that open processes that are easily used facilitate this hijacking. TELs and caps do not necessarily represent a public groundswell.[20] Also, while they clearly have some positive

---

17. Warren Deschenaux, "Maryland Fiscal Discipline Is the Budget Limit," *Public Budgeting & Finance* 17, no. 1 (1997): 99–105; Marcia Howard, "State Tax and Expenditure Limitations: There Is No Story," *Public Budgeting & Finance* 9, no. 2 (1989): 83–90.

18. Jerome Rothenberg and Paul Smoke, "Early Impacts of 2 1/2 in Massachusetts," *Public Budgeting & Finance* 2, no. 4 (1982): 90–110; Bruce Wallin, "Tax Revolt in Massachusetts: Revolution and Reason," *Public Budgeting & Finance* 24, no. 4 (2004): 34–50.

19. Barry Poulson, "Surplus Expenditures: A Case Study of Colorado," *Public Budgeting & Finance* 22, no. 4 (2002): 18–43.

20. Smith, 2004.

functions, they have some major weaknesses.[21] Voters normally have less information available to them than legislators, so the budget decisions may be made in relative ignorance of the consequences; the timing of referenda can disrupt budgeting during a fiscal year by causing massive uncertainty; and politicians looking for winning issues bypass the legislature. The major concern, though, is that citizens respond to the appeal of tax reductions made by these politicians often in the belief that there will be no service reductions as a result. They are responding to the offer of getting something for nothing, a formula that cannot possibly be sustained over the long run.

Capital budgeting. There is a third major difference between the state and national governments with respect to budgeting, namely that the states generally have separate capital budgets, and the federal government does not. One reason is that it is easier to define capital projects at the state level, as states are responsible for state roads and bridges, many public buildings, parks, prisons, and state university physical plants. At the federal level, capital shades over into the idea of investment, and human capital blends in with bricks and mortar, or tanks and ships. A second reason is that states are forbidden to borrow to close a budget gap; if capital and operating budgets were merged, it would be impossible to distinguish borrowing for capital construction, which is generally permitted, from borrowing for operating deficits, which is not permitted. A third reason is that a capital budget can be a powerful tool to help states adapt to the cycles of the economy. States can borrow for capital projects during the downswing of the business cycle and pay back when revenues are more readily available during the upswings. When states pay for capital projects with cash, they can adjust the amounts to the business cycle by spending more during booms and less during busts.[22] The states' capital budgeting processes have attracted the attention of authors writing for PB&F.

Articles in PB&F on capital budgeting point out the variety of techniques that states use to fund capital projects, including federal grants, and hence the consequences on state budgets and state borrowing of reductions in these grants. When states encounter fiscal stress, they may use what remains of these grants more to close operating gaps than for capital, and the cash capital outlays are also likely to be reduced, sometimes leaving capital underfunded at the state level.[23] One wonders what an appropriate and sustainable level of capital spending is and how budgeteers would know they had reached this level. While some researchers worry about oversupply of pork-type projects, those writing about capital budgeting in PB&F seem to worry more about systematic reasons for undersupply of capital and the need for and cost of borrowing.

The articles on capital budgeting also stress the variation between state capital budgets, their lack of inclusiveness, and the generally weak tests for the prioritization of capital projects. They argue that poor measures of depreciation make it impossible to charge capital consumption to appropriate accounts or to consider net gains in assets. Such

---

21. Krishna Tummala and Marilyn Wessel, "Budgeting by Ballot, Initiatives in the State of Montana," *Public Budgeting & Finance* 3, no. 1 (1983): 66–82.

22. The national government can push capital expenses off into the future by stretching out purchases of very expensive planes or ships. This is done sometimes to keep within spending caps, but it has not been identified as an adaptation to cycles of boom and bust in the economy.

23. John Peterson, "Creative Capital Financing in the State and Local Sector," *Public Budgeting & Finance* 2, no. 4 (1982): 73–89.

articles express a longing for a technical evaluation of capital that makes more sense in a business environment in which capital produces revenue streams. While authors in PB&F may lament the lack of measures of depreciation and hence question whether state capital budgets are anything more than a listing of capital projects, they do not examine the way in which projects are actually prioritized or how those prioritization techniques change from one administration to the next, or from a rich environment to a lean one, leaving open some key research questions.[24]

Similarities to the Federal Government

A second cluster of state budgeting articles explores issues that resonate across levels of government because structures, functions, or processes are similar enough to create a comparative focus. The states may provide examples for the national government, or the national government may create a kind of yardstick against which state level processes or institutions can be measured. The comparative framework suggests some questions to ask, and relevant dimensions to explore. At the same time, intergovernmental fiscal relations link the federal and state levels, and also the state and local levels, creating a number of parallel issues. The national government provides grants to the states, and also mandates the performance of some functions or implementation of some policies, sometimes with too little money to accomplish the goals. The states, similarly, share some revenue with their local governments and also sometimes mandate services, service levels, or policy implementation. Just as there is a question about centralization at the federal level, there are also questions about state centralization. These patterns of relationships between the national government and the states and the states and their local governments comprise the actual workings of fiscal federalism at any given moment, in all its messy complexity.

The articles in PBF that deal with these topics can be divided into four loose groups, addressing budget process, budget reforms, tax expenditures, and intergovernmental fiscal relations. The budget process articles ask the questions who makes what budget decisions with what effect on the final determination of the budget, what roles do different actors play. The articles about budget reforms include what reforms have been adopted and how they have been implemented and adapted over time. The articles that discuss tax expenditures focus less on the process of granting tax breaks than on ways of making them visible and controlling them, as well as the difficulties in tax expenditure reporting and the limits of utilization. Finally, the articles on intergovernmental relations focus on grants from the federal level to the states and state responses to declines in the amounts, shifting program responsibilities, and unfunded mandates and fiscal noting.

Budget process issues. At the state, as at the national level, the balance of budgetary responsibilities between the legislature and the executive has shifted over time. Most states

24. Henry Thomassen, "Capital Budgeting for a State," *Public Budgeting & Finance* 10, no. 4 (1990): 72–86; Lawrence Hush and Kathleen Peroff, "Variety of State Capital Budgets," *Public Budgeting & Finance* 8, no. 2 (1988): 67–79.

have some form of executive budget process, and the governors generally have strong veto powers, which they sometimes use extensively. The nature of these veto powers and how they have been used has been of intense interest over the years, in part because the president has coveted (and briefly obtained) such powers.[25] Federal grants to the states used to bypass the legislature, but when the new federalism shifted responsibility to the states while reducing the dollar amounts of the grants, legislators got more involved in appropriating the federal monies.

When the balance between the governor and the legislature is too far slanted to the governor, the result has been to bring informal negotiations between the governor and legislature behind closed doors. Alternatively, the legislature may participate in the formation of the governor's budget proposal which they later will have to act on, but in which they can make few changes. New York State, one of the most extreme executive budgeting states, has exemplified both of these adaptations.[26]

The theory behind shifting budget power increasingly to the governor has been that the governor will control the agencies, simultaneously trimming down their budget requests and imposing his or her policy concerns on the budget proposal. The legislature is assumed to be profligate, if not corrupt, and undisciplined, so its role is minimized. Those assumptions may have been justified at one time, but the more contemporary view is that governors may take an advocacy or a guardian role and that legislatures may take the opposite role from the governor. The role of the agency heads is also more nuanced than simply always asking for more.

Legislators sometimes play an active oversight role. How active they are in budgeting may depend on whether there are cuts pending, or whether the legislative majority party is different from that of the governor. If they feel they need to play a more active role, they often do. But when they do not play an active oversight role, program and financial auditors may pick up some of the slack, a role that legislators are reportedly uncomfortable with. Legislators may try to intervene to block or influence investigations that might prove embarrassing, or they may ignore the audits completely.[27]

The articles in PBF have asked what the role of the executive budget office is in an effort to understand the role of the governor in controlling department budget requests and promoting his or her policy preferences. Researchers have asked about the orientation of the executive budget office and the decision-making rules of the staff. This literature finds variation between the states and within states over time, in terms of how policy oriented the budget office is. The questions asked parallel concerns at the national level about whether and how the Office of Management and Budget can simultaneously maintain neutral competence and serve a president who is partisan and help accomplish his policy prior-

25. Robert Lee, "State Item Veto Issues in the 1990s," *Public Budgeting & Finance* 20, no. 2 (2000): 49–73; Thomas Lauth, "The Line Item Veto in Government Budgeting," *Public Budgeting & Finance* 16, no 2 (1996): 97–111; Louis Fisher, "The Item Veto Act of 1996: Heads Up from the States," *Public Budgeting & Finance* 17, no. 2 (1997): 3–17.

26. Howard F. Miller, "Behind the State Budget," *Public Budgeting & Finance* 1, no. 4 (1981): 68–75.

27. Karen Schuele Walton and Richard E. Brown, "State Legislators and State Auditors, Is there an Inherent Role Conflict?, *Public Budgeting & Finance* 10, no. 1 (1990): 3–12.

ities.[28] Goodman and Clynch later confirmed that the budget analysts make decisions using both political and technical information.[29]

Finally, though the governor and the budget office are supposed to curtail the demands of the agency heads through top-down guidance in the budget process, one article questions whether the agencies actually try to maximize their budget requests in the first place, or whether agency heads judge their success by a variety of criteria, with budget maximization relatively low on the list. The portrait that emerges of the motives of agency heads is a much more moderate one than the model of powerful executive in control of the budget would require. The agency heads ideally want to maintain programs and get a little more for urgent new needs. They value and work to preserve relations with the budget office and governor on one hand and the legislature on the other, and these goals lead them to moderate their requests. They fight when they need to protect existing staff from cut backs.[30]

Budget reform issues. The budget literature has sometimes seemed consumed by following whatever budget reforms, in process or format, are currently in progress. The pages of PB&F reflect the historical concerns from early pieces on the implementation of zero-based budgeting and its more moderate relative, target-based budgeting (sometimes called redirection) to articles on various phases of performance measurement and performance budgeting. Among the conclusions from this literature are (1) that reforms continue to evolve after adoption, sometimes becoming something quite different than initially intended, and (2) that many states adopt reforms when they are popular but some of them drop them after a few years of experimentation. A third conclusion is that performance measurement is viewed as useful for management purposes, but not necessarily for budgeting or allocation guidance.[31]

Robert Lee speculated that one possible reason for what he called "backsliding" is that reforms may be adopted only because they are popular or for symbolic reasons rather than because they are needed to solve some recurrent problem, and in those cases there is little

---

28. James Gosling, "State Budget Office and Policy Making," *Public Budgeting & Finance* 7, no. 1 (1987): 51–65; Kurt Thurmaier and James Gosling, "The Shifting Roles of State Budget Offices in the Midwest: Gosling Revisited," *Public Budgeting & Finance* 17, no. 4 (1997): 48–70.

29. Doug Goodman and Edward Clynch, "Budgetary Decision Making by Executive and Legislative Budget Analysts: The Impact of Political Cues and Analytical Information," *Public Budgeting & Finance* 24, no. 3 (2004): 20–37.

30. Sydney Duncombe and Richard Kinney, "Agency Budget Success: How It Is Defined by Budget Officials in Five Western States," *Public Budgeting & Finance* 7, no. 1 (1987): 24–37.

31. Jerry Mccaffery, "The Transformation of Zero Based Budgeting: Program Level Budgeting in Oregon," *Public Budgeting & Finance* 1, no. 4 (1981): 48–55; David Sallack and David N. Allen, "From Impact to Output: Pennsylvania's Planning-Programming Budgeting System in Transition," *Public Budgeting & Finance* 7, no. 1 (1987): 38–51; Henry M. Huckaby and Thomas P. Lauth, "Budget Redirection in Georgia State Government," *Public Budgeting & Finance* 18, no. 4 (1998): 36–45; Meagan M. Jordan and Merl M. Hackbart, "Performance Budgeting and Performance Funding in the States: A States Assessment," *Public Budgeting & Finance* 19, no. 1 (1999): 68–89; Katherine Willoughby, "Performance Measurement and Budget Balancing: State Government Perspective," *Public Budgeting & Finance* 24, no. 2 (2004): 21–39.

motivation to institutionalize the reforms. If the data collected is not used for decision making, it may eventually cease to be collected at all.[32]

Tax earmarking and tax expenditures. Tax earmarking means designating all or a portion of a particular revenue source for a specific, narrowly defined purpose. It is the opposite of a general tax that may be spent on any need. Earmarking constrains budgeting and makes it more difficult to balance the budget, but is often necessary when public distrust is high and the public fears that general taxes will be either misspent or spent for things they consider of lower priority. Most governments have a mix of earmarked and unearmarked revenues. The exact mix and changes over time may reflect differences in the level of public trust.

The articles in PB&F do not discuss earmarking in general, probably because budgeters do not have good data sources with which to track earmarking at the state level. Several articles discuss specific cases of earmarking, however. Charles Spindler looked at earmarking lottery revenue for education, to see whether earmarking a new source of revenue increased funding, or whether the state merely substituted earmarked for unearmarked revenue. Spindler found considerable substitution, perhaps adding to the public mistrust that leads to earmarking revenues in the first place.[33] Genie Stowers looked at a different function of earmarking, to protect programs against cutbacks.[34]

Earmarking is a strategy to protect a program from cuts or to help pass a new or increased tax in the face of massive public distrust. By comparison, tax expenditures are a way of adjusting the tax burden on classes of people or businesses after a tax has passed or has been increased. To some extent, tax breaks are used to head off a tax protest, reducing the burdens of those most negatively affected by the tax. Tax expenditures provide breaks or reductions in the taxes owed by businesses or individuals, without changing the structure of the tax itself. They may be used to increase the equity of a tax, to lure in businesses or encourage business expansion, or to do favors for powerful constituents.

For many states, tax expenditures have seemed free, and hence have been widely distributed by the state. How much is too much? Is this a tool that should be encouraged or discouraged? One approach to answering this question has been to compare an individual state's tax expenditures with the federal government's tax expenditures. This comparison emphasizes that the impact of tax expenditures depends on the tax structure as well as to whom and for what tax breaks are granted. Where states differ in tax structure from the federal government, one should expect the impact of tax expenditures would also differ. For example, the graduated nature of the federal income tax means that tax expenditures typically benefit the well to do considerably more than poorer people, a feature that has made some people oppose tax expenditures at the federal level. At the state level, however, state income taxes may be much less steeply graduated, and some are not graduated at all,

---

32. Robert Lee and Robert Burns, "Performance Measurement in State Budgeting: Advancement and Backsliding from 1990 to 1995," *Public Budgeting & Finance* 20, no. 1 (2000): 38–54; Robert Burns and Robert Lee, "The Ups and Downs of State Budget Process Reform: Experience from Three Decades," *Public Budgeting & Finance* 24, no. 3 (2004): 1–19.

33. Charles Spindler, "The Lottery and Education: Robbing Peter to Pay Paul," *Public Budgeting & Finance* 15, no. 3 (1995): 54–62.

34. Genie Stowers, "Earmarking as a Strategy against Budget Constraints: The San Francisco Children's Amendment," *Public Budgeting & Finance* 15, no. 4 (1995): 68–85.

which results in less upward bias of benefits from tax breaks, unless they are limited to wealthy businesses.[35]

Regardless of the impact of tax breaks on different income groups, some state officials feel they may be giving away too much revenue in the form of tax breaks. State officials want the freedom to give tax breaks, but also want to curtail the dollar value of additional breaks. Making the cost of tax breaks more visible in the form of tax expenditure reports that estimate the amounts lost each year seemed like a reasonable approach to helping instill some discipline. Some reformers also hoped that if tax expenditures were more visible, they could become part of the expenditure budget. Decision makers would be able to spend money on a program through direct outlays or through tax expenditures, or a combination of both, depending on what made more sense in context. One study of tax expenditure reports found that they were used in revenue decisions and policy deliberations, but not in expenditure decisions.[36]

While the idea is clear in principle, it is exceedingly difficult to measure tax breaks in practice, in part because what is a structural change and what is an exception to an existing structure is obscure. John Mikesell wrote a recent summary of the status of tax expenditure reporting in the states. He found that a majority of states reported tax expenditures in some way, but that many did not have a reasonable and consistent set of workable definitions underlying their reports. The huge variation between reports from different states makes it virtually impossible to compare amounts of revenue foregone across the states.[37]

Intergovernmental revenues. A number of articles in PB&F address intergovernmental finance and the states. Some address the shift of functions and reduction in funding to the states that marked the early Reagan presidency; some document the increase in problematic unfunded mandates from the federal government to the states. They also discuss the states' practice of giving unfunded mandates to their own local governments, and the process of trying to curtail this practice. On the one hand, continuing revenue limitations and recessions cause a decrease in state revenues that tempt state governments to pass on burdens to the local governments and to preempt local revenue sources for state use; but on the other hand, the states are responsible for the fiscal well-being of the local governments, if the local governments encounter serious fiscal stress, the states are responsible for bailing them out. The result of these two opposing pressures has varied from state to state, but in general, states have tried to buffer their local governments from extreme cuts. When Wisconsin encountered major budget gaps, both cyclical and structural, the governor threatened to terminate state aid to local governments, but in fact, did not do so.

One extraordinary finding was reported in a mini-symposium in 1984, namely that state legislatures became more active in making decisions on grants after the Reagan era devolution and budget cuts. Though there was less money to go around, and hence the decisions were probably not fun, the legislature became more involved in appropriating

---

35. Kyle I. Jen, "Tax Expenditures in Michigan: A Comparison to Federal Findings," *Public Budgeting & Finance* 22, no. 1 (2002): 31–45.

36. Jean Harris and S. A. Hicks, "Tax Expenditure Reporting: The Utilization of an Innovation," *Public Budgeting & Finance* 12, no. 3 (1992): 32–49.

37. John Mikesell, "Tax Expenditure Budgeting, Budget Policy, and Tax Policy: Confusion in the States," *Public Budgeting & Finance* 22, no. 4 (2002): 34–51.

grants, although up until that point, grants had pretty much been the domain of the governor. Legislatures may get more involved when programs are threatened with cuts than they do when new apparently free grant money is delivered from the federal government.[38]

QUESTIONS ONLY LIGHTLY TOUCHED ON IN PB&F

While the articles in PB&F on state budgeting have introduced a variety of different topics, many of them need some follow up. Other issues have not been raised in the pages of this journal, but might provide profitable lines of inquiry.

One set of issues that could be further explored is the cascade of actions and reactions that occur when states pass tax limits or pass tax breaks reducing the tax yields for the local governments and then filling in with state revenues for some or all of the revenue losses. There was scant mention of the fiscal centralization that results from such activities, and almost no tracking of the monies that states pay local governments to replace property taxes. What happens to those funds during a recession when state money becomes scarce? This problem is becoming more acute as states avoid tax increases during recession and emphasize cuts in spending instead. The Wisconsin case where shared revenues were threatened with termination raised the issue, but it has not been addressed for other states. More broadly, what is the extent of state centralization and what are the consequences of it? How do state payments to local governments hold up during recessions, what is the range of state behavior, and what contributes to one pattern or another?

A second issue only lightly touched on in the articles in PB&F is the idea of a budgetary base. Lauth introduced this issue years ago in an article that bears following up now. In practice, the budget base is a much more nuanced concept than originally appeared in the incrementalist literature. It is impossible to budget without some kind of base, so the questions arise, how is base budget defined, is the definition and use of base consistent from agency to agency, does it change over time, and if so, in response to what kind of pressures? Is the budget base explained anywhere in budget documents? Is the base not examined, as incrementalism argues, or partially examined, or episodically examined? Is it examined often enough? If anything, the importance of tracking how the concept of base is used has increased since Lauth's seminal article.[39]

Another issue that could be profitably investigated is the amount of discretion the governor has. The articles in PB&F have been so focused on comparing the governor's budget power versus the legislature's, and on the policy or technical orientation of the budget office, that the question of how much discretion the governor actually has to

38. Fred Doolittle, "State Legislatures and Federal Grants, an Overview," *Public Budgeting & Finance* 4, no. 2 (1984): 7–23.

39. Thomas Lauth, "Explaining the Budget Base in Georgia," *Public Budgeting & Finance* 7, no. 4 (1987): 72–82.

implement policy has been overlooked. How much of the budget is so locked up in entitlements, in debt repayment, in constitutional requirements and TELs, that there is little discretion for the governor. Does the amount of discretion exercised by the governor influence the amount of policy analysis done by the budget office, and could a reduction in governor's discretion explain Robert Lee's intriguing finding that program analysis was declining in some state's budget offices?[40]

The movement toward smaller government and limited taxation is well under way; one of its major strategies is to lock in policy preferences so they are nearly impossible to reverse later. To the extent that this policy locking is going on, discretion should be diminishing in the governor's office and consequently in the budget office. Why do policy analysis if there is no revenue with which to implement that policy, if the scope of public policy is diminishing? A secular decline in discretion may be exacerbated by recession and somewhat masked by boom, so the key research question is can we see a long-term trend backward to the days when budget offices were more mechanical and less policy oriented? If not, then what are the policies that budget offices are working on? In any given state, in any given fiscal environment, how much discretion is there, is it increasing or decreasing, and who gets to use it, and how is it maintained or recreated, and for how long? Are policy windows opened less wide and less often than in the past?

There was very little discussion in PB&F about the relationship of the agencies with the legislature, whether they submit their budget proposals to the legislature at the same time as they do to the governor, and if so, what the legislature does with these requests. Do these requests bypass the governor and budget office in more than a routing sense, does the legislature still use the governor's proposal as the basis for budget examination, is this a distinction without a difference, or does the simultaneous submission actually empower the legislature to second guess the governor, to support the agencies in those matters that are of concern to the legislators?

What are the legislators' budgetary concerns? When they get involved in the budgetary decision making, to what extent are they just interested in distributive pork projects, or protecting constituents from program cuts, and to what extent are they interested and active in formulating or debating public policy? There is almost nothing in these articles on legislative budgeting, when it occurs, and what it means. One piece on New York State raised the question about whether the legislative body should participate in the executive budget hearings arguing that they should not.[41] But in states like New York, where the legislature has been radically disempowered with respect to the budget, if the legislature has no input into the governor's budget proposal, it has almost no input into the budget.

These articles in PB&F made very little mention of ethics. One article dealt with the issue broadly, arguing that ethics statements and guidelines specifically dealing with

---

40. Robert D. Lee, Jr., "The Use of Program Analysis in State Budgeting: Changes between 1990 and 1995," *Public Budgeting & Finance* 17, no. 2 (1997): 18–36.

41. Miller, 1981.

budgeting were insufficient. What is considered ethical among budgeteers? How do particular values clash and with what outcomes? Is it ethical to hold a hearing on the budget after the decisions have been made? How are such hearings rationalized? Is it ethical to replace general funds for education with lottery revenues earmarked for education when the lottery was approved with the idea that it would increase education spending? What about the ethics of contracting or the ethics of internal borrowing from pensions, or external borrowing to close a budget gap? How do budgeteers feel about these issues, how do they deal with such issues when arise, and what do they do if they are pressed into doing something they consider ethically questionable? How well insulated are budget offices from pressures to do unethical things? Should they be buffered better than they are?

Budgeting is partly about accountability, and in recent years performance measurement has increased, and audits have expanded from purely financial to performance auditing as well. These issues raise a host of ethical concerns, including the integrity of the performance data and rewarding some agencies for misleading or selective information, withholding information that could be used against the governor or administration by the opposition party, or that could be used to cut budgets for programs that aid dependent populations. What about the ethics of leashing inspector generals (IGs), setting up offices to find and prevent corruption and waste, but limiting or directing their investigations in ways that will prevent embarrassment to the administration? Is this viewed as an ethical breach?

There were no articles in PB&F on corruption at the state level, despite its occasional burst into the news. When does corruption occur, or grow, and when does it decline, in response to what pressures or structures or conditions? Is there a level of ordinary corruption that is so common it is not viewed as corruption at all? What is considered below the line or above the line, by whom? Is there a difference between what is specified in organizational guidelines and what is informally accepted by public employees? How much serious corruption is there? How does it affect the budget? For example, if a state gets a reputation for dishonest bidding procedures, and potential bidders drop out, how much does that cost a state in increased expenditures? Presumably, the cost of kickbacks is recouped by businesses in higher prices to the state, how much does this cost the taxpayers? Is the scope of corruption increasing as the public sector increases the amount of contracting and the size and duration of contracts? Is there an acceptable level of corruption, below which the cost of monitoring exceeds the gains from increased integrity? Are there particular institutions that work better to keep government honest? Does the creation of an IG system with independence and broad powers help?

There was very little mention of the state-level IGs, though some 20-plus states have at least some IGs. There is enormous variation from one state to the next in whether they have any IGs, have one or a few for specific agencies, or have a whole system of IGs that covers the whole state or nearly the whole state government. These IG offices have different degrees of independence as well as differing scope of authority. What does this variation mean? Do the states without IGs have fewer scandals or higher trust levels from the public and hence feel no need to set up a watchdog agency, or do they have other institutional means of monitoring and dealing with corruption, waste, fraud, or abuse? Does having an IG system in place reduce waste, fraud, and abuse? Does the system work? How would anyone know? Of particular interest is a full-blown IG system with broad investigative powers that reports only to a department head and may be fired at will—a sort of fully owned and leashed junkyard dog.

The idea of an IG office that has broad powers of investigation but whose appointed head may be fired at will suggests a symbolic role for the IGs, to raise public support without exposing the administration to bad publicity from adverse findings. What other elements of budgeting at the state level are primarily symbolic and how do they work?

Scholars and practitioners made almost no mention of the issue of secrecy in the pages of PB&F. The issue was mentioned briefly in 1981, when one practitioner noted that if executive branch budget hearings become public the real decision making would just move elsewhere.[42] Secrecy was of relatively little concern in the early years of PB&F, when budget processes were generally available to public scrutiny, the documents were improving in terms of ability to communicate with the public, and the trend seemed to be toward more openness and more citizen participation.

In recent years, secrecy has become an important issue. With increases in tax expenditures—revenues that are never collected and so generally do not appear in the budget—and increases in contracting, transparency is diminishing in many places even without the specific intent to make decisions out of public view. Creative capital finance and complex rescue schemes are sometimes too difficult for the public to follow. And when budget gaps are closed through sleight of hand, pushing expenditures off into future years, borrowing internally from pension funds, and selling future revenue streams from tobacco settlements at discounted rates, the public cannot possibly penetrate what is going on or how much the decisions cost. How should secrecy in budgeting be measured, what are its dimensions, and what causes it to increase or reduce its scope? When is secrecy a by-product of other policies and when is it an explicit decision to exclude particular information from budget documents or release information in totally disaggregated fashion, or charge disproportionate fees for freedom of information requests? What causes budgeting to occur behind closed doors, and how much of the decision making goes on there? What causes the formal process to continue in public while the actual one becomes less visible?

While several articles in PB&F deal with contracting at the state level, they do not deal with the aspect of contracting that influences the openness of the budget process. Budgeteers have not yet worked out a way of making larger and more significant contracts appear in the budget, so even if the rest of the budget is open and clear, the more contracting a state does, the less the public knows about operations.

One additional topic that was skimmed over lightly in these past 25 years of articles in PB&F is partisanship and its effect on budgeting. Some of the articles address the way budget staff make decisions, and how they include policy guidance and concerns, but

---

42. Miller, 1981.

they tend to skirt the broader issue of party and particularly, party contention. One article raised the curious term "fiscal brinksmanship," the process of the minority party trying to make the majority party look bad or force it to make difficult decisions that will create enemies. The result of fiscal brinksmanship might be to lower taxes, a highly popular move, forcing the administration to wrestle with spending cuts (a highly un-popular move) to rebalance the budget. This phenomenon requires further exploration, especially perhaps when the result is to violate the norms of budgetary balance. Beyond that, whether the governor controls comfortable margins in both house of the legislature, or whether he or she is of the opposite party from the legislative majority may influence the budget process, such as whether budget agreements are negotiated behind closed doors with legislative leaders, how many legislative prerogative projects must be granted to get support for budget legislation, and whether the governor exercises his or her veto against legislative add-ons. It is difficult to begin to unravel how the budget process works in many states without understanding something about partisan politics.

The authors writing in PB&F have done only a relatively limited amount of looking at budgeting over time, and hence have not spent much time theorizing about how processes work themselves out over time, or what lengthens or shortens the arc of the pendulum when processes shift back and forth between extremes. As a group, we tend to see each crisis as a stand-alone event rather than looking for the potential turnaround points. But with 25 years of solid research in hand, it is time to begin to theorize about our findings. Which of the processes we have observed are truly cyclical, reoccurring in nearly the same manner at fixed or variable intervals, and which ones are sets of actions and reactions which leave budget processes and outcomes in a different position than they were initially, that change the playing field? Which processes are sticky, hard to reverse? What does equilibrium consist of, have we seen any examples of this kind of stability, when and how does it occur, what destabilizes an existing equilibrium? Is equilibrium to be sought after, is it good?

We have also done little theorizing about what is necessary in a budget process. Are there minimum conditions necessary for budget processes to be stable or to facilitate democracy, in terms of accountability, predictability, minority rights and participation, openness, sufficient time for and information for decision making? What kind of and how much historical information should be available to budgeteers? How can researchers and practitioners distinguish between changes to the budget process that shift power here or there for short-term political and policy gains and changes that help strengthen the norms of balance or accountability and transparency? What kind of template can we use to compare budget processes over time and between states that will focus on meaningful and interpretable differences?

SUGGESTED RESEARCH STRATEGIES

Reviewing 25 years of articles on state budgeting in PB&F reveals some patterns and suggests some ways that the field as a whole can make future research more efficient, cumulative, and explanatory. Most of the research reported in PB&F is based on emerging policy problems—something happens, or is proposed, and researchers go out to investigate it. The federal government adopts an item veto, researchers go to look at the experience of the states with item vetoes. A number of states are planning to put TABOR amendments on the ballot, so researchers pay more attention to the state or states that have already adopted this measure and try to learn from it or them. The federal government shifts responsibility for some programs to the states while cutting funding to pay those programs—researchers monitor the response of the states.

If some issues reoccur with some frequency, then researchers get to revisit the topic and build on what they learned in the last round, comparing, for example, reactions with prior recessions to current ones. During a recession when states are desperate to close budget gaps, research increases on rainy-day funds, their functioning, and their appropriate size.[43] When the level of mandating goes up or its expense becomes problematic, researchers examine the extent of mandating and the effectiveness of controls developed to combat unfunded mandates.[44]

There have been some major exceptions to the responsive model of choosing research topics, some efforts to maintain data over time and look for changes. This kind of monitoring effort can be difficult to maintain because it is not clear what will turn up, and the year-to-year changes may be minor or so disaggregated it is difficult to see patterns. Sometimes, though, these monitoring articles have raised significant issues. Robert Lee's surveys monitoring budget reforms and their implementation over time turned up a period of retrenchment of particular budget reform adoptions, which he called backsliding.[45] Once such a finding is brought to light and named, researchers ought to go in and figure out what is happening, what it means. Perhaps because Lee promised to explore his own findings, others have not, leaving readers hungry for some answers. Does the reason for adoption or the match between existing problems and the reform influence the institutionalization of reforms? What makes states more vulnerable to passing fads of budget reform? Of the ones that persist over time, how much do they change, do they in essence become something else in order to suit new administrations, while maintaining the same name or format? It is easy to understand how

43. Russell S. Sobel and Randall G. Holcombe, "The Impact of State Rainy Day Funds in Easing State Fiscal Crises during the 1990–1991 Recession," *Public Budgeting & Finance* 16, no. 3 (1996): 28–48; James W. Douglas and Ronald Keith Geddie, "State Rainy Day Funds and Fiscal Crises: Rainy Day Funds in the 1990–1991 Recession Revisited," *Public Budgeting & Finance* 22, no. 1 (2002): 19–30; Yilin Hou, "What Stabilizes State General Fund Expenditures in Downturn Years, Budget Stabilization Fund, or General Fund Unreserved Undesignated Balance?", *Public Budgeting & Finance* 23, no. 3 (2003): 64–91; Yilin Hou, "Budget Stabilization Fund: Structural Features of the Enabling Legislation," *Public Budgeting & Finance* 24, no. 3 (2004): 38–64.
44. Catherine Lovell and Hanria Egan, "Fiscal Notes and Mandate Reimbursement in the 50 States," *Public Budgeting & Finance* 3, no. 3 (1983): 3–18.
45. Lee and Burns, 2000.

some complicated reform that requires lots of effort and results in data that is not used in decision making could be abandoned, but less easy to see why simpler reforms might be left by the wayside. Abandonments might indicate processes that redistribute power in ways that were not agreed to by the parties and which only become clear over time. In any case, these abandonments are puzzling, and unraveling the puzzle is likely to create greater understanding not only of the reforms but also of state budgeting and institutions.

The field needs some more proactive monitoring of key issues, such as the relative powers of the legislature and executive and intergovernmental relations, including state centralization, mandating, both funded and unfunded, and shared revenues. It would be useful to keep data on state levels of earmarking over time. Some of this used to be done by Advisory Commission on Intergovernmental Relations, but with the demise of that federal agency, many of the key issues are no longer monitored, and hence changes cannot be observed.

A second recommendation is that we need more and better typologies of states in order to help pick case studies. Too often individual state studies are ignored because it is unclear what they represent, the extent to which they are unique and the extent to which they can be generalized. In lieu of functioning typologies that outline the key features of states that influence budgeting, researchers often grab whatever they can find, the size of the state, for example, or its taxable wealth, or divided government. In what ways do these characteristics influence budgeting in a state? Other features may be better indicators. For example, the level of earmarking of state revenues varies enormously from state to state. Because it often reflects public distrust of government, it might be a useful way to characterize states. What other features of budgeting might cluster along with this one? Or we could group states on a continuum from most extreme legislatively dominated to most extreme executive dominated. What differences in budgeting would one expect from states characterized in this fashion? Or perhaps states should be characterized in terms of the scope of services they provide. Political scientists have sometimes grouped states by the level of contestation between political parties. Does the degree of dominance of the majority party substantially influence budgeting, and if so, in what ways? At the level of nations, comparative researchers have worked out corruption indexes, would it make sense to do the same for the states? If so, how would those indexes correlate with descriptions of budgeting in the state or other measures of public trust?

If we can design a series of relevant typologies, researchers can pick the one that makes the most sense for the dependent variable of interest. Do states that are higher or lower on the corruption index also score higher or lower on a secrecy index or on an index of symbolic politics in budgeting? Are states with more balanced powers between the legislature and the governor more open than states with less balanced powers? Are they more efficient? Are states that have high gubernatorial powers also high in secrecy? Most important if researchers are comparing the budget adaptations of California and New York, they would be less likely to say these are two big and rich states, and hence similar in some key way, when one of them is out on the extreme of disempowering the legislature in budgeting and the other much closer to a balanced powers model.

If something happened in one state, we would not have to reason backward, searching for possible antecedents of the events in question. We could reason forward. For example, we could monitor the high tax level states, predicting certain things about them, perhaps that they are likely to give away more tax breaks, and hence are more likely to have adopted tax expenditure reporting, or they are more likely to have adopted TELs, formally or informally. If those predictions do not pan out, they set up research questions that can help us get deeper into the material. What was wrong with our original model, what did it not include that turned out to be significant, and is that factor likely to become stronger or more important in the future? Was our model generally predictive, but off on a few outliers? If so, what was it about those outliers that gave them a different look?

Third, it should be useful to add to our institutional focus a perspective that pays attention to functions and how they are performed. It may matter less whether the budget office does policy analysis than whether policy analysis is performed at all, and if so, by whom, with what effect. The question of whether the budget office does policy analysis assumes that the budget office is the item of concern, rather than whether the function of analyzing policy is performed, by whom, and how it is integrated into the budget. After we know who, and how much of it they do, we can ask what difference it makes where the function is performed or whether it is performed at all.

Consider a second example of how this expanded view might work. The traditional institutional view of IGs would focus on that office. If one adds a more functional approach, one would also ask what agencies perform similar or identical functions in one state that IGs play in another state. If those functions are adequately performed by other offices, maybe that state does not need an IG system. Trying to evaluate the efficacy of IG offices between states that have them and those that do not is likely to founder completely if the states that do not have IGs have other institutions that perform the same functions. Also, this focus makes it clearer that in examining IGs, one needs to look at what range of functions out of the total possible they are performing, and whether other agencies in the state are performing the rest. Which ones remain uncovered and with what effect?

The same reasoning applies to evaluating the effects of rainy day funds. Rainy-day funds may not be necessary if other funds or year-end balances play the same or similar role, or if the state has a good balance of elastic and inelastic revenue sources making rainy-day funds less necessary, or if the state borrows internally during recessions (say from pension funds) and pays back during booms. How a state manages the economic cycles of boom and bust is a better research question than does the state have a rainy-day fund and if so, did they manage to get through the recession more easily than states without rainy-day funds or severely underfunded ones. What would be useful here is an index of prevention of and perhaps a second and related one of preparation for recessions. One component of that preparation might be rainy-day funds. A state might score low on prevention, with highly elastic revenue sources, no provision for returning excess revenues, and a habit of program expansion or tax cuts during booms, but also score reasonably high on preparation for recession-related gaps, with buffer funds fully funded, or flexible fund structures that allow shifting of revenues, and a pattern of borrowing, internally and externally, during recession and paying back during boom. Or vice versa, a state might be high on prevention but low on preparation. The problematic states would be the ones in between, with low prevention and low preparation for response.

Taking a broader perspective about how particular functions are accomplished not only allows the stringing together of small problems, but suggests a way of tracking evolution over time toward problem solutions, and a way of monitoring what moves a state along that sequence and what holds it up. For example, consider the issue of tax expenditures and the granting of tax breaks. By itself, this issue is important in states, it represents a major source of revenue loss. But by itself, it is difficult to see what the other alternatives are that the state did not choose. Tax expenditures are particular breaks to particular groups of individuals, either to improve equity of an inequitable tax, or to stimulate the economy during recession, or just to satisfy political demands and fend off blame for possibly losing an industry or business. But there are alternatives to tax expenditures, such as revising the tax structure so that it is less burdensome on particular groups and more equitable, or implementing tax and or spending limits that reduce the tax burdens for everyone. Which of these options or what combination of options does any given state pick? The literature suggests that tax limitations are not necessarily triggered by the level of taxation, but they may be in some states. Considering tax expenditures, tax levels, and equity-based tax reforms together gives much more theoretical and explanatory power than considering any of these issues by themselves.

Finally, in generating research questions, we need to pay more attention to what is not there. What about the states that do not have IG systems? What about the states that do not report their tax expenditures? What about the states that do not pass along unfunded mandates to the local governments or cut their shared revenues during recession? What about the states that have low levels of earmarking? What about the states that do not run "gaps" during recessions? What about states that do not have TELs? How about states that have "backslid" on budget format or process reforms?

What can we learn from these states and their experiences? Are they managing their economy better, are they richer or more prosperous, less corrupt, or better managed, do they have more or less party contestation? Have they reformed their taxes and so have less need of tax expenditures, have they found a formula that helps them resist the demands of major industries for tax breaks, are their tax systems more equitable, or do they just not collect much in the way of taxes? Are there models or typologies we can develop to explain what is happening in the states that seem to defy the trends?

In 25 years, budgeteers have described the major trends in state budgeting in PB&F. Most of this research has been episodic, driven by current events. Depth is better in those areas where problems reoccur and researchers can look over developments that occurred over time, but we have much left to do. There are a number of topics we have barely touched, and our research strategies could use some improvement. The field is poised for takeoff, but we may need some more infrastructure before much of it happens, in the form of trend monitoring and typology building. If we can do that, our studies will be more proactive, we will be able to predict and test explanatory models, and we will be able to accumulate results from different studies.

Chapter 3

Congressional Budgeting at Age 30: Is It Worth Saving?*

ROY T. MEYERS and PHILIP G. JOYCE

The congressional budget process is now 30 years old. We review this history to describe why the process was adopted, how it has evolved, and what it has produced. In the early years, the process institutionalized but did not prevent the creation of a significant deficit. During the 1990s, the process was improved and the deficit was converted to a surplus. Since 1999, both the budget process and budget discipline have greatly eroded. We propose some technical and organizational changes that might improve the process, but in the end, what is most needed are leaders who will promote fiscal responsibility for the federal government.

INTRODUCTION

The vaudevillian Jimmy Durante often complained that "Everyone wants to get inna the act!" Regarding the Act whose history and effects we cover in this article—the Congressional Budget and Impoundment Control Act of 1974 (CBA)—everyone seems to have an opinion of whether it has been a success or not. And much like tastes in humor differ widely, from people who guffaw at broad slapstick to those who are mildly amused by subtle wit, there is no consensus on the Congressional Budget Act.

We do not intend that this article will produce such a consensus. Instead, we will describe some of the major developments of the past 30 years, and make some observations that could help readers think about the future of the congressional budget process. For some readers, there will be ironic humor in what we present—either as illustrations of the foibles of humans trying to deal with complicated problems, or as depressing "bad jokes."

Roy T. Meyers is Professor of Political Science and Director of the Sondheim Public Affairs Scholars Program at the University of Maryland, Baltimore County, MD. He can be reached at *meyers@umbc.edu*. Philip Joyce is Professor of Public Policy and Public Administration at the George Washington University. He can be reached at *pgjoyce@gwu.edu*.

*This chapter was originally published in *Public Budgeting & Finance*, Vol. 25, Silver Anniversary Edition (2005): 68–82.

THE CONGRESSIONAL BUDGET ACT OF 1974: WHY THEN OR AT ALL?

The CBA was somewhat of an accident of history. Budgeting in Congress had long been problematic. In fact, it was difficult to call what happened in Congress "budgeting," given that most definitions of budgeting have something to do with the planned allocation of scarce resources. Instead, Congress passed laws that affected the fisc in a disconnected manner, with no "bottom line" and no coordination between committees aside from informal party leadership meetings or floor debates.

Budgetary conflicts during the latter 1960s and early 1970s were accurately described by Schick as "the 7-year war."[1] The Great Society and the Vietnam War had created a classic "guns AND butter" problem, and insufficiently tight monetary policy led to higher inflation. While inflation partially covered deficits through bracket creep increases in revenues, it also widened deficits through its effects on entitlements. In the run-up to the 1972 election, Congress and the president held a bidding war over Social Security, which produced a huge increase in the benefit base, plus future indexing of benefits through a technically flawed, overly generous cost-of-living adjustment. Unforeseen were the looming oil embargoes and macroeconomic stagflation.

But given the powerful pull of the status quo in American politics, traditional congressional budgeting may have continued unabated. What intervened was President Nixon's postlandslide hubris. He impounded funds that had been appropriated by Congress, in some cases over his veto. This challenge to the legislative power of the purse was politically foolish—its unmatched spending power makes Congress admired cross-nationally and helps protect incumbents from strong electoral challenges. Ironically, it was Nixon who then signed the CBA into law in 1974, as by then he was so weakened by Watergate that he was barely holding on to the position that he would soon vacate under threat of impeachment.

The 1974 midterm election that followed Nixon's resignation triggered, completion of congressional restructuring that had begun in the late 1950s. Then, Congress was seen as a "club" ruled by its longest-serving and typically most conservative members.[2] Fenno and Wildavsky portrayed committees and chairs as effective protectors of the status quo. But the civil rights movement and the 89th Democratic Congress challenged these traditional forces, which were further weakened in 1975 when chairs became subject to the Caucus, subcommittees were empowered, and "sunshine" became the standard. That is, just as Congress was asserting its budgetary authority against an imperial presidency, it was also decentralizing power and opening its actions to public view—neither of which made it easy to budget.[3]

---

1. Allen Schick, *Congress and Money* (Washington, DC: The Urban Institute, 1980).

2. Donald R. Matthews, *U.S. Senators and Their World* (New York: Random House, 1960); Robert A. Caro, *Master of the Senate* (New York: Alfred A. Knopf, 2002).

3. Nelson W. Polsby, *How Congress Evolves* (New York: Oxford University Press, 2004); John Elwood, "The Great Exception: The Congressional Budget Process in the Age of Decentralization," in *Congress Reconsidered*, eds. L. C. Dodd and B. L. Oppenheimer, 3rd ed. (Washington, DC: Congressional Quarterly, 1985), 315–342.

Like most legislation, the CBA represented compromise. Enacted to end a war, it set out a new field on which players could variously reach agreements and express conflicts—and perhaps even go to war again. And, of course, they did.

THE CONGRESSIONAL BUDGET ACT—AS WRITTEN AND AS PRACTICED

The federal budget process has been adapted regularly to reflect contemporaneous concerns. In their work on American political development, Orren and Skowronek describe such changes with the social science jargon "intercurrence." Stripped of some of its complications, this concept means that institutions are internally contradictory because they have been designed over time by people with different goals and understandings.[4]

In the case of the CBA, a common way of describing this confusing reality is that it layered new institutions over existing ones, rather than starting from scratch with a new design. That is, to the existing appropriations, authorizations, and revenues committees, and the standard legislative processes they led, the CBA added budget committees and a formal budget process. To the existing support agencies of the General Accounting Office (GAO) and the Congressional Research Service, the CBA added the new Congressional Budget Office (CBO).

"Layered" suggests a geological process of sedimentation, and after 30 years there are other geological metaphors that describe subsequent budgetary practices. For example, it was not long into CBA implementation that there was a volcanic shift in American politics, from a state—California—that knows such events. Proposition 13 and the subsequent election of Ronald Reagan created a new foundation for the budget process—antitax politics—and the basis for Republican dominance of the nation's politics.[5]

This development was especially important given the already built-in growth in spending from entitlements; the two together created a structural deficit, much like a fault zone with two clashing tectonic plates. The resulting tension has yet to be released by a policy earthquake. However, political and economic conditions have caused important metamorphic adaptations of the budget process. These changes can be grouped into three distinct "fiscageological" periods:

- The Bedrock Period—1974–1980, during which the structure and institutions of the Congressional budget process were established.
- The Orogenic[6] Period—1981–1997, which shifted the budget process to focus on eliminating the deficit, a goal that was finally achieved at the end of this period.

---

4. Karen Orren and Stephen Skowronek, *The Search for American Political Development* (New York: Cambridge University Press, 2004).

5. Sheldon Pollack, *Refinancing America: The Republican Antitax Agenda* (Albany: State University of New York Press, 2003).

6. For those readers who are wistfully hoping we meant to refer to "erogeny," we must inform you that "orogeny" is the process of mountain formation.

- The Erosion Period—1998–2005, which saw the elimination first of the consensus goal of a balanced budget, and then the destruction of the procedures that had helped balance the budget.

The Bedrock Period (1974–1980)

The early years of the budget process were predictably characterized by jockeying for position between old institutions and new. After all, the revenue and appropriations committees had never intended that the new budget process would threaten their views from the summit. The Budget Committees were expected to be relatively weak, particularly in the House because its membership would be rotated and drawn largely from other committees. In the Senate, as many Senators already sat on influential committees, this reduced their desire to serve on the novice Budget Committee.

Nor was the process generally expected to produce major changes in budget outcomes. While deficits were nearly universally decried, there was nothing about the process—such as constitutional spending caps and revenue floors—that would "guarantee" smaller deficits. Nonetheless, the budget process was to have a small bias toward deficit reduction, for although the Budget Committees were relatively weak, newly established budget procedures enabled these committees to press for lower deficits. The Budget Committees were to begin each year by asking other committees for their recommendations ("views and estimates"). They then were to develop a concurrent budget resolution—a congressional plan for the budget that would not be sent to the president, as would a regular law. The resolution was to set targets for aggregates (spending-budget authority and outlays, revenues, deficit/surplus, and debt) and for budget functions (sectors of the budget, such as "natural resources"), after a floor debate on priorities and a conference between the House and Senate.

These functional targets would be "crosswalked" (i.e., transformed in categorization) to committee jurisdictions—a difficult task as budget functions and committee jurisdictions were not well aligned, and as committees did not want the Budget Committees to usurp their authorities over policy decisions. The targets would be enforced by a combination of independent information and procedural hurdles. The CBO would provide cost estimates for legislative proposals, and help the Budget Committees keep a running tab of the budgetary impacts of legislation, known as "scorekeeping." The main procedural tool was the parliamentary point of order, the traditional mechanism for resolving turf battles between appropriations and authorization committees.

In 1946, Congress had first attempted a comprehensive budget process reform; it completely failed.[7] This time, Congress did much better; by the beginning of the 1980s, most of the provisions of the CBA were institutionalized. Congress annually adopted a

---

7. Ralph K. Huitt, "Congressional Organization and Operatings in the Field of Money and Credit," in Commission on Money and Credit, *Fiscal and Debt Management Policies* (Englewood Cliffs, NJ: Prentice-Hall, 1963).

budget resolution. CBO's economic projections, cost estimates, and analyses acted as a counterweight to the numbers coming out of the Office of Management and Budget (OMB). The leadership of the Budget Committees, particularly Senator Edmund Muskie (D-ME), led serious debates on priorities, and Congress symbolically challenged presidential budget policies, particularly in last year of the Carter administration. Yet the congressional budget process still was not very important, particularly in making large changes to the policy status quo.

The Orogenic Period (1981–1997)

In contrast, during most years from 1981 to 1997, the congressional budget process was supremely important, so much so that it was not uncommon to hear complaints (with some justification) that policy making had become overly "fiscalized." How did the pre-1980 molehill become the post-1981 mountain range?

Here again we have irony, for the next step in strengthening congressional budgeting began with another assertive president. In this case, President Reagan, not Congress, challenged the status quo, by reducing individual income tax rates, scaling back domestic discretionary spending, and pushing a large defense buildup. Reagan exploited the new congressional budget process to enact these policies. Consider reconciliation. A relatively unimportant procedural device in the original CBA, it was envisioned as part of the second budget resolution, which was intended to adjust spring wishes to fall political reality. In 1980, however, the Budget Committees experimented with reconciliation as a method of putting teeth into the budget resolution. Just one year later, the second budget resolution was dropped and reconciliation enabled reductions in mandatory spending; it also effectively cut discretionary appropriations by reducing authorization ceilings—an approach that has not been repeated.[8]

Once the procedure of reconciliation became more important, it became the preferred way of enacting major policy changes. As the CBA establishes limits on debate for reconciliation bills, reconciliation can be used by a small majority (i.e., less than 60 votes) to stop filibusters and other dilatory tactics used by Senate minorities. As a result, not only was much of the initial Reagan program enacted using reconciliation, but so were the less publicized 1982 and 1984 tax *increases* that were enacted to partially offset the 1981 tax cut. Further, the 1990, 1993, and 1997 deficit reduction actions were enacted using reconciliation, as was the 1996 welfare reform legislation.

As important as reconciliation was, its influence should not be overestimated. While reconciliation could be used by the Budget Committees to pressure authorizing and revenue committees to consider deficit reductions, these committees could also resist.

---

8. Allen Schick, *Reconciliation and the Congressional Budget Process* (Washington, DC: American Enterprise Institute, 1981); Committee on the Budget, U.S. House of Representatives, "A Review of the Reconciliation Process," October 1984; Richard Doyle, "Congress, the Deficit, and Budget Reconciliation," *Public Budgeting & Finance* 16, no. 4 (1996): 59–81.

Even during this orogenic period, it was not uncommon that reconciliation savings included in first drafts of budget resolutions were watered down during markup, and that the assumptions implicit to reconciliation directives in enacted budget resolutions were ignored by targeted committees. And while reconciliation helped the congressional majority adopt a strong position within Congress, this did not ensure success against a combative president. In 1995–1996 the new Republican majority, emboldened by the apparent public endorsement of the "Contract with America," attempted to enact large changes to Medicare and Medicaid through reconciliation. They failed, as Bill Clinton used his persuasive powers to convince the public that the changes envisioned in the reconciliation bill were reckless bad ideas.[9]

A decade earlier saw the failure of another ambitious plan. After a majority of Senators firmly grasped the "third rail" by proposing entitlement savings (including in Social Security), President Reagan and Speaker Tip O'Neill jointly threw the switch when they refused to go along. In anger and frustration, Congress then adopted "Gramm–Rudman–Hollings" (GRH), formally known as the Balanced Budget and Emergency Deficit Control Act. GRH set fixed deficit targets, with a balanced budget required by five years, and created a "sequestration" enforcement procedure that would be automatically triggered if these targets were breached. Sequestration was dubbed by Senator Rudman as "a bad idea whose time has come."[10] In fact, the entire law was flawed and should never had been adopted. Its fixed targets quickly became too ambitious as a weaker-than-expected economy and a lack of budgetary control created larger baseline deficits. Sequestration was an empty threat: it would cut mostly discretionary spending when mandatory spending was not controlled by reconciliation, and Congress could stop sequestration simply by changing the law. Deficit targets applied not to actual deficits, but to the projected deficits in the president's budget and budget resolution. This inspired much gimmickry; the "rosy scenario" of the early 1980s was replicated in the latter 1980s, just with bigger and scarier numbers.[11]

While the 1981–1989 period was one of building the deficit mountain, 1990–1997 was a time of tearing it down. A large decline in the stock market eventually led Congress and President George H. W. Bush to meet at Andrews Air Force Base for a "budget summit," and by the end of 1990, significant policy and procedural responses were in place. In place of GRH's balanced budget target without any policies to attain that position, the bipartisan Omnibus Budget Reconciliation Act of 1990 enacted tax increases and spending cuts that significantly reduced deficits. Another big cut in the deficit followed the 1992 election prodding of deficit hawk Ross Perot, who received the largest percentage of the popular vote by a third-party candidate since Eugene Debs; without any Republican support, in

9. David Maraniss and Micheal Weisskopf, *Tell Newt to Shut Up!* (New York: Simon & Schuster, 1996).

10. Senator Warren Rudman, as quoted in Edward Wehr, "Congress Enacts Far-Reaching Budget Measure," *Congressional Quarterly Weekly Report* 43 (1985), p. 2604.

11. Joseph White and Aaron Wildavsky, *The Deficit and the Public Interest* (Berkeley: University of California Press, 1989).

1993 the Democrats enacted a large reconciliation bill that relied heavily on tax increases. In 1997, another, smaller reconciliation bill made changes in Medicare, which had begun to loom large in the baseline; many of these savings were "given back" in succeeding years.[12]

The 1990 procedural response to large deficits, the Budget Enforcement Act, exemplified a lesson that was learned through the GRH debacle—procedures work best when they hold policy makers accountable for things that they can control (policies) rather than holding them responsible for events that they cannot control (such as the size of the economy in a given year).[13] For the first half of the 1990s, caps limited total discretionary spending to roughly their 1991 level; post–Cold War savings in defense offset increases for domestic spending. The PAYGO rule required that any mandatory spending increases and tax cuts be offset by savings in these areas.

By fiscal year 1998, these policy and process changes contributed substantially to the development of the first budget surplus in roughly three decades. The budget process itself did not force elected leaders to eliminate the budget deficit; instead, Presidents George H. W. Bush and Clinton, and Congress, decided to exercise responsible fiscal leadership, and then redesigned and honored the budget process to enable this result. There was also a significant amount of luck involved. President Bush had the *bad* luck to have his political courage "rewarded" by a recession, which apparently, but not really, eroded all of the deficit reduction that had been gained in 1990. His reward was complete by 1992, when conservative Republicans put minimal effort into his reelection campaign because the president had abandoned his blustering "Read my lips—No new taxes!" pledge from the 1988 nomination convention. On the other hand, President Clinton and the Republican Congress had the *good* fortune to have their deficit reduction actions accompanied by the unprecedented sustained peacetime growth, and the investment bubble, of the late 1990s.[14]

The Erosion Period (1998–2005)

The great French caricaturist Daumier once drew Sisyphus pushing a boulder labeled "budget" up a steep incline. Perhaps the endless task of making difficult budget decisions is suitable punishment for the typical misdeeds of politicians. But in 1998, good deeds were rewarded; a full four years ahead of the schedule projected when the 1997 budget resolution was enacted, the federal budget came into surplus. The boulder had been pushed to the top of the incline, and then seemed about to rise far above it, like a hot air balloon. This "balloon" was an illusion created by the overheated economy and optimistic baseline con-

---

12. Daniel J. Palazzolo, *Done Deal? The Politics of the 1997 Budget Agreement* (New York: Chatham House, 1999).

13. See "The Budget Process and Deficit Reduction," Chapter 6 of Congressional Budget Office, *The Economic and Budget Outlook: Fiscal Years 1994–1998* (January 1993). For a less charitable interpretation, see Richard Doyle and Jerry McCaffery, "The Budget Enforcement Act: The Path to No-Fault Budgeting," *Public Budgeting & Finance* 11, no. 1 (1991): 25–40.

14. Philip G. Joyce and Roy T. Meyers, "Budgeting during the Clinton Presidency," *Public Budgeting & Finance* 21, no. 1 (2001): 1–21.

The Evolution of Public Finance and Budgeting

ventions. But the boulder did stay at the top of the incline for several years, until cascading rivers of black ink undermined its supports.

Budget surpluses were a positive development for the country, but were tremendously surprising. Their arrival created an existential crisis in the budget process: if the goal is no longer to reduce deficit x percent by year Z, what should the goal be? (Luckily for the Concord Coalition, at least, this crisis was short lived.)

The last year of the Clinton presidency provided a temporary answer. To prevent the Republicans from cutting taxes, Clinton campaigned to "Save Social Security First." Unfortunately, the administration framed its position as protecting trust fund surpluses, especially with Vice President Al Gore's campaign mantra about a "lockbox," which would protect Social Security surpluses. As they did not make the better argument that running general budget surpluses would build future debt capacity—good for the economy and Social Security—they failed to build a lasting political consensus.

A temporary agreement did emerge, however, around the goal of balancing the budget excluding the Social Security surpluses; both 2000 presidential campaigns embraced this goal. Once in office, President George W. Bush promised that his policies—tax cuts and increased spending (e.g., for a prescription drug benefit)—would cost only the non-Social Security surplus. CBO and OMB projections of the effect of the tax cut issued in the summer of 2001 were watched closely to determine whether this magic line had been crossed.

September 11 changed all that in a hurry. While there was some indication even prior to that date that the tax cuts and the economic downturn were putting the stated goal in jeopardy, the rapid agreement between the president and Congress to provide $40 billion of immediate assistance to victims blew the lid off of the fictional lockbox. This immediate cost was then dwarfed by the commitment to improve homeland security and by the war in Afghanistan. As the economy weakened, the Republicans promoted the supposed stimulative effects of their tax cuts, even though most of the cuts were to occur later. In the short time that it took for the administration's attention to turn to Iraq, which was supposed to be a nearly costless war, prudence was demolished as the primary goal of budgetary policy. By postulating a condition of continual "crisis," the government declared that large budget deficits (beyond those offset by trust fund surpluses) were completely acceptable.[15] Or as Vice President Dick Cheney repeatedly commented during the campaign, "Reagan proved that deficits don't matter." Cheney would be right if he was referring to the short-term political effects, but most economists argue that sustained, large budget deficits create significant economic dangers.[16]

---

15. See Philip G. Joyce, "Federal Budgeting after September 11th: A Whole New Ballgame, or Is It Déjà Vu All over Again?", *Public Budgeting & Finance* 25 (2005): 15–31.

16. Laurence Ball and N. Gregory Mankiw, "What Do Budget Deficits Do?" National Bureau of Economic Research Working Papers (1996).

To continue with the metaphor of erosion, these policy changes resemble another California geological phenomenon—the massive mud slide. Swept away by these policy changes were the budget procedures that contributed to deficit elimination: the discretionary spending caps and PAYGO were intentionally allowed to expire at the conclusion of fiscal year 2002. Keeping them would have forced difficult policy choices, and after the extraordinarily competitive and disputed election of 2000, the Republicans decided not to risk being blamed for such choices, as were Clinton and the congressional Democrats after 1993.

But the demise of these procedures did not occur all at once. From the beginning, the discretionary caps had an exception for emergencies. During most of the 1990s, contrary to the fears of some, almost all declared "emergencies" were legitimate ones, such as for major hurricane damage. But those fears came true once budget surpluses materialized. The best example was the declaration of the 2000 census as an emergency, which presumably would surprise the authors of the U.S. Constitution, which requires a decennial census.

Mandatory spending offers even more telling examples. During the 1990s, PAYGO had effectively warded off tax cuts and additions to entitlements with the uncomfortable question "How are you going to pay for that?" But eventually this constraint could not prevent a political majority from doing something big. One evasion technique was to create accounting illusions with the 10-year horizon for budget projections. This term period was an extension of, first, a three-year period, and then a five-year one, to prevent costs from being pushed into the years immediately following the end of the projections. The reported costs of the Bush tax cuts were artificially lowered from the intentions of the sponsors by assuming tax increases in the latter years of the projection period as the tax cuts reached their formally scheduled expiration dates. Another technique for enabling deficit-increasing legislation was to lowball likely mandatory costs, as happened with the Medicare prescription drugs legislation. But by this time PAYGO's de facto demise had been overtaken by its intentional de jure lapsing.

The decline in effectiveness of the caps and PAYGO was matched by a more general decline in the budget process. Reconciliation was not used from 1998 to 2005, and for three of the past seven fiscal years (1999, 2003, and 2005), Congress has been unable to enact a budget resolution at all. In order to understand the magnitude of this failure, consider that a budget resolution had been enacted in each of the 23 fiscal years from the first year that the CBA took effect (1976–1998).

The current policy effects of these procedural inadequacies would be well recognized by David Stockman, who in 1981 projected "deficits as far as the eye can see."[17] But President Bush's big fiscal mistake makes the Reagan-era mistake look like chump change. Some might argue that this comparison is exactly wrong, given that current deficits are smaller now as a percentage of GDP than they were in the 1980s. But this interpretation is very misleading because budget accounting does not recognize the

---

17. For a description of how we got there the first time, see David Stockman, *The Triumph of Politics: How the Reagan Revolution Failed* (New York: Harper Collins, 1986).

The Evolution of Public Finance and Budgeting

huge backloaded costs of Bush administration initiatives, which are especially worrisome now that spending pressures in health care and Social Security are nearer at hand. And Reagan did support some deficit reductions, while George W. Bush learned the lesson of his father's defeat all too well: rather than confronting fiscal problems, his administration cynically won its reelection by mortgaging the future. Their rhetorical claims of fiscal responsibility are completely contradicted by the numbers that show the effects of Bush administration policies will be a continuation of large deficits for the foreseeable future.[18]

While there are other individuals in positions of responsibility, such as Congressman John Spratt (D-SC) and Comptroller General David Walker, who attempted to make the country's current choices transparent, they were largely voices in the wilderness. Most Democrats in Congress and on the campaign trail did not exactly distinguish themselves with truth telling. Nor did Federal Reserve Chairman Alan Greenspan, who boldly called in 2001 for tax cuts lest the entire public debt be paid down too quickly. He recently admitted that his secondary suggestion of "triggers" (which would cancel tax cuts should forecasted surpluses fail to materialize) was ignored by tax cutters, who saw his main message as an unambiguous green light for their tax-cuts-at-all-cost approach.

It was common at the creation of the CBA to argue that the law's purpose was to reassert congressional authority, not bias policy toward balancing the budget—that is, the process was to be "budget neutral." An alternative view was that the process was designed to constrain government's tendency to be imprudent, or that it *should* serve that function. We take the latter position. We also believe that if American citizens were encouraged to understand budgetary realities, they would quickly conclude that their country has an unsustainable policy. That this policy was enabled by September 11 is no excuse; rather, it is a warning to expect the unexpected in an interconnected world. That was a message learned recently by many living next to the Indian Ocean, when a huge tsunami was produced by an earthquake in the Sunda trench. A continuation of U.S. budgetary policy poses an incalculable but real risk of a different kind of devastation—a dollar strike or its equivalent that would destabilize the world economy.[19]

WHAT SHOULD BE NEXT?

So if not this federal budget process, then what? Unfortunately, the lesson from the past 30 years is not very comforting: the perception of unacceptable budget policies may or may not force budget process innovations. And when they do, these innovations sometimes work and sometimes are mammoth failures. Further, we are under no illusions

---

18. Congressional Budget Office, *An Analysis of the President's Budgetary Proposals for Fiscal Year 2006* (Washington, DC, March 2005); Ron Suskind, *The Price of Loyalty* (New York: Simon & Schuster, 2004).

19. Robert E. Rubin, Peter R. Orszag, and Allen Sinai, "Sustained Budget Deficits: Longer-Run U.S. Economic Performance and the Risk of Financial and Fiscal Disarray," paper presented at the Allied Social Science Associations Annual Meetings, January 4, 2004.

about the extent of interest and ability within Congress to enact comprehensive reforms. Budget process debates of recent years have been perfunctory, confused, and not necessarily oriented toward fiscal responsibility; when some Republicans recently suggested that PAYGO should apply to spending but not tax cuts, we did not conclude that a new era of fiscal responsibility had begun.

Nevertheless, we do think we can learn a bit from the past 30 years that might be useful in the future; so here are our capsule observations. Each of us will offer more extended and comprehensive arguments in future publications.

First, we would rule out three options that are commonly suggested:

Back to the Good Old Days, Version 1

Some of the CBA provisions, as amended, obviously did not work and were thus discarded. As the entire budget process now seems broken, it may be the case that it should never have been expected to work and should therefore be abandoned. The Congressional Budget Act could be a fragile edifice attempting to hold back the sea—the sea defined as the institutional inability of Congress to make comprehensive policy; complete erosion is a natural end for sand castles.

The most prominent advocate of this perspective is Lou Fisher, who suggests that Congress was better off without a budget process.[20] His thesis is that Congress cannot be expected to take the lead in pursuing policies—increasing taxes and cutting spending—that inflict pain on constituents. In the years prior to the enactment of the Budget Act, the president played this role. But the ambition of the Congress in budget making actually encouraged presidential irresponsibility as the president can now blame Congress rather than taking responsibility for his own proposals; this in turn encourages congressional irresponsibility.

Our difficulty with Fisher's argument is not in description but prescription. We remain convinced that having the appropriations committees in charge would not be an improvement; that they could not control the budget prior to 1974 was one reason why the CBA was enacted. We come down on the side of having a strong congressional budget process—run by budget committees with comprehensive jurisdictions and effective enforcement tools—and look for other mechanisms to reduce the potential for institutional blame shifting.

Constitutional Rules

In line with the substantial theoretical literature which argues for constitutional rules rather than discretion for elected officials, in the late 1980s and early 1990s Congress flirted with a balanced budget amendment to the Constitution.[21] Offered consistently in both the House and the Senate, the amendment reached its high water mark in 1995,

---

20. Louis Fisher, "Federal Budget Doldrums: The Vacuum in Presidential Leadership," *Public Administration Review* 50 (1990): 693–700.

21. For an empirical analysis of the fiscal rules literature, see George Kopits and Steven Symansky, "Fiscal Policy Rules," International Monetary Fund, Occasional Paper 162, 1998.

when it achieved the necessary two-thirds approval in the House and fell only one vote short in the Senate. But this was always an ill-conceived attempt to constitutionalize fiscal policy. As critics of the amendment pointed out at the time, annual balance is not a useful rule for federal budgeting, given the periodic necessity of engaging in counter-cyclical fiscal policy.[22] Even more ill advised was the rule pushed by House Republicans that would have required constitutional supermajorities to enact tax increases. While we agree that a consensus on an overall goal for budgetary policy is absolutely crucial to effective federal budgeting, the notion that this can be done by enshrining an undesirable goal in the constitution strikes us as especially daffy.

Back to the Good Old Days, Version 2

Then there is the argument that a return to the strictures of the Budget Enforcement Act—the caps and PAYGO—will reproduce the responsible budget outcomes of the 1990s. It is possible that a reestablished PAYGO could hinder continuation of tax cuts that are now scheduled to expire—if that is the desire of Congress. But the magnitude of the current deficit gap will require much more action. A hard freeze on discretionary spending would likely make a large contribution only if the nation substantially downsizes its military ambitions. Because the greatest deficit growth is because of huge scheduled increases in mandatory spending for Medicare and Medicaid, which PAYGO would not control, we instead will need to consider large reconciliation savings for these well-established health-care programs—a challenging task when quality and access outcomes for the United States do not look good compared with many developed countries.

An Alternative Reform Agenda

By rejecting these suggestions, we do not mean to suggest that congressional budgeting is worth saving "as is." Instead, we hope that Congress could build on the strengths of the existing process, but also make improvements designed to address its weaknesses. With that in mind, we offer a number of observations.

The greatest strength of the congressional budget process has been the improved informational basis of budgeting, from CBO especially, but also from the budget committee staffs and GAO (recently renamed the Government Accountability Office). We confess that we are hopelessly biased here, given that both of us have worked for CBO, yet we think our view that CBO is the success story of the budget process is widely shared by expert observers: CBO has surely eclipsed OMB as the best source of reliable numbers for the federal government.[23]

The development of the credibility and independence of CBO has not been accidental. It came about because of inspired leadership in the face of demanding clients. At a

22. See Philip Joyce and Robert D. Reischauer, "Deficit Budgeting: The Federal Budget Process and Budget Reform," *Harvard Journal on Legislation* 29, no. 2 (1992): 429–453.

23. See Walter Williams, *Honest Numbers and Democracy: Social Policy Analysis in the White House, Congress and in Federal Agencies* (Washington, DC: Georgetown University Press, 1998).

number of times in its history, such as when President Reagan took office, when it analyzed the Clinton health plan, or after the Republicans took over Congress in 1994, it was faced with the threat of retaliation for unwanted analyses, but escaped relatively unharmed because of the intelligence and strong backbones of its leaders and staff, and the support of key congressional leaders and staff.[24]

Some members of Congress will always be tempted to use CBO for short-term political advantage. One way to prevent them from being successful would be to provide a stronger conceptual basis for CBO's work (and that of OMB). The budget agencies now use outdated budget concepts that are modified versions of those recommended by the 1967 President's Commission on Budget Concepts. A new commission could recommend improvements, so that budget agencies would have an easier time resisting scandalous gimmicks such as the recent proposal to lease fuel tankers from Boeing. A commission could also reduce confusion about how the budget process could deliberate about desirable macrobudgetary goals.[25]

Expanding use of performance information is a related challenge. Sustained effort to implement the 1993 Government Performance and Results Act has dramatically increased the quantity and quality of program performance information. However, there is not much evidence that this information has had a material impact on budget decisions, especially in Congress, where a taste for pork barrel is, believe it or not, even more widely satisfied than in the past. Mitch Daniels, the first OMB director of the Bush administration, became persona non grata with the Republican Congress when he criticized this behavior. OMB also created the Program Assessment Rating Tool (PART), through which programs must document their effectiveness; PART results are readily accessible on the Web. While we will wait for the results of systematic research about whether PARTs have been biased by partisan motives, we are impressed by the detail and transparency of the PARTs. However, we will criticize the PARTs—which are aptly named—because they unfortunately have not been applied to tax preferences. More generally, the budget process has completely failed to systematically address tax expenditures, the number and cost of which have exploded since the simplification-intending 1986 Tax Reform Act.[26]

Of course, continued expansions in the supply of quality information will not necessarily elicit more demand for such information from elected officials. It may be possible, however, to stimulate demand by reinvigorating the priority-setting role of the budget process. Budget resolutions originally focused on allocations to the various budget functions, but only with great difficulty as budget functions and committee jurisdictions were misaligned. Then, as the deficit grew, procedural controls emphasized

---

24. One of the authors (Joyce) is currently completing a book on CBO. Its working title is *The Congressional Budget Office: Truth, Power, and Consequences.*

25. Roy T. Meyers, "It's Time for a Second Commission on Budget Concepts," paper given at the 3rd Annual Congressional Budget Office Director's Conference, September 14, 2004.

26. See Philip Joyce, *Linking Performance and Budgeting: Opportunities in the Federal Budget Process,* IBM Center for the Business of Government, 2004.

The Evolution of Public Finance and Budgeting

jurisdictional distinctions between mandatory and discretionary spending. The process now does not enable trade-offs between different budget functions, nor comparisons within budget functions of different forms of allocations (i.e., discretionary spending, mandatory spending, and tax expenditures).

Two reforms—one relatively easy and one tremendously hard—could help complete the transition to performance budgeting. The budget resolution debate could be preceded by release of an annual report of national indicators for all of the functional areas in the budget, an approach that is already used by some state governments. This report—a real "state of the nation"—would be more useful than each president's mind-numbing list of legislative proposals; it would provide an accounting of the nation's problems and successes, which should focus on the budget debate. The federal government already collects a tremendous amount of quality information; while some indicators would need data improvements, the main challenge for Congress would be agreeing on which of many indicators should be featured in this report. But these choices would themselves be useful for setting budget priorities. For example, budget resolutions are now debated without any formal acknowledgment of the current child poverty rate and recent trends in that rate. Is this defensible? GAO has quietly recommended the adoption of a congressional "performance resolution" to accompany the budget resolution; this strikes us as a useful and desirable first step.[27]

The harder nut is reorganization. Over the past few decades, reorganization has received almost no serious consideration—the public administration consensus has been that bureaucratic reorganization results in excessive costs, and the political science consensus has been that the political status quo is too strong. Yet we have a new Department of Homeland Security, and earlier this year House Majority Leader Tom DeLay engineered an internal reorganization and consolidation of the House Appropriations Committee's subcommittees. A broader reorganization of the committee system could better align it with budget functions—e.g., there could be a committee on health policy, rather than the current situation in which there are three separate committees dealing with Medicaid, Medicare, and the operating budgets of the rest of HHS. A possible drawback of this approach is that current structural redundancies promote useful competition. However, much of the current competition is surely dysfunctional, such as turfing between authorization and appropriations committees, and excessive delays in the legislative process.

We also believe that Congress should tie its budget process more closely to that of the executive branch. The CBA asserted independence of the presidency, but unrealistically so. The historical evidence is not strong that Congress can force presidents to be fiscally

---

27. David M. Walker, "Effective Oversight and Budget Discipline Are Essential—Even in a Time of Surplus," testimony before the U.S. Senate Committee on Budget (February 1, 2000), pp. 22–23; Marc Miringoff and Marque-Luisa Miringoff, *The Social Health of the Nation* (New York: Oxford University Press, 1999); Government Accountability Office, "Informing Our Nation: Improving How to Understand and Assess the USA's Position and Progress," Washington, DC, November 2004.

prudent, or that Congress is strongly motivated to do so. Of course, the Constitution requires the branches to agree if appropriations and reconciliation legislation is to pass (the exception of a veto-proof majority in Congress is theoretically possible but highly unlikely). If the congressional budget were to be considered not as a concurrent resolution, but as a joint resolution that would require the president's signature, this might encourage earlier discussions, and then compromises over budget differences between the branches.[28]

In the end, however, what the budget process needs most is leaders who are morally committed to exercise political responsibility. Citizens are often confused by policy details, and especially by the technical complexity of budgets. They frequently reward ambitious politicians for serving free lunches, even though citizens know in the abstract that this practice is unwise. Breaking this cycle will require those engaged in partisan competition for office to act differently: to educate citizens about budgetary realities and to constrain themselves when making budgetary decisions. An improved budget process may help politicians to succeed with this strategy, but cannot motivate them to choose it in the first place. Returning to our "fiscageological" metaphors, we may need a political earthquake.

28. Roy T. Meyers, "The Budget Resolution Should Be Law," *Public Budgeting & Finance* 10 (1990): 103–112.

The Evolution of Public Finance and Budgeting

Chapter 4

Public Financing in Developing and Transition Countries[*]

ROY BAHL and SALLY WALLACE

The widespread adoption of fiscal decentralization laws during the past 25 years can be mostly tracked to economic efficiency gains and nation-building objectives. Subnational governments (SNGs) in industrialized countries account for about twice the share of total government expenditures as in developing countries. Transition countries also assign more expenditure responsibilities to SNGs than do the developing countries. There has been little growth in the SNG expenditure or tax shares over the past three decades. We confirm the basic hypotheses that the SNG expenditure share is significantly higher in countries with higher incomes, larger populations, and a lower degree of corruption.

INTRODUCTION

Among the developments in public finance and budgeting over the last 25 years, those in the developing and transition countries are some of the more dramatic changes. The political and economic shifts from planned states to new market economies and the push for economic growth called for new tax policies, new relationships between the private and public sector, new systems of budgeting, and new relationships among levels of government. The focus of this paper is on the latter, intergovernmental fiscal relations, with an emphasis on trends in developing and transition countries. The theory that the decentralization of fiscal decisions can lead to better governance has gained great currency in the past 25 years. In the developing and transition countries, there has been widespread adoption of fiscal decentralization laws. In many industrialized countries, the interest in fiscal decentralization has deepened. In this review paper, we outline the reasons for this political enthusiasm, track the progress of fiscal decentralization over the

Roy Bahl, Professor of Economics, Andrew Young School of Policy Studies, Georgia State University, 14 Marietta Street, N.W. Atlanta, GA 30303. He can be reached at *rbahl@gsu.edu.*

Sally Wallace, Associate Professor of Economics, Andrew Young School of Policy Studies, Georgia State University, 14 Marietta Street, N.W. Atlanta, GA 30303. She can be reached at *swallace@gsu.edu.*

[*]This chapter was originally published in *Public Budgeting & Finance,* Vol. 25, Silver Anniversary Edition (2005): 83–98.

past quarter century, present some empirical work that addresses the question, "Why do countries decentralize?" and discuss the reasons why this policy direction might or might not accelerate. Our concern in this analysis is with the fiscal role of subnational governments (SNGs). We define SNG finances as the sum of provincial (state) and local government taxing and spending.

WHY DECENTRALIZATION? THEORY AND RHETORIC

The appeal of fiscal decentralization as a policy strategy is broadly about the political economy of governance, and about the economic and political gains and losses that can march along with this approach to reform. Underneath this political motivation is an underlying set of country-specific factors that make decentralization a more or less desirable policy reform. If one is to understand the reasons why fiscal decentralization has been such an important policy topic over the last quarter century, one must begin by understanding what has moved so many countries to adopt this governance strategy. We try and answer the question, "Why decentralization?" by referring first to the underlying theory about what the gains should be, and second to the rhetoric that has accompanied decentralization programs in countries around the world.

The Theory

The theory of fiscal decentralization is drawn from economics. Most students of this subject begin with Oates' decentralization theorem, "in the absence of cost savings from the centralized provision of a [local public] good and of interjurisdictional externalities, the level of welfare will always be at least as high (and typically higher) if Pareto-efficient levels of consumption are provided in each jurisdiction than if any single, uniform level of consumption is maintained across all jurisdictions."[1] The story is a compelling one: local voters will be happier if they choose the level and mix of government services to be provided. The more diverse the preferences within a country, the greater the efficiency gains from assigning these functions to local governments.

In theory, revenue mobilization might also increase as a result of decentralization, for two reasons.[2] First, if the local population is successful in getting the package of service they want, they might be more willing to pay. Second, because local governments have a comparative advantage in assessing and collecting some taxes, overall revenue mobilization might be increased by decentralizing certain taxing powers.

The theoretical underpinnings for decentralization were developed in a context of governance in industrialized economies. Bahl and Linn make the case that the efficiency

---

1. Wallace Oates, *Fiscal Federalism* (New York: Harcourt Brace, 1972), 54.
2. Roy Bahl and Johannes F. Linn, *Urban Public Finance in Developing Countries* (Oxford, UK: Oxford University Press, 1992).

gains from fiscal decentralization may not be captured as fully in developing countries, for several reasons. First, the absence of open elections at the local level in some countries limits the extent to which the local population can reveal its preferences for public services.[3] Second, local governments may not be able to reach desired levels of spending or revenues because of their limited administrative abilities. Finally, there are legal constraints, i.e., local governments may not have been assigned the "right" expenditure responsibilities or adequate taxing powers.

The Rhetoric[4]

Few countries choose to get carefully focused on the question of "Why decentralization?" Many countries never take the step of developing a White Paper that specifically identifies the problems that might be resolved with fiscal decentralization. But there is almost always a "rhetoric"—delivered in speeches, policy papers, in the press, by interest groups, donors, and the government—from which one might tease out the underlying reasons.

In fact the justification varies from country to country. Various advocates will see decentralization as primarily an economic, political, social, management, or even a military strategy. The way these national leaders see it will pretty much drive the way they design it. This also explains why the rhetoric in support of fiscal decentralization is so varied, and perhaps even why there is such a gap between the rhetoric and the real impact of successful decentralization.

In many cases, the rationale for decentralization matches up well with the problems that the country is facing, suggesting that fiscal decentralization policy is more than a political strategy. Russia's fiscal decentralization developed shortly after the breakup of the Soviet Union and looks very much like one designed to head off separatist movements. South Africa's movement of decision-making power to over 800 local governments is exactly what one would have expected in the aftermath of apartheid. Indonesia's decentralization followed the economic chaos that came with the Asian crisis, and was a reaction to what was perceived to be overcentralization.

Many would like to believe that fiscal decentralization is an effective strategy for stimulating economic development. Intuitively, the argument is reasonable. The government closest to the local or regional economy is in the best position to decide on matters such as the best regulatory environment for local business, the right infrastructure investments to make, the proper structure of taxation, and in general, the enabling

---

3. Even with local elections, the introduction of decentralization policies may be more likely when the party system is organized at the state versus the central level. See Eliza Willis, Christopher Garman, and Stephan Haggard, "The Politics of Decentralization in Latin America," *Latin America Research Review* 3, no. 1 (1999): 7–55.

4. For a more detailed discussion of these same arguments for fiscal decentralization, see Roy Bahl and Jorge Martinez, "Sequencing Fiscal Decentralization" (Washington, DC: World Bank, July 1, 2005), especially Annex A.

environment best suited to develop the local economy. Lady Ursula Hicks had this in mind in her 1961 book, *Development from Below*, which was one of the early arguments for stronger local government in developing countries.[5] Whatever the reason, the search for empirical evidence on the relationship between decentralization and economic development has not produced conclusive evidence.[6] The absence of statistical proof is not damning of the economic development argument, and may be because of the problems with separating the impacts on economy from the impacts on everything else. In this context, McNab develops the interesting point that the effects of decentralization on economic development are indirect, i.e., decentralization impacts technical efficiency, income inequality and corruption, which in turn affect economic growth.[7]

The growing number of countries with democratically elected SNGs clearly has stimulated interest in fiscal decentralization. Those interested in the politics of policy development might argue that this factor has been paramount in stimulating at least the rhetoric and probably the demand for fiscal decentralization. And, it is not all rhetoric. Elected politicians at the SNG level push hard for some powers to shape budgets (although they are much more enthusiastic about having power to spend than they are about having power to tax). Even in China, provincial leaders (who are appointed by the central government) lobby for a greater flow of resources to their provinces. Tanzi makes the same argument with respect to the centrally appointed *prefets* in France and Italy.[8]

It should be recognized that politically driven decentralization processes do not guarantee that government fiscal decisions will end up being made closer to the people. The current cases of India and Spain demonstrate that most of the fiscal powers on the expenditure and revenue sides of the budget can remain at the state or provincial level, with these governments acting as centralized regimes toward their local governments.

Another important part of the rhetoric is that centralization is an inefficient management approach, especially in large countries. Fiscal management, i.e., supervision of a substantial part of the budgetary affairs of every SNG, can be costly and can lead to poor public service outcomes when countries are very large. It can also create significant ill will on the part of local officials and their constituencies who feel burdened by the

5. Ursula K. Hicks, *Development from Below: Local Government and Finance in Developing Countries of the Commonwealth* (Oxford, UK: Clarendon Press, 1961).

6. Tao Zhang and Heng-fu Zou, "Fiscal Decentralization, Public Spending, and Economic Growth in China," *Journal of Public Economics* 67, no. 2 (1998): 221–243; Hamid Davoodi and Heng-fu Zou, "Fiscal Decentralization and Economic Growth: A Cross-Country Study," *Journal of Urban Economics* 43 (1999): 244–257; Justin Yifu Lin and Zhiqiang Liu, "Fiscal Decentralization and Economic Growth in China," *Economic Development and Cultural Change* 49, no. 1 (2000): 1–22; Jorge Martinez-Vazquez and Robert M. McNab, "Fiscal Decentralization and Economic Growth," *World Development* 31, no. 9 (2003): 1597.

7. Robert McNab, "An Empirical Examination of the Outcomes of Fiscal Decentralization." (Ph.D. dissertation, Georgia State University, Andrew Young School of Policy Studies, Economics Department, 2000).

8. Vito Tanzi, "Fiscal Federalism and Decentralization: A Review of Some Efficiency and Macroeconomic Aspects," in *Annual World Bank Conference on Development Economics, 1995* (Washington, DC: The World Bank, 1995): 295–316.

central bureaucracy. A relatively few central officials cannot make the important fiscal decisions for every local government, on a case-by-case basis. There are just too many complications and too many special circumstances for this to be a viable approach in large countries. China and India have populations in excess of one billion, and China has nearly 60,000 SNGs, while India has nearly a quarter million; Brazil has a land area greater than 8.4 million square kilometers; Indonesia is composed of 6,000 inhabited islands and Russia has 11 time zones. How could such countries be managed efficiently from a national capital, by a relatively few senior officials? Yet, as late as the mid-1990s, the budget of each of the 89 regional governments in Russia was being approved in Moscow on the basis of face-to-face negotiations. Some form of decentralized governance would seem an imperative in large countries.

The problems with centralized control are not limited to large countries. Even in small nations, the combination of a poor transportation and communications network can make the national capital very remote. In Nepal, for example, many of the 4,000 local governments are several days journey from Kathmandu.

Fiscal decentralization is a strategy that sells because people want different things from their local governments. Centralization, on the other hand, implies some degree of uniformity in the government services delivered, and in the revenue-raising powers given to SNGs. But there is a resentment of enforced uniformity, and various regions within countries have pushed hard for autonomy to choose a package of services that better fits their demands. Countries with interregional variations in language (e.g., India, Sudan), ethnic background (e.g., Indonesia, Nigeria), or climate and terrain (e.g., Russia) are good candidates for fiscal decentralization. Even countries that are relatively homogenous in population mix and climate may be pressured for different service standards in urban and rural areas, or in regions with different economic bases. Local populations apparently can recognize the potential economic efficiency gains.

There has been an undercurrent of sentiment against big government in the last two decades, and a loss in confidence in the ability of the public sector to adequately and efficiently serve the population. Some of this sentiment has taken the form of a push to privatization of what heretofore had been seen as public sector activities. As Tanzi[9] points out, the enthusiasm about placing greater reliance on the market has been accompanied by the parallel view that less power should be in the hands of the central government. This sentiment has made fiscal decentralization an easier sell in the last two decades.

Another explanation for the increased demand for fiscal decentralization in recent years is the improved management and administrative capacity of local governments. The rap on SNGs has always been their inability to recruit quality staff to deliver services effectively, or to manage money. Although many of the same criticisms are leveled today, there can be no doubt that great numbers of provincial and local governments have "grown up" in terms of their management and administrative capacity. Affordable

---

9. Tanzi, Ibid.

microcomputer systems, improved education, and the greater relative attractiveness of employment in the SNG sector have all contributed to this. When SNGs feel ready, they bring pressure for more fiscal autonomy and this is a factor contributing to the increased demand for fiscal decentralization.

Once countries reach a certain threshold, decentralization policy gains a significant amount of momentum. Local elections, improved administrative capacity, and "local nationalism" can make the demand for fiscal decentralization irresistible. If it is not given in a formal way, it may be taken using "backdoor" approaches. A good example is Chinese local governments who were denied formal taxing powers but levied informal (often illegal) taxes, which were kept in off-budget accounts. Local governments did take on more fiscal autonomy on the revenue and the expenditure side, and this was in response to a demand for local services that higher level governments were unwilling to fund. But this "backdoor" approach brought inefficiencies in terms of how the funds were raised and in terms of spending from segmented, extra budgetary accounts.[10] It may be far better to structure a program of fiscal autonomy than to have it taken on an ad hoc basis.

Perhaps the most compelling rhetoric has to do with service delivery. The level and quality of local public services provided in most developing countries is appalling. "The job is not getting done anyway, let's try another approach" is an argument that gets great deal of sympathy and support. There seems to be a feeling in some camps that more local control over expenditure decisions can make things better. The Inter-American Development Bank,[11] commenting on the policy agenda for Latin America, put it this way: "Policy makers in the region are becoming aware of the potential offered by externalities and interdependence existing between fiscal decentralization, the effectiveness of social spending, and greater local political participation." There are at least intuitive arguments to support this. SNGs are better positioned to determine the location of capital investments, they may be able to better control the performance of employees working at the local level, and they might be better at maintaining the local public capital.

Local voters feel more likely to be "heard" by local politicians and bureaucrats than by central politicians and bureaucrats. It is also true that the local population is more aware of the decisions made by local bureaucrats than they are of decisions made by central government officials, and hence are more likely to hold local officials accountable for services provided.[12] Khemani reports results for India that show local voters holding local officials more accountable for economic performance than they do officials of

---

10. Christine P. Wong, ed., "Overview of Issues in Local Public Finance in the PRC," in *Financing Local Government in the People's Republic of China* (Hong Kong: Oxford University Press, 1997); Roy Bahl, *Fiscal Policy in China: Taxation and Intergovernmental Fiscal Relations* (San Francisco: The 1990 Institute, 1999).

11. Inter-American Development Bank, "Fiscal Decentralization: The Search for Equity and Efficiency," *Economic and Social Progress in Latin America* (Washington, DC: Inter-American Bank, October 1994).

12. Elinor Ostrom, Larry Schroeder, and Susan Wynne, *Institutional Incentives and Sustainable Development: Infrastructure Policies in Perspective* (Boulder, CO: Westview Press, 1993).

higher-level governments.[13] There is, of course, the risk that decentralization will fail to improve the level and quality of public services, but the risks associated with doing nothing are often perceived as a worse alternative, a continuation of the dismal performance of the centralized approach to service delivery.

Finally, decentralization may be a part of the strategy to hold countries together, or of a strategy for nation building. Some countries have been formed out of unnatural partners and have dissolved when the opportunity arose, e.g., Czechoslovakia and Yugoslavia. In some cases, the fall of strong central regimes has prompted a call to move governance away from the central level and has stimulated fiscal decentralization initiatives. Indonesia, South Africa, and Russia are cases in point. Other troublesome partnerships have played to special autonomy measures to try and hold the country together. Nigeria, the Philippines, and Sudan fall into this category. We also may note that even in the case of reunifications, decentralization plays an important role as in Vietnam, Germany, and China-Hong Kong.

This survey suggests that countries express their interest in fiscal decentralization in many different ways. Likely this has to do with the political selling of fiscal decentralization. In fact, however, most of the rhetoric about the benefits of fiscal decentralization can be tracked to two rationales: economic efficiency gains and nation building. The decentralization theorem, it seems, is an important guide for thinking about devolving budgetary powers to SNGs.

THE EMPIRICAL EVIDENCE

The great number of countries pursuing some form of decentralization policy indicates the popularity of this development strategy. We turn now to a discussion of the actual implementation of decentralization policy, as measured by fiscal data. As will be shown below, the evidence about the progress is mixed.

Trends

The most commonly used comparative measure of fiscal decentralization is the SNG share of total government expenditures. This measure ignores the degree of discretion given to SNGs, but it does show the extent to which the financing of government services is passed through their budgets.[14] Although this measure is flawed as an indicator of the

---

13. Stuti Khemani, "Decentralization and Accountability: Are Voters More Vigilant in Local vs. National Elections?" *World Bank Policy Research Working Paper No. 2557* (2001).

14. The point that the subnational government expenditure share is a measure that overstates true fiscal decentralization is developed in some detail in Robert D. Ebel and Serdar Yilmaz, "On the Measurement and Impact of Fiscal Decentralization," in *Public Finance in Developing and Transitional Countries: Essays in Honor of Richard Bird*, eds. Jorge Martinez-Vazquez and James Alm, *Studies in Fiscal Federalism and State-Local Finance* (Cheltenham, UK: Edward Elgar, 2003), 101–119.

extent to which SNGs influence resource allocation, it is suggestive of the importance of the SNG sector in government finance.

This expenditure decentralization ratio and an analogously defined tax decentralization ratio are reported in Table 1.[15] The results presented here are not surprising in showing that SNGs in industrialized countries account for about twice the share of total government expenditures as in developing countries. Industrialized countries are characterized by more stable economies, less regional inequality, and more developed infrastructure, and these are all factors that encourage the choice of more fiscal decentralization. Transition countries assign more expenditure responsibilities to SNGs than do the developing countries, but they give relatively little fiscal discretion to the lower-level governments.

What is surprising is that on average, there has been little growth in the SNG expenditure or tax shares over the past three decades. This time pattern holds true for both industrialized and developing countries.

Although some countries have greatly decentralized their fiscal structures over this time period, the average performance suggests a quite stable level. Recent research has shown that there has been little change, on average, in the claim of intergovernmental transfers on the tax revenues of those higher-level governments making the transfers.[16]

We can say less about the decentralization of taxing powers because the International Monetary Fund's (IMF) *Government Finance Statistics* (GFS) *Yearbook*, from which these data are drawn, appears to misclassify transfers as local taxes in some country cases. Definitional problems not withstanding, these data show that the SNG tax share is about twice as high in industrialized than developing countries, and that there has been little change in these shares in the past 30 years. These is no evidence of a significant movement to shift the locus of taxing powers to lower-level governments.

Intercountry Variations

Why do some countries choose to decentralize their financing structure more than others? Researchers have studied this question over the past 25 years and have reached similar conclusions about the determinants of cross-country variations in the expenditure decentralization ratio.

The statistical approach followed is more or less the same in all of these studies. The dependent variable is the expenditure share of SNGs, and data on this variable are taken

---

15. This table is an updated version from Roy Bahl and Sally Wallace. "Fiscal Decentralization: The Provincial-Local Dimension," *Public Finance in Developing and Transitional Countries: Essays in Honor of Richard Bird: Studies in Fiscal Federalism and State-Local Finance*, series ed. Wallace E. Oates (Cheltenham, UK: Edward Elgar, 2003).

16. Roy Bahl and Sally Wallace, "Intergovernmental Transfers: The Vertical Sharing Dimension," ISP Working Paper No. 04-19, Atlanta, GA: International Studies Program, Andrew Young School of Policy Studies, Georgia State University, 2005.

TABLE 1
Fiscal Decentralization Indicators

	1970s		1980s		1990s–2000s		
	Developing Countries	OECD Countries	Developing Countries	OECD Countries	Developing Countries	OECD Countries	Transition Countries
SNG tax as a share of total government tax	10.68 (43)	17.91 (24)	8.87 (33)	18.18 (23)	10.61 (28)	18.39 (21)	22.41 (23)
SNG expenditure as a share of total government expenditure	13.42 (45)	33.68 (23)	12.09 (41)	31.97 (24)	12.97 (54)	32.68 (24)	30.32 (24)

Sample sizes are given in parentheses.
SNG, subnational government; OECD, Organisation for Economic Co-operation and Development.

from the *IMF Government Finance Statistics Yearbook*.[17] The independent variables are specified to match the theoretical expectations about the determinants of expenditure decentralization. Various studies have used cross-sections of data for a given year or an average over a span of years, or have used panel data.[18]

Most of the results in previous studies square with theoretical expectations.[19] The size of a country, measured either as population or land area, seems to be a significant determinant of the degree of expenditure decentralization. Per capita gross domestic product (GDP), usually standing as an index of economic development is associated with a higher level of decentralization.[20] The extent to which a country is at war or is threatened by war appears to be associated with more centralization.[21] Some researchers have found that ethnic diversity drives up the level of decentralization, a result that squares with theoretical expectations, and others have found a positive effect of urbanization.

In this analysis we update the empirical work from the newer issues of *GFS*, specify the model in a slightly different way than has been done in the past, and use a more extensive data set than has been the case in some studies. We simulate a cross-section by using average values of these data for the period covering the 1990s to the present.

The dependent variable, as in previous studies, is the expenditure decentralization ratio. By 2002 (the latest year for which data are available), this ratio ranged from 70 percent in China to less than 3 percent in a number of developing countries. The sample includes 87 countries and is comprised of transition, developing, and industrialized nations. This large sample allows us to compare the determinants of decentralization among countries with a variety of underlying differences in economic and political institutions.

We specify five determinants of expenditure decentralization. Population size and land area are used as independent variables to measure the size effect, and a positive association with expenditure decentralization is expected. Per capita GDP (in US$) and a dummy variable for developing countries are used to measure the level of economic development, with an expected positive marginal effect in each case. We use ethnic fractionalization as an index of population heterogeneity and expect a positive relationship with expenditure decentralization.[22] Transparency International's index of corrup-

---

17. International Monetary Fund, *Government Finance Statistics Yearbook* (Washington, DC: IMF, 2003).

18. Leonardo S. Letelier, "Explaining Fiscal Decentralization," *Public Finance Review* 33, no. 2 (2005): 155–183.

19. A very good review of the literature is provided by Letelier, Ibid., 155–183.

20. Michael Wasylenko, "Fiscal Decentralization and Economic Development," *Public Budgeting and Finance* 7, no. 4 (1987): 57–71; Ugo Panizza, "On the Determinants of Fiscal Centralization: Theory and Evidence," *Journal of Public Economics* 74, no. 1 (1999): 97.

21. Roy W. Bahl and Shyam Nath, "Public Expenditure Decentralization in Developing Countries," *Environmental Planning C: Government and Policy* 4, no. 4 (1986): 405–418; Letelier, 155–183.

22. Alberto Alesina, Arnaud Deevleeschauwer, William Easterly, Sergio Kurlat, and Romain Wacziavg, "Fractionalization," *Journal of Economic Growth* 8, no. 2 (2002): 155–194.

TABLE 2
Ordinary Least-Squares Estimates of the Determinants of Expenditure Decentralization[b]

	Equation (1)	Equation (2)
Constant	− 2.89	1.30
	(2.10)	(1.82)
Per capita	0.21	
GDP (in US$)[a]	(2.62)	
Dummy variable for less-developed countries		− 0.88
		(2.83)
Population[a]	0.32	
	(6.25)	
Land area[a]		0.21
		(4.53)
Ethnic fractionalization	0.32	− 0.05
	(0.80)	(0.13)
Corruption	− 0.43	− 0.89
	(2.76)	(1.11)
Transition country	1.05	0.19
Dummy variable	(5.37)	(0.60)
$\bar{R}^2$	0.47	0.40
N	86	87

[a]In logarithms.
[b]Expenditure decentralization is defined as the subnational government share of total government expenditures. GDP, gross domestic product.

tion is an independent variable with an expected negative relationship with the expenditure decentralization ratio, i.e., we expect more corruption to be associated with less decentralization.[23] We argue that decentralization is less likely to be a policy strategy in centralized countries where corruption is entrenched. We introduce a dummy variable for transition countries to control for differences in the functions of government.

The results of this estimation, presented in Table 2, confirm the basic hypotheses about the determinants of fiscal decentralization. The expenditure share is significantly higher in countries with higher incomes, in large countries, and in countries with a lower degree of corruption. The results are robust with respect to alternative measures of country size or income level. We also find that, cetera paribus, the SNG expenditure share is higher in transition countries. Between 40 and 50 percent of the cross-country variation can be explained.

23. Transparency International, *Global Corruption Report* (Berlin: Transparency International, 2005). We calibrate the corruption index so that a larger number implies more corruption.

THE CONSTRAINTS TO DECENTRALIZATION[24]

The trend of decentralization in developing and transition countries is not necessarily what one might expect. The more-or-less constant expenditure share of SNGs in developing countries over the past three decades raises the question about why countries have not decentralized more than they have. In fact, there are some significant constraints to fiscal decentralization that have held back the growth of SNG finance, and that may continue to constrain fiscal decentralization. In the case of transition countries, the limited time frame of the data does not allow us to say much about changes in the level of decentralization. We may note, however, that the level of expenditure decentralization is much higher than that in developing countries, and is more on par with the decentralization level in Organisation for Economic Co-operation and Development countries.

The economies of less-developed countries tend to be more exposed to external shocks, e.g., movements in international financial markets, or changes in world prices for a primary export product or in energy prices. In such cases, central governments will want to hold on to the major instruments of fiscal policy so as to have flexibility in controlling the overall level of the deficit. If SNGs play a larger role in the fiscal system—as, for example, accounting for a larger share of expenditures, taxes, or borrowing—the central government will have less flexibility to deal with fiscal imbalance. There is also the issue in many countries of SNGs not facing a hard budget constraint (and/or being subjected to an overassignment of expenditure responsibilities) and passing their deficits to higher-level governments. Brazil and Argentina are the cases most often cited as the example of fiscal decentralization compromising macroeconomic stability.

This same argument could be made in transition countries, especially in the early 1990s as a result of the fall of the Soviet Union. The centrally planned economies of countries such as Ukraine, Kazakhstan, Uzbekistan, Kyrgyzstan, Georgia, Armenia, and the like were especially vulnerable after the dissolution of the Soviet Union. Theoretically, we might expect that this would have led to high levels of centralization to allow the government control of the levers of the economy. However, aside from cases such as Latvia, Estonia, and the Czech Republic, the dismal fiscal condition of the central government and high level of public expenditures resulted in an off-loading of expenditure responsibilities to the SNGs.

Some research disagree with the proposition that macroeconomic stability is a constraint to the enactment of fiscal decentralization program.[25] If business cycles are regional, some SNGs may even be better positioned to absorb external shocks than are

---

24. Bahl and Linn, 385–427; Roy Bahl, "Fiscal Decentralization as Development Policy," *Public Budgeting and Finance* 19, no. 2 (1999): 59–75; Remy Prud'homme, "On the Dangers of Decentralization," *World Bank Economic Review* 9 (1995): 201–219; Tanzi, 295–316.

25. Paul Berndt Spahn "Decentralized Government and Macroeconomic Control," *Infrastructure Notes* FM-12 (Washington, DC: World Bank, 1997); David Sewell, "The Dangers of Decentralization According to Prud'homme: Some Further Aspects," *World Bank Research Observer* 11 (1996): 143–150.

central governments. Some would go so far as to say that in certain circumstances SNGs can play a role in stabilization policy.[26]

Another constraint to substantial decentralization has to do with infrastructure planning and service delivery. In developing countries the basic system is not yet in place—trunk roads, power grids, ports, universities, etc.—and this pushes infrastructure decisions to a higher-level government, which is more capable of accommodating externalities. Moreover, there is the fear that the delivery of infrastructure—construction and maintenance—is beyond the reach of many provincial and local governments. At least in the poorest countries, this argument supports continued centralization. Some of this capacity did exist at the lower levels of government in centrally controlled economies such as the Russian Federation. Therefore, this constraint to fiscal decentralization was not as pronounced in many transition countries.

A third constraint is equalization. Most developing and transition countries face greater inequalities among regions than do industrialized countries. Because they have access to the more productive tax bases, central governments are in a better position to accommodate these inequalities through the tax-transfer system than are SNGs. Moreover, fiscal decentralization, if it includes significant local government taxing powers, is inherently counterequalizing in that it favors wealthier jurisdictions. In practice, the counterequalizing fears associated with overassignment of taxing powers to local governments has not materialized in most countries, either because taxing powers have not been handed down to any great extent or because compensating equalization transfers have been introduced. In any case, central governments do not appear to have used their fiscal discretion to pursue regional equalization.[27] Prud'homme, however, reports on several cases where a centralized fiscal system led to fiscal redistribution among the regions.[28]

A fourth constraint is bureaucratic. Central control of finances means that line ministries are responsible for much of the portfolio of service delivery, or at least for identifying targets for spending and disbursing funds. Under a decentralized system, the SNGs will assume this responsibility and the control of the central bureaucracy will be dramatically reduced. Those bureaucrats, who will lose power, and perhaps even jobs, form a powerful lobby for centralization. This pull to centralization holds for developing, transition, and industrialized countries.

It is commonly argued that fiscal decentralization in the form of greater expenditure assignments to SNGs in developing countries (and more recently in the case of transition countries) would compromise the quality of public services delivered. A number of

---

26. Edward Gramlich, "Federalism and Federal Budget Protection," *National Tax Journal* 40, no. 3 (1987): 299–313.

27. For evidence on Brazil, see Teresa Ter-Minassian, ed, "Brazil," *Fiscal Federalism in Theory and Practice* (Washington, DC: International Monetary Fund, 1997): 450–456. On the Philippines, see Richard M. Bird and Edgard R. Rodriguez, "Decentralization and Poverty Alleviation. International Experience and the Case of the Philippines," *Public Administration and Development* 19 (1999): 299–319.

28. Prud'homme, 201–219.

arguments have been made in support of this proposition:[29] (a) the quality of SNG civil servants is weak because career opportunities are more limited than at the central level; (b) public expenditure management systems (e.g., treasury, accounting, and auditing) are weak; and (c) opportunities for bribery and nepotism are likely to lead to waste. These are old arguments but still powerful constraints to decentralizing policy.

A relatively new issue in this literature is the relationship between decentralization and corruption. One school of thought is that decentralized systems are more corrupt, in part because local politicians are more susceptible to pressures from local interest groups.[30] If local voters are not sophisticated enough to hold local officials accountable, corruption will go unchecked. This suspicion may be more perception than reality. Tumennasan argues that the greater accountability of local government officials and interjurisdictional competition are deterrents to corruption, and estimates a negative relationship between decentralization and corruption.[31] Fisman and Gatti[32] and Gurgur and Shah[33] reach a similar conclusion. Nevertheless, the fear that decentralization breeds more corruption is often enough to cause countries to hold on to centralized fiscal systems.

CONCLUSION AND FUTURE IMPLICATIONS

Fiscal decentralization has become entrenched as a part of development strategy in much of the world. Transition countries have adopted decentralization as a natural part of the switch from planned to market-based economic systems. With only rare exceptions is fiscal decentralization abandoned once it gains some momentum. However, as we point out in this paper, it has stalled in developing and developed countries in the last quarter of this century, and it has stalled at the very time that the hype has been greatest. By the early 2000s, the average share of government expenditures made by SNGs was about the same as in the 1970s in developing countries. The same may be said for industrialized countries, but the level is about twice as high. The share in many transition countries, while exploding in the 1990s, has also plateaued.[34]

What might the future hold? Are there factors at work that suggest that SNG fiscal shares will now begin to increase? Or to fall? Of course, futures are not predictable, and

---

29. Tanzi, 295–316, Prud'homme, 201–219.

30. Ibid., 201–219.

31. Bayar Tumennessan, "Fiscal Decentralization and Corruption in the Public Sector" (Ph.D. dissertation, Georgia State University, Andrew Young School of Policy Studies, Economics Department, 2005).

32. Raymond Fisman and Roberta Gatti, "Decentralization and Corruption: Evidence across Countries," *Journal of Public Economics* 83 (2002): 325–345.

33. Tugrul Gurgur and Anwar Shah. "Localization and Corruption: Panacea or Pandora's Box?" *World Bank Policy Research Working Paper 3486* (2001).

34. We emphasize that these are averages and hide the cases of some countries where there were significant increases and others where the subnational government fiscal share fell.

one cannot see with any degree of certainty the major changes in attitudes toward governance that are coming. However, one could argue persuasively that the next quarter century will not see changes of the magnitude of the last quarter century: e.g., the breakup of the Soviet Union, the end of apartheid, or the replacement in many countries of long-time central government domination with democratic governance. As fiscal decentralization is often driven by big events such as these, we might speculate that major impetuses for enhanced provincial and local government finance will not be on the scene. On the other hand, there probably will be significant international financial disruptions, China and India's continued emergence on the world economy will have ripple effects, and many countries will remain in the throes of internal strife. And, as has been discussed in this paper, all of these factors provide an impetus for various types of fiscal federalism reforms and for more fiscal decentralization.

There are factors that might suggest a continued stall, and hold some countries from decentralizing further. Continued struggles with fiscal balance may cause some central governments to continue to exercise caution in committing large vertical shares to SNGs. Trade liberalization and international competition will limit tax-policy choices, and pressures to maintain budget balance will continue to argue for reducing subsidies of all kinds. Social needs and infrastructure needs might continue to crowd out decentralization, by raising its opportunity cost. In other words, there could be more pressure than before for central governments to hold on to their revenue collections. This pressure will be especially great in the poorest countries.

On the other hand, there are five factors that suggest an increase in the financing share of SNGs. First, the issue itself will not go away. Most of the reasons why countries argue a decentralization strategy, as surveyed in this paper, go back to the issue of economic efficiency gains, i.e., getting government fiscal decisions closer to the people. Higher-level governments have been responding to the call by SNGs for more say about the tax and expenditure decisions that affect them. Moreover, there is evidence of concern about whether the electoral processes for local officials give local constituencies enough voice. Second, the "determinants" analysis carried out in this paper and that from earlier studies suggests that fiscal decentralization is a strategy that goes hand in hand with economic development. As income rises, so does the share of fiscal activity managed by SNGs. As the GDP gap between the rich and the poor countries closes, so will the fiscal decentralization gap.

A third reason to expect increases in the fiscal share of lower-level governments is the possibility that more taxing powers will be passed down, particularly to those SNGs with the administrative wherewithal to administer a tax system. This increased provincial and local taxing power could roll out into increased spending by these governments as locals reacted to their newfound power to tax and choose their expenditure mix. Fourth, SNGs have increased their capacity to both deliver services and administer certain types of taxes. With a current groundswell of reaction against big government, central governments might be more willing to pass at least more spending responsibility to state and local governments and "get them on the learning curve" with respect to delivering local services.

Finally, there is the issue of the flypaper effect with respect to central government taxes, i.e., central government taxes have "stuck where they hit." The rate of central revenue mobilization increased in many countries, but the rate of pass through to lower level governments did not. Much of the increase in the revenue mobilization of the past quarter century, particularly that in emerging economies, has been because of the introduction of the VAT and to ensuing rate increases in the VAT. These revenues were guarded by most central governments, and until recently, the VAT was thought of as unsuitable as a provincial-level tax. Central governments in most countries were wary of committing a large share of this revenue bonanza to SNGs.[35] The next round of VAT adjustments will more likely be base broadening and administrative cleanup, and there may be less hesitance to pass a guaranteed share of revenues through to SNGs.

---

35. There were exceptions to this general rule, and some countries have earmarked a percent of value-added tax (VAT) collections for revenue sharing with lower-level governments.

Chapter 5

United States Revenue Policy: Stability within the Rhetoric of Reform[*]

JOHN L. MIKESELL

The past quarter century has produced little change in the government revenue share of gross domestic product in the United States. The federal share has fallen, but the state and local share has increased. There has been no great change among revenue sources, certainly nothing like the flight from the property tax that characterized the prior decade. Several issues have dominated revenue policy discussions over the last quarter century. These include the role of the property tax, realignment of the federal tax base away from income, tax simplification, and base broadening. There have been no definite solutions to date.

INTRODUCTION

The public revenue system, the mix of revenue laws that define how the cost of government services is intended to be distributed and administrative structures that implement those policies, plays a crucial but usually quiet role in the operation of a modern democratic state. Should the system fail to produce revenue consistent with the adopted scale of government services, the fiscal sustainability of the government and its supporting economy is at peril. If administrative structures do not faithfully implement the adopted tax policy, the intentions of that policy in terms of revenue yield, economic impact, or cost distribution will not be carried out. The two elements of the system—the policy and its administration—form inseparable components of the fiscal whole. Failure in either element can cause havoc for revenue production and, ultimately, for the provision of fundamental governmental services.

Over the past quarter century in the United States, both revenue policies and their administration have changed and there continue vibrant discussions about making further

John L. Mikesell is Professor of Public Finance and Policy Analysis, School of Public and Environmental Affairs, Indiana University, Bloomington, IN. He can be reached at *mikesell@indiana.edu*.

[*]This chapter was originally published in *Public Budgeting & Finance*, Vol. 25, Silver Anniversary Edition (2005): 99–126 as John L. Mikesell, "Changing Revenue Policy in the United States: An Overview of the Record and Perennial Puzzles."

changes. It has been an era mostly of economic expansion, although the recessions at the beginning of the 1980s (two of them), at the beginning of the 1990s, and of mid-2001 were not easy for the revenue systems of many governments. It was also an era in which tax policy makers had to begin paying attention to what was happening not only in neighboring localities and states but in economies all around the globe. And technology created new markets, new goods, new ways of doing business, and new ways to collect taxes, not to mention new ways for those wishing not to pay taxes to fulfill those wishes. The sections that follow will consider the path of the public revenue system over that period and a number of the main policy challenges that have shaped development of the policy and continue to be unresolved. Few are likely to be conclusively resolved in the near future.

CHANGING REVENUE PATTERNS

The revenue system, in terms of how revenue bases have been tapped, has been generally stable in the last quarter century, as data presented later will demonstrate. The primary bases are the same and there has been no serious switching between taxpayer active and taxpayer passive means of collecting taxes levied on these bases. This may be the result of political paralysis: after the tax revolt era of the 1970s, few lawmakers seemed much interested in fundamental restructuring because restructuring almost inevitably means higher burdens on some elements of the private economy (and lower burdens on others) and elected officials are not interested in bearing the political vengeance of those elements with higher burdens, no matter how important the change might be for fundamental revenue policy. Politicians remember the fate of President George H. W. Bush after he violated his "no new taxes" pledge and are intensely shy about tax increases for anyone, anytime, no matter the potential contribution of the resulting tax revenue to fiscal sustainability. It is better to leave the system alone than it is to create the opposition that any restructuring inevitably produces. Simply reducing taxes for everyone—a politically popular approach—has a practical limit defined by demand for government services, after all, but tax restructuring with some shifting of burdens is politically dangerous. Distribution models are easy enough to create now that interest groups can quickly create scenarios that identify who pays more and who pays less with any restructuring and can mobilize the losers, no matter the fundamental soundness of the policy change.

The general political inclination toward tax system stability is reinforced by the incremental nature of tax policy. There is no standard review and reconsideration cycle for tax systems, certainly nothing like the annual review and approval that spending appropriations require. In large measure, the tax laws in place next year are those from this year, unless explicit legislative change has occurred or, infrequently, unless there is an expiration clause in the tax law.[1] Hence, taxation is a nearly pure incremental system—with minimal or no policy change to the tax structure base in most years. That

---

1. Real property taxes are an exception. Usually the property tax rate must be adopted each year, although the tax itself and its underlying policies remain in place.

The Evolution of Public Finance and Budgeting

presumption that any new laws will become "part of a stable and semi-permanent legal structure"[2] is critical not only for providing a basis for fiscal stability but also for providing the citizenry a solid basis for economic and legal transactions. Just as tax legislation with retroactive application can create havoc for economic enterprise, an unstable tax law erodes the certainty of contract that is critical for growth and development. Transitions can be traumatic for fairness and efficiency. Therefore, it is for good reason that it takes a near-cataclysmic event to produce a major restructuring of revenue policy. Even the significant rewriting of the Internal Revenue Code in 1986—a dramatic broadening of the income tax base and reduction of statutory rates—left federal revenue policy still income base driven and not moved toward a consumption base, something that research leading up to that restructuring was seriously suggesting.[3]

Revenue policy is even more permanent than government spending programs, which have been regularly criticized for their rigidity. But, with revenue laws, there is sound reason for stability. And, at the federal level, tax fundamentals have been remarkably stable. Brownlee identifies only five distinct tax regimes since 1789: from 1789 to the Civil War (low rate import duties), from 1862 to World War (WW) I (higher rate import duties, excises on alcohol, tobacco, and some luxury goods), 1916–1931 (individual and corporate income taxes, consumer excises), 1932–1940 (more excises, higher income tax rates on high-income earners), and 1941 to the present (individual income tax on the masses).[4] These few change points all were associated with total war or Depression; without such events, the change in systems can be expected to be gradual and that is exactly the record of the past quarter century. It historically has taken a major shock to dislodge the basic tax structure. Because there were no major shocks during the past 25 years, not even the shock of a Proposition 13 or even the problems of any prolonged recession, the absence of major change in revenue policy is not surprising. But it will be seen later that there are perennial issues that have haunted the years and may be coming to a resolution in the near future.

Public Revenue in the National Economy

Total government receipts from the private economy have been around 35 percent of gross domestic product (GDP) for the past quarter century. Figure 1 shows the pattern of federal, state, local, and total government own-source receipts as a percentage of GDP

---

2. John Buckley, "Estate Tax Repeal: More Losers than Winners," *Tax Notes* (February 14, 2005): 833. As Buckley points out, one of the unfortunate developments of the recent decade has been passage of major federal tax laws that have uncertainty-creating gimmicks inserted to exploit budget scoring rules to reduce the apparent revenue consequences of the laws and thereby reduce tax system stability. Nevertheless, the basic rule of stability remains across all levels of government: the system is permanent, unless specific provisions have been adopted to alter that permanency.

3. David Bradford and the U.S. Treasury Tax Policy Staff, *Blueprints for Basic Tax Reform*, 2nd ed. (Arlington, VA: Tax Analysts, 1984).

4. W. Elliott Brownlee, *Federal Taxation in America: A Short History*, 2nd ed. (Cambridge, UK: Cambridge University Press, 2004).

FIGURE 1
Total, Federal, State, and Local Government Own-Source Receipts as Percent of Gross Domestic Product, 1980–2004

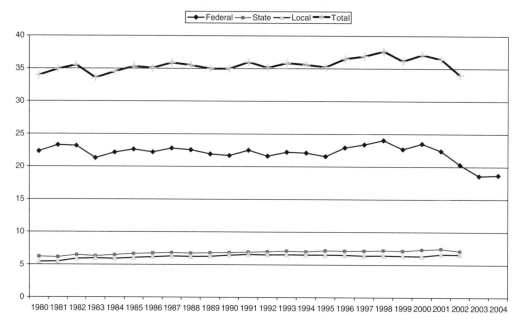

from 1980 to 2004.[5] State and local government receipts show a general upward trend over the period, as receipts relative to economic activity rose. However, the pattern of federal receipts is more complicated. The share was broadly constant at around 23 percent of the economy until the mid-1990s, at which point the share rose until 1998. From that year onward, the trend has been toward lower shares—falling below

---

5. The data require some discussion. First, the federal collection data go beyond receipts (taxes—income taxes, excises and customs duties, social security system payroll taxes, and death taxes—and certain miscellaneous receipts, the largest component being Federal Reserve System profits) to include payments from the public that are treated in budget accounts as offsetting receipts and collections from the public and get netted against outlays rather than being counted as collections from the private sector (the largest two components are postal service charges and Medicare insurance premiums). To omit these components would exclude a large share of user charge revenue and provide a misleading picture of federal receipts. Second, the state and local government collections data extend beyond the narrow Census data reports that distinguish between general operations of government and operations of utilities (water, electric, transportation, etc.) and state monopoly liquor stores. This distinction, if honored here, would cause an understatement of the extent to which these governments charge for services they provide. Hence, the analysis here includes utility and state liquor store revenue with other charges by these governments (university tuition, hospitals, solid waste and sewerage charges, lotteries, etc.). Finally, data reporting periods for federal, state, and local governments do not exactly match. Because data are not available for concurrent fiscal years, the reports here must be considered approximations.

20 percent for 2003 and 2004. Because federal receipts are roughly two-thirds of the total, the pattern for total receipts generally follows that of the federal government. In the period, the consistent growth of both state and local receipts has little discernable impact on the path of total receipts. The total share is a bit lower at the end of the quarter century than it was at the beginning—and this is driven by the behavior of federal receipts.

Changes in Federal Revenue

Not all components of the federal revenue system have followed the same path. Table 1 tracks the flow of individual revenue categories to the federal budget from fiscal 1980 to 2004 as a percentage of GDP and Table 2 tracks shares of total receipts from the public for major categories for those years. The changes are in both the relative amounts collected from the public and the distribution of those collections across the main sources. In these tables, offsetting receipts and collections are included as part of the federal revenue system, a treatment that does not match federal budget reports but is consistent with the fundamental logic of government finance that balances direct charges against taxes as methods for supporting governmental services. These are best considered revenues, not negative outlays, in tracking federal claims on the private economy.

Table 1 shows that the total federal tax burden as a share of total economic activity has declined somewhat from fiscal 1980 to fiscal 2004, from 18.97 percent of GDP to 16.27 percent. The larger decline, however, appears in total receipts from the public. When miscellaneous receipts and offsetting receipts and collections are added in, the fall in the total share is from 22.31 percent of GDP in fiscal 1980 to 18.72 percent of GDP in fiscal 2004. Each individual category of receipts has fallen with the exception of social security tax collections, which rose from 5.79 to 6.35 percent.

These patterns of decline have not been consistent through the years. In particular, the individual income tax rose consistently as a share of GDP through the latter half of the 1990s, with the booming economy, peaking at 10.35 percent of GDP in 2000. From that high, the decline has been continuous, to 7.00 percent in 2004. Corporate income tax collections hovered around 2 percent of GDP in the last half of the 1990s, a level last experienced in 1980 and 1981, but then fell to 1.22 percent in 2003, the lowest level in the quarter century, only to recover to 1.64 percent in 2004. Social security collections gradually rose through the period, although did decline somewhat after 2001. Of course, the actuarial condition of the social security trust funds—both the Old Age Survivor and Disability Insurance (OASDI) and Medicare funds—would indicate that the yields still are insufficient to support the system in the long term. Offsetting receipts show erratic variation generally around 4 percent of GDP until 1998, at which point they fall to a plateau of around 2.15–2.25 percent through 2004. Total receipts peaked at 24.04 percent of GDP in 1998 and have consistently fallen since.

Table 2 focuses on category shares of total federal receipts from the public. The individual income tax and social security contributions continue as the largest sources of total federal receipts—over 70 percent of the total in 2004. However, while the individual

TABLE 1
Federal Receipts as a Percentages of GDP, 1980–2004

	Individual Income Tax	Corporate Income Tax	Social Security	Excise Taxes	Estate and Gift	Customs	Total Taxes	Miscellaneous	Offsetting Receipts and Collections from the Public	Total Receipts from the Public
1980	8.96	2.37	5.79	0.89	0.23	0.26	18.97	0.47	2.87	22.31
1981	9.35	2.00	5.97	1.34	0.22	0.26	19.59	0.45	3.23	23.28
1982	9.23	1.53	6.25	1.13	0.25	0.27	19.15	0.50	3.52	23.17
1983	8.39	1.08	6.07	1.03	0.18	0.25	17.44	0.45	3.38	21.28
1984	7.76	1.48	6.22	0.97	0.16	0.30	17.33	0.44	4.37	22.14
1985	8.06	1.48	6.39	0.87	0.15	0.29	17.69	0.45	4.46	22.61
1986	7.92	1.43	6.44	0.75	0.16	0.30	17.46	0.45	4.27	22.18
1987	8.08	1.80	6.52	0.70	0.16	0.32	18.36	0.42	4.01	22.78
1988	8.00	1.89	6.67	0.70	0.15	0.32	18.14	0.41	3.99	22.54
1989	8.25	1.91	6.65	0.64	0.16	0.30	18.35	0.43	3.12	21.91
1990	8.14	1.63	6.62	0.62	0.20	0.29	17.99	0.49	3.20	21.68
1991	7.88	1.65	6.67	0.71	0.19	0.27	17.78	0.40	4.32	22.50
1992	7.63	1.61	6.63	0.73	0.18	0.28	17.49	0.44	3.68	21.61
1993	7.75	1.79	6.51	0.73	0.19	0.29	17.55	0.30	4.37	22.21
1994	7.70	1.99	6.54	0.78	0.22	0.28	17.84	0.33	3.93	22.10
1995	7.98	2.12	6.55	0.78	0.20	0.26	18.27	0.39	2.90	21.56
1996	8.40	2.20	6.52	0.69	0.22	0.24	18.60	0.33	3.99	22.91
1997	8.88	2.20	6.50	0.69	0.24	0.22	19.03	0.31	4.05	23.39
1998	9.46	2.15	6.53	0.66	0.23	0.20	19.66	0.37	4.01	24.04
1999	9.64	2.02	6.70	0.77	0.30	0.20	20.02	0.38	2.27	22.68
2000	10.35	2.14	6.72	0.71	0.30	0.21	20.86	0.44	2.21	23.51
2001	9.90	1.50	6.91	0.66	0.28	0.19	19.83	0.38	2.20	22.40
2002	8.27	1.43	6.76	0.65	0.26	0.18	17.86	0.33	2.14	20.33
2003	7.33	1.22	6.58	0.62	0.20	0.18	16.14	0.32	2.14	18.60
2004	7.00	1.64	6.35	0.60	0.21	0.18	16.27	0.28	2.16	18.72

Source: Budget of the United States Government: Historical Tables Fiscal Year 2005 and 2006 at *http://www.gpoaccess.gov/usbudget/fy05/hist.html*
Budget of the United States Government (1982–1995) [Doc. ed.]. Annual United States, Y 1.1/7:(CONG-SESS- NOS.)/V.1.
GDP = gross domestic product.

The Evolution of Public Finance and Budgeting

TABLE 2

Federal Receipts as Percentage of Total Receipts from the Public, 1980–2004

	Individual Income Tax	Corporate Income Tax	Social Security	Excise Taxes	Estate and Gift	Customs	Total Taxes	Miscellaneous	Offsetting Receipts and Collections from the Public
1980	40.14	10.62	25.95	4.00	1.05	1.18	85.05	2.09	12.86
1981	40.16	8.59	25.66	5.74	0.95	1.14	84.17	1.94	13.89
1982	39.84	6.58	26.96	4.86	1.07	1.18	82.66	2.17	15.17
1983	39.44	5.05	28.53	4.82	0.83	1.18	81.97	2.13	15.90
1984	35.04	6.68	28.11	4.39	0.71	1.34	78.26	2.01	19.73
1985	35.67	6.54	28.27	3.84	0.68	1.29	78.27	1.98	19.75
1986	35.71	6.46	29.05	3.37	0.71	1.36	78.72	2.05	19.24
1987	37.02	7.91	28.61	3.06	0.71	1.42	80.57	1.84	17.59
1988	35.51	8.36	29.59	3.12	0.67	1.43	80.48	1.80	17.72
1989	37.67	8.73	30.37	2.91	0.74	1.38	83.77	1.97	14.27
1990	37.54	7.52	30.56	2.84	0.92	1.34	82.98	2.25	14.76
1991	35.04	7.35	29.66	3.18	0.83	1.19	79.02	1.77	19.21
1992	35.30	7.44	30.68	3.38	0.83	1.29	80.93	2.02	17.05
1993	34.88	8.04	29.31	3.29	0.86	1.29	79.00	1.33	19.66
1994	34.83	9.00	29.60	3.54	0.98	1.29	80.73	1.48	17.79
1995	37.00	9.84	30.37	3.60	0.93	1.21	84.74	1.79	13.47
1996	36.66	9.60	28.45	3.02	0.96	1.04	81.16	1.42	17.42
1997	37.99	9.39	27.78	2.93	1.02	0.92	81.35	1.31	17.33
1998	39.34	8.96	27.15	2.74	0.94	0.85	81.75	1.55	16.70
1999	42.49	8.92	29.56	3.40	1.34	0.89	88.30	1.69	10.02
2000	44.01	9.08	28.61	3.02	1.27	0.87	88.74	1.88	9.38
2001	44.20	6.72	30.85	2.94	1.26	0.86	88.51	1.68	9.81
2002	40.70	7.02	33.23	3.18	1.26	0.88	87.87	1.61	10.52
2003	39.42	6.55	35.41	3.35	1.09	0.99	86.80	1.71	11.49
2004	37.41	8.76	33.92	3.23	1.15	0.98	86.95	1.51	11.54

Source: Budget of the United States Government: Historical Tables Fiscal Year 2005 and 2006 at *http://www.gpoaccess.gov/usbudget/fy05/hist.html* Budget of the United States Government (1982–1995) [Doc. ed.]. Annual United States, Y 1.1/7:(CONG-SESS- NOS.)/V.1.

income tax collections share in 2004 is slightly smaller in 2004 as compared with 1980—37.41 against 40.14 percent—social security collections are considerably greater—33.92 versus 25.95. The upward trend for these collections paused from 1995 to 1998 but otherwise was continuous through the quarter century. The corporate income tax share modestly increased from 1983 to 2000, from 5.05 to 9.08 percent, as restructuring closed some important avoidance avenues, but then declined. The share was 8.76 percent by 2004, the highest it had been since 2000. A final important pattern is that shown by offsetting receipts. While there have been fits and starts in that share over the years, since about 1985 the path has been generally downward. In 1985, the share was 19.75, but had declined to 9.38 percent in 2000. It has reversed a bit, to 11.54 by 2004. This pattern is an important one. These offsetting collection revenues, reflective of the concept that users of services ought to bear costs of their provision, have not kept pace with overall receipts and appear to be part of a movement away from the direct user-pays concept of government finance. Whether planned or intentional, this is an important change in government finances.

The smaller revenue sources showed some modest changes recently, with lower shares for excises and customs duties and higher shares for estate and gift taxes. There were no dramatic shifts for these taxes, however.

Changes in State and Local Government Revenues

A number of changes have also appeared in how state and local governments finance the services that they provide. These changes are detailed in Tables 3–6. As in the analysis of federal collections, the changes are analyzed both in terms of relative amounts collected from the private economy and in terms of the distribution of collections across the main revenue sources. The receipts reports include the operations of utilities and state liquor stores with taxes and charges by general state and local government operations. The complete receipts data are available only through 2002.

While both state and local collections from the private sector as a percent of GDP are higher in 2003 than in 1980, those percentages have reached their present levels by divergent paths. For states, the trend has been persistently upward, except from 2001 to 2003, when the share fell from 7.45 to 7.00 percent, principally because of an absolute decline in individual income tax collections. That drop was a distinct exception as the share rose from 6.21 percent in 1980 to 7.09 percent in 2002. The path is different for local governments. The local share rose from 5.43 percent in 1980 to 6.57 percent in 1990, fell through the 1990s to 6.32 percent in 2000. It was a bit lower in 2002 and 2003. Even with the decline through the 1990s, the share in 2003 is above that in 1980 by more than a percentage point, a considerable relative change in share. The trend has been for greater state and local tax, charge, and sales revenue as a share of GDP. That, of course, is in contrast to the downward trend at the federal level previously noted.

Shares in the revenue structure show more substantial change and several are of particular importance. The first is in the relative significance of retail sales and individual income taxes in the state revenue structure. For most of the second half of the 20th

TABLE 3

State Taxes, Charges, and Sales Revenue as Percentage of GDP, 1980–2003

	Property	General Sales	Selective Sales	Individual Income	Corporate Income	Other	Total Taxes	Charge and Miscellaneous Revenue	Utility and Liquor Sales	Total
1980	0.10	1.55	0.88	1.33	0.48	0.57	4.91	1.15	0.15	6.21
1981	0.09	1.48	0.84	1.31	0.45	0.61	4.79	1.20	0.15	6.14
1982	0.10	1.55	0.87	1.40	0.43	0.65	5.00	1.33	0.15	6.48
1983	0.09	1.52	0.86	1.41	0.37	0.60	4.85	1.31	0.15	6.30
1984	0.10	1.59	0.85	1.50	0.39	0.58	5.00	1.33	0.14	6.48
1985	0.09	1.65	0.85	1.51	0.42	0.59	5.10	1.42	0.14	6.66
1986	0.10	1.68	0.84	1.51	0.41	0.57	5.11	1.50	0.13	6.74
1987	0.10	1.68	0.85	1.60	0.44	0.54	5.21	1.48	0.12	6.81
1988	0.10	1.70	0.84	1.57	0.42	0.53	5.17	1.45	0.11	6.74
1989	0.10	1.70	0.82	1.62	0.44	0.51	5.18	1.51	0.11	6.80
1990	0.10	1.72	0.82	1.66	0.37	0.51	5.18	1.56	0.11	6.85
1991	0.10	1.72	0.84	1.66	0.34	0.52	5.18	1.63	0.11	6.92
1992	0.11	1.70	0.87	1.66	0.34	0.52	5.20	1.70	0.10	7.00
1993	0.12	1.72	0.90	1.68	0.36	0.53	5.32	1.67	0.10	7.09
1994	0.12	1.74	0.89	1.66	0.36	0.51	5.28	1.62	0.10	6.99
1995	0.13	1.79	0.87	1.70	0.39	0.51	5.40	1.68	0.09	7.17
1996	0.13	1.78	0.85	1.71	0.38	0.50	5.35	1.67	0.09	7.12
1997	0.12	1.78	0.83	1.75	0.37	0.50	5.35	1.69	0.09	7.13
1998	0.12	1.78	0.82	1.83	0.36	0.51	5.41	1.71	0.09	7.21
1999	0.13	1.77	0.81	1.86	0.33	0.49	5.39	1.64	0.09	7.12
2000	0.11	1.78	0.79	1.98	0.33	0.50	5.50	1.74	0.09	7.32
2001	0.10	1.77	0.78	2.05	0.31	0.51	5.53	1.82	0.11	7.45
2002	0.09	1.71	0.79	1.77	0.24	0.50	5.10	1.83	0.15	7.09
2003	0.10	1.68	0.81	1.66	0.26	0.50	5.00	1.84	0.15	7.00

Source: U.S. Bureau of Census, Governments Division and U.S. Department of Commerce, Bureau of Economic Analysis.

TABLE 4
Local Government Tax, Charge, and Sales Revenue as Percentage of GDP, 1980–2003

	Property	General Sales	Selective Sales	Individual Income	Corporate Income	Other	Total Taxes	Charge and Miscellaneous Revenue	Utility and Liquor Sales	Total Tax, Charges, and Sales
1980	2.35	0.29	0.14	0.18	0.00	0.13	3.10	1.56	0.77	5.43
1981	2.30	0.30	0.13	0.18	0.00	0.13	3.03	1.63	0.81	5.47
1982	2.42	0.31	0.14	0.16	0.03	0.12	3.18	1.83	0.88	5.90
1983	2.43	0.32	0.14	0.15	0.03	0.12	3.20	1.87	0.91	5.97
1984	2.35	0.32	0.14	0.14	0.04	0.13	3.14	1.86	0.90	5.89
1985	2.36	0.35	0.15	0.15	0.04	0.14	3.19	1.93	0.93	6.05
1986	2.41	0.36	0.15	0.16	0.04	0.15	3.25	1.98	0.93	6.16
1987	2.46	0.36	0.15	0.16	0.04	0.16	3.34	2.02	0.93	6.29
1988	2.49	0.36	0.16	0.16	0.04	0.16	3.36	1.95	0.92	6.23
1989	2.50	0.35	0.16	0.16	0.04	0.16	3.36	1.98	0.92	6.26
1990	2.58	0.37	0.16	0.16	0.03	0.16	3.47	2.08	0.90	6.45
1991	2.70	0.37	0.16	0.17	0.03	0.15	3.58	2.09	0.91	6.57
1992	2.71	0.36	0.16	0.17	0.03	0.15	3.58	2.05	0.88	6.52
1993	2.73	0.36	0.16	0.17	0.03	0.15	3.61	2.06	0.88	6.55
1994	2.67	0.37	0.17	0.17	0.04	0.16	3.57	2.05	0.89	6.51
1995	2.62	0.38	0.17	0.17	0.03	0.17	3.53	2.11	0.88	6.52
1996	2.55	0.38	0.17	0.17	0.03	0.16	3.46	2.15	0.87	6.49
1997	2.51	0.38	0.17	0.17	0.04	0.16	3.42	2.11	0.85	6.39
1998	2.51	0.38	0.17	0.18	0.04	0.16	3.44	2.14	0.84	6.42
1999	2.46	0.39	0.17	0.18	0.03	0.17	3.40	2.11	0.84	6.36
2000	2.43	0.41	0.17	0.17	0.04	0.17	3.39	2.10	0.83	6.32
2001	2.50	0.44	0.18	0.18	0.04	0.17	3.50	2.22	0.88	6.60
2002	2.57	0.41	0.18	0.16	0.03	0.18	3.53	2.17	0.87	6.57
2003	2.61	0.41	0.18	0.16	0.03	0.18	3.56	2.13	0.83	6.51

Source: Same as Table 3.

The Evolution of Public Finance and Budgeting

TABLE 5
State Tax, Charge, and Sales Revenue as Percent of Total, 1980–2003

	Property Tax	General Sales Tax	Selective Sales Tax	Individual Income Tax	Corporate Income Tax	Other	Total Taxes	Charge and Miscellaneous Revenue	Utility and Liquor Sales
1980	1.67	24.90	14.24	21.40	7.69	9.18	79.08	18.57	2.35
1981	1.54	24.17	13.72	21.30	7.37	9.90	77.99	19.60	2.41
1982	1.48	23.87	13.49	21.67	6.64	9.97	77.11	20.55	2.34
1983	1.47	24.06	13.57	22.33	5.90	9.56	76.89	20.77	2.34
1984	1.52	24.57	13.05	23.14	6.09	8.90	77.27	20.61	2.12
1985	1.42	24.77	12.70	22.64	6.27	8.80	76.59	21.38	2.03
1986	1.45	24.89	12.48	22.44	6.11	8.49	75.86	22.24	1.90
1987	1.43	24.66	12.45	23.53	6.42	7.99	76.48	21.73	1.79
1988	1.47	25.29	12.53	23.29	6.30	7.87	76.75	21.56	1.68
1989	1.45	25.06	12.03	23.83	6.40	7.46	76.24	22.14	1.62
1990	1.47	25.09	11.92	24.18	5.47	7.49	75.63	22.81	1.56
1991	1.50	24.88	12.15	23.94	4.91	7.52	74.89	23.54	1.56
1992	1.51	24.26	12.50	23.68	4.92	7.40	74.26	24.25	1.48
1993	1.65	24.28	12.69	23.75	5.13	7.46	74.96	23.61	1.43
1994	1.70	24.87	12.71	23.68	5.19	7.33	75.48	23.14	1.38
1995	1.79	24.93	12.18	23.68	5.48	7.18	75.26	23.44	1.30
1996	1.79	25.06	12.00	24.01	5.27	7.09	75.22	23.51	1.27
1997	1.74	24.90	11.66	24.49	5.19	7.06	75.04	23.72	1.24
1998	1.69	24.63	11.32	25.40	4.93	7.07	75.04	23.74	1.22
1999	1.76	24.89	11.36	26.16	4.66	6.87	75.71	23.09	1.20
2000	1.53	24.27	10.81	27.07	4.52	6.87	75.08	23.75	1.17
2001	1.38	23.76	10.43	27.57	4.20	6.82	74.16	24.38	1.46
2002	1.31	24.18	11.13	24.99	3.38	7.05	72.03	25.79	2.18
2003	1.36	24.04	11.62	23.70	3.60	7.08	71.50	26.28	2.22

Source: U.S. Bureau of Census, Governments Division.

TABLE 6
Local Government Tax, Charge, and Sales Receipts as Percentage of Total, 1980–2003

	Property	General Sales	Selective Sales	Individual Income	Corporate Income	Other	Total Taxes	Charge and Miscellaneous Revenue	Utility and Liquor Sales
1980	43.30	5.39	2.58	3.29	0.00	2.45	57.01	28.88	14.18
1981	42.12	5.40	2.33	3.23	0.00	2.34	55.42	29.80	14.78
1982	41.06	5.34	2.39	2.65	0.54	2.03	54.00	31.06	14.94
1983	40.69	5.32	2.41	2.53	0.52	2.07	53.55	31.24	15.21
1984	39.96	5.46	2.44	2.45	0.66	2.28	53.25	31.55	15.20
1985	39.09	5.75	2.47	2.53	0.60	2.26	52.69	31.98	15.33
1986	39.06	5.78	2.45	2.53	0.58	2.36	52.75	32.17	15.08
1987	39.12	5.75	2.46	2.59	0.65	2.51	53.08	32.15	14.77
1988	40.00	5.71	2.50	2.58	0.65	2.52	53.96	31.34	14.69
1989	39.92	5.58	2.50	2.62	0.60	2.49	53.71	31.68	14.61
1990	40.04	5.77	2.47	2.56	0.49	2.45	53.77	32.21	14.02
1991	41.04	5.65	2.47	2.55	0.48	2.29	54.49	31.74	13.77
1992	41.56	5.59	2.50	2.56	0.49	2.26	54.96	31.50	13.54
1993	41.71	5.55	2.50	2.55	0.51	2.31	55.13	31.46	13.41
1994	40.99	5.65	2.55	2.54	0.57	2.47	54.77	31.49	13.73
1995	40.18	5.79	2.59	2.55	0.48	2.58	54.17	32.29	13.54
1996	39.34	5.86	2.59	2.62	0.53	2.43	53.37	33.16	13.46
1997	39.28	5.90	2.63	2.66	0.58	2.51	53.57	33.08	13.35
1998	39.10	5.96	2.63	2.76	0.59	2.55	53.60	33.32	13.08
1999	38.70	6.15	2.61	2.81	0.54	2.72	53.53	33.20	13.27
2000	38.41	6.56	2.66	2.76	0.57	2.70	53.65	33.26	13.08
2001	37.86	6.59	2.70	2.73	0.54	2.56	52.99	33.64	13.37
2002	39.13	6.29	2.67	2.49	0.44	2.68	53.70	33.06	13.24
2003	40.05	6.25	2.71	2.45	0.42	2.71	54.58	32.64	12.78

Source: Same as Table 5.

The Evolution of Public Finance and Budgeting

century—from fiscal 1947 to fiscal 1997—the retail sales tax was the largest single tax source of state government as its growth financed the expansion of state programs through the post–WW II era and beyond. However, strong growth in individual income tax receipts in the last years of the 1990s (and adoption of the tax in Connecticut) caused income tax receipts to exceed sales tax receipts in fiscal 1998. The two taxes continue as the twin buttresses of state government finance.[6] The income elasticity of the individual income tax is significantly greater than that of the retail sales tax. As a result, the tendency is for income tax revenue to increase more quickly than retail sales tax revenue during economic expansion—like that of most of the 1990s—unless legislative changes intervene.

Second, the state corporate income tax diminishes in importance as a revenue source. The decline is from 7.69 percent of total tax, charge, and sales revenue in 1980 to 3.60 percent in 2003. States appear to have focused on corporate taxes in their efforts to attract economic activity, with many exemptions, credits, and other preferences to make their tax environments friendlier to business activity. More recent is the movement toward single-sales or double-weighted-sales factor corporate profits apportionment, replacing the traditional sales-property-payroll factor, as a method for making state tax climates more welcoming for business and, as a result, reducing state corporate income tax revenue. Also, new business organization structures designed to provide the untaxed pass-through of business profits to owners in the manner of a partnership while providing some of the protections and provisions of the corporate form have added to the decline in the taxable corporate base. To the extent such pass-through income is taxed by a state, it will be in the individual income tax, rather than in the corporate income tax. There has always been an air of strong doubt about the case for state corporate income taxes, so the decline in their importance as a revenue source may not be a cause for great concern, except for the extent to which reductions have been provided haphazardly, and the extent to which the cost of government services significant to economic activity has not been generated by the revenue system. The root causes of the decline are almost certainly more a part of competition for economic activity, in the belief that tax climate is crucial for economic expansion, than it is based on the fundamental principles that may or may not provide logical support for such a tax.[7]

Third, there has been a decline in shares of both selective excise tax and revenues from miscellaneous other taxes. For the former, from 14.24 percent of the total in 1980 to 11.62 percent in 2003 and for the latter, from 9.18 to 7.08 percent. These taxes, some levied on a specific rather than ad valorem basis, simply have not grown at the pace of the income and general sales taxes. Even when inflation is not rampant, their yields cannot keep up because of the low income elasticity of their bases.

---

6. The sales tax returned to its top position, at least for the time being, in 2003 and stayed there by a narrow margin in 2004. Barring structural changes, the individual income tax is likely to pass the sales tax again in a few years.

7. A good analysis of the logical positions on taxation of business appears in Thomas Pogue, "Principles of Business Taxation," in *Handbook of Taxation,* ed. Bart Hildreth and James Richardson (New York: Marcel Dekker, 1999), 191–204.

Finally, there has been a significant increase in the extent to which charges and miscellaneous revenues contribute to total state revenues. The share increased from 18.57 percent in 1980 to 26.28 percent in 2003. Substantial increases in higher education tuition are important contributors to this increase. The share of charge and miscellaneous revenue in state finances is now greater than the share of offsetting receipts and collections is in federal finances, which was not the case at the beginning of the 1980s. This change is consistent with the antitax philosophy that drives most legislatures.

A number of significant changes also are apparent in the revenue systems of local government. First, the property tax continues as the most important tax source for local governments, 43.3 percent of total tax, charge, and sales revenue in 1980 against 40.05 percent in 2003. There is a slight decline in share—but nothing like the decline in the 1970s when the property tax revolt and the spirit of California's Proposition 13 was in full flower. The share was 56.6 percent in 1971–1972, so the decline in share from then until 1980 was dramatic.[8] From that point, the property tax has retained its critical position as the fiscal foundation of local government finances.

Second, the general sales tax continues as second-ranking tax in terms of revenue to local government, increasing modestly from 5.39 percent in 1980 to 6.25 percent in 2003. A much larger increase in share occurred in the previous decade: the share was 3.7 percent in 1972. This source was important to local governments as they avoided the politically unpopular property tax during the 1970s. The contribution from local income taxes is somewhat lower in 2002 than it was in the early 1980s. These taxes just have not caught on as a local tax source.

Third, changes in the shares of charge and miscellaneous revenue and utility revenue generally cancelled each other out. Charge and miscellaneous revenues increased from 28.88 percent of total tax, charge, and sales revenues in 1980 to 32.64 percent in 2003; utility revenue fell from 14.18 percent in 1980 to 12.78 percent in 2003. The combined share for charge and sales revenues was 43.06 percent in 1980 and 45.42 percent in 2003. A movement toward having users bear a larger share of the cost of government services was stronger during the 1970s: the combined share was 32.3 percent in 1972, so there was a significant shift in the 1970s. However, of the three tiers of government, the local is more reliant on charges than either state or federal governments—and the differences are even more distinct if school districts are excluded from the local government tallies.

Some Revenue Patterns for All American Governments

One distinction about the revenue system that continues over the past quarter century is the American devotion to the income base. The individual income tax dominates the federal revenue system, followed closely by the narrow-base income (payroll) tax that

8. King-Meadows and Lowery find the limits adopted during the tax revolt era did reduce the size of government. Tyson King-Meadows and David Lowery, "The Impact of Tax Revolt Era State Fiscal Caps: A Research Update," *Public Budgeting & Finance* 16, no. 1 (1996): 102–112.

The Evolution of Public Finance and Budgeting

supports the federal social insurance system. More federal revenue comes from the corporate income tax. At the state level, although the system is more balanced than the federal one, the individual income tax still produces about one-quarter of all revenue and is the first or second largest tax source in virtually all the states. This domination is apparent through the years and shows up in international comparisons. Using International Monetary Fund statistics to allow a uniform comparison, the most recent data show the United States to raise 73.7 percent of its tax revenue (all levels of government) from income and social security payroll taxes, compared with a median for high-income member countries of the Organisation for Economic Co-operation and Development (OECD) of 64.7 percent.[9] That is a significant difference for a major tax source. This difference is supported by dramatically lower reliance on revenue from taxes on goods and services in the United States, 15.2 percent of tax revenue, against a median of 28.3 percent in these OECD countries. Much of this revenue in other countries comes from national value-added taxes, the development of which must rank as the most significant fiscal innovation of the last half of the 20th century. The United States is the only OECD country now that does not levy such a tax, but its effectiveness at raising revenue with few distortions and at low cost has stimulated no groundswell of interest in adopting the tax here. The federal establishment is suspicious and state and local governments worry about impacts on their use of the consumption base. Maybe it will, however, be the answer to one of the perennial puzzles discussed later.

A second distinction in the revenue system is limited use of charge and sales revenue to support government activities. In spite of considerable public opposition to tax increases, improved technology for metering and controlling usage of services (necessary to impose an effective direct charge), and great support for market-oriented solutions to public problems, the last quarter century shows no great swing toward direct charges as an element of government finance. While lotteries have become a standard component of state fiscal systems, increasing from 10 states in 1980 to 40 states plus the District of Columbia in 2005, revenue from them remains a minor component of state receipts and other charge and sales revenue have not grown dramatically. This is a component of a market approach to government operations that seems not to have taken hold in the United States.

PERENNIAL AND PERSISTENT PUZZLES IN REVENUE POLICY

A number of issues have been important in revenue system structure and administration during the past quarter century. Most have been with tax systems even longer than that. It is not an exercise in futility to continue their exploration because, over time, some progress may be possible, even as lawmakers generally insist that two steps forward be

---

9. International Monetary Fund, *Government Finance Statistics Yearbook 2003.*

accompanied by at least one step back when the issue is taxation. Some of the more significant areas will be reviewed here.

The Role of the Property Tax

The fine review of the property tax by Glenn Fisher, in its title, raises the possibility that the property tax is the "worst tax."[10] That is what the annual polls conducted by the now-defunct Advisory Commission on Intergovernmental Relations showed the popular view to be. In each polling cycle, either the federal individual income tax or the local property tax ranked as the popular choice as the worst tax then levied. Possibly the opposition to the property tax was at its most fervent during the late 1970s, when Proposition 13 in California focused national attention on the tax and stimulated movement to constrain the burden of the tax, if not remove it entirely from the portfolio of revenue options. That brought the precipitous decline in the role that the property tax played in state and local revenue portfolios that was previously noted—from 56.6 percent of local government revenue in 1971–1972 to 43.4 percent in 1980. But popular opinion about property taxation is not likely to have improved and few lawmakers are eager to be seen as supporting greater reliance on the tax. Indeed, schemes to reduce reliance on property taxes as a means for finance of local government are perennial proposals in most state legislatures.

The property tax can be difficult to defend. As Frederick Stocker, a tax economist who generally supports the use of property taxes (as does Glenn Fisher), observes, the property tax in most states "resembles a structure built by a mad architect, erected on a shaky foundation by an incompetent builder, and made worse by the well-intentioned repair work of amateur tinkerers."[11] In practice, the tax typically has low elasticity to economic activity, causes considerable horizontal disparity in tax burdens, places noticeable burden on housing, may discourage economic development, places disproportionate burden on real-property-intensive economic activity, and is costly to administer properly, to name only a few from its lists of offenses.

Nevertheless, in spite of all its perceived problems, the real property tax appears the ideal source of independent revenue for local governments and, with the will to impose proper design and administration, most of those objections can be remedied. If there is a desire for a degree of local revenue autonomy to support decentralization of government operations to get public decisions closer to the people for more responsive government, there are no serious alternatives. The real property tax base is immobile, can equitably and efficiently be administered even at the somewhat more leisurely pace that characterizes local administration, can be implemented to encourage economic development,

---

10. Glenn W. Fisher, *The Worst Tax? A History of the Property Tax in America* (Lawrence: University Press of Kansas, 1996).

11. Frederick C. Stocker, *Proposition 13: A Ten Year Perspective* (Cambridge, MA: Lincoln Institute of Land Policy, 1991), 1.

and is difficult to evade. As the only substantial tax source that is collected by a taxpayer passive format, its administrative cost is relatively high, but compliance is simple because the work is done by trained tax authorities with virtually no requirements placed on the property owner. The fruits of good quality local government services show up as higher property values, thus establishing a link between services provided and payment of the tax—and a good number of services financed from property tax revenue provide direct protective services to the property. Hence, there are strong efficiency, equity, and administrative grounds for use of the real property tax as the fiscal foundation of local government operations.

Maybe the slowed pace of declining property tax reliance reflects the implicit realization of the necessary role of the property tax in a modern system of government finance in a democracy. Or it may reflect the reality that there are few meaningful alternatives for providing local revenue autonomy. The property tax has problems, but not so many as with any broad-based alternatives for its replacement or with narrower specialty taxes. Sokolow, however, raises an important issue. The property tax limitations starting at the end of the 1970s have diminished "local fiscal discretion while increasing the state role in local finance increases."[12] While his analysis focused on the western states, similar observations can be made throughout the country. In essence, the constraints on the property tax emerging from public dissatisfaction have diminished local fiscal autonomy and increased fiscal centralization—even as the principle of subsidiarity, in other words, that government decisions should be made at the lowest feasible unit of government is spreading as a guiding standard throughout the rest of the world.[13]

Even as Americans object to the burdens of the real property tax, countries that are establishing new systems of government and government finance after years of nondemocratic or nonmarket-oriented government control are looking to the property tax as a means of finance for local government, as are other countries looking to decentralize their systems of local government finance. That is true in South Africa where Bell and Bowman have explored its application as the means of support of the new local governments and it is true in countries making the steps away from the central plan, as Zorn, Tesche, and Cornia have explored for Bosnia.[14] Kelly has shown how Kenya can work to improve the operations of its property tax with a collection analysis model that can be

---

12. Alvin D. Sokolow, "The Changing Property Tax in the West: State Centralization of Local Finances," *Public Budgeting & Finance* 20, no. 1 (2000): 97.

13. Mullins and Joyce provide a broader examination of the effects of the tax and expenditure limitation movement on state and local fiscal structures, including a helpful categorization of types of limits on property taxes. Daniel R. Mullins and Philip G. Joyce, "Tax and Expenditure Limitations and State and Local Fiscal Structure: An Empirical Assessment," *Public Budgeting & Finance* 16, no. 1 (1996): 75–101.

14. Michael E. Bell and John H. Bowman, "Local Property Taxation in South Africa: Current Performance and Challenges for the Post-Apartheid Era," *Public Budgeting & Finance* 17, no. 4 (1997): 71–87; and C. Kurt Zorn, Jean Tesche, and Gary Cornia, "Diversifying Local Government Revenue in Bosnia–Herzegovina through an Area-Based Property Tax," *Public Budgeting & Finance* 20, no. 4 (2000): 63–86.

applied to many revenue mobilization programs.[15] And there are similar applications in developing and transition countries worldwide. Even some European countries are reconsidering the property tax as a means for local finance as they seek to move public decision making closer to the general public. Careful analysis of all the options available for creation of modern systems of taxation have led these and other countries to the conclusion that local fiscal autonomy and utilization of a real property tax are synonymous.

Without the broad base available from the real property tax, local governments are almost certain to be fiefs of higher governments, no matter the rhetoric. It is a lesson that Americans might well reflect on as politicians continue to run on antiproperty tax platforms. How would limiting local autonomy help make government more efficient and responsive to the interests of the citizenry? And there is another dilemma in property tax administration. Information technology, including modern geographical information systems, sophisticated mapping, and computer modeling, make high-quality property tax administration more feasible and less expensive with each passing year and assessors now are much more capable of keeping assessed values in line with the market value of property on an annual basis. Yet political animosity to property taxation remains high and sentiment to move the property tax base away from current market value to some other standard (usually a version of the acquisition value scheme created by California's Proposition 13 in 1978) is strong. Indeed, such changes have been adopted for at least some types of property in Michigan and Florida and are regularly proposed in other states. Just as closer matching of assessed values to current market values of property is becoming a good possibility for any jurisdiction, a revolt against the use of property values, particularly current market values, is growing. The considerable disparities and distortions that characterize property taxation in California seem destined to repeat themselves in a number of other states unless some strategy can be found to change the political dynamic.

Realigning the Federal Tax System

As observed earlier, the income base dominates the finances of the federal government. For some years, many observers have believed that this amounts to overreliance and that, at a minimum, some of that income-based burden should be shifted to a general consumption base. Others have argued that income simply should not be used as a tax base at all. The argument will not disappear, most recently surfacing as part of the discussions of the President's Advisory Panel on Federal Tax Reform in 2005. Regardless of whether realignment will occur soon or not, it is assured that discussion will not subside. And here is the sneaky part. The existing federal individual income tax is already something of a hybrid income—consumption tax, in light of the many preferences already in the system for saving (the many preference programs for retirement savings, the exclusion of capital gains on home sales, medical savings account deductions, tuition

---

15. Roy Kelly, "Designing a Property Tax Reform Strategy for Sub-Sahara Africa: An Analytical Framework Applied to Kenya," *Public Budgeting & Finance* 20, no. 4 (2000): 36–51.

savings programs, etc.). A realignment to a consumption base would not be as drastic as it might appear on first consideration, although the means of administering a new consumption tax might be considerably different than the current system based on individual annual reports.

The economic case is straightforward. Movement from income to consumption as a tax base would encourage saving and capital formation and higher saving and investment would allow improved economic expansion and modernization. Because an income tax causes both income saved and return from that saving to be taxed, there is a tax advantage to consumption now relative to delayed consumption, i.e., saving. International comparisons show the United States to have extremely low personal savings rates—and heavy reliance on income taxation relative to consumption taxation. While there are other confounding factors, the nature of our federal tax system may be a contributing influence to this lower savings rate and reduced economic potential. The several federal income tax attempts to provide some tax relief for personal saving are elements grafted onto the basic income tax, certainly not anything fundamental.

There is a strong philosophical/equity argument for consumption taxation as well. The tax base serves as the standard for distributing the cost of government across elements of the private economy and needs to be driven by the capacity of each private entity to bear a portion of that total cost. Private consumption is each entity's own assessment of how much private goods and services it can afford to purchase—household consumption indicates the share of total consumption in the economy it can afford, based on its own assessment of current, anticipated future, and accumulated household resources. In a market-based economy, such a self-assessment of household affluence would appear to be the ideal standard for determining shares of the cost of government as well. That is the essence of the consumption base—driving shares of the cost of government according to shares of private consumption. And there is an important fundamental justice argument as well. Nicholas Kaldor made the point effectively many years ago: "An Expenditure base would tax people according to the amount which they take out of the common pool, and not according to what they put into it. . . . It is only by spending, not by earning or saving, that an individual imposes a burden on the rest of the community in attaining his own ends."[16]

Suppose the federal government is to follow the economic logic and proceed toward consumption taxation.[17] It has three fundamental alternatives: (i) a personal consumption tax operated in the same fashion as the present income tax although with full (or at

---

16. Nicholas Kaldor, *An Expenditure Tax* (London: George Allen and Unwin, 1955), 53.

17. These comments do not include the major transition issues that would be involved if a consumption tax were to completely replace the income taxes. For instance, what to do about the many people who have lived their economic lives under an income tax, have managed to save enough for their retirements, and now face having consumption based on those savings taxed at rates high enough to replace income tax yield? Such people would correctly feel extremely unfairly treated by their government. But what to do for their transition?

least fuller) deduction for personal savings;[18] (ii) a value-added tax generally modeled on the extremely successful European system; or (iii) a retail sales tax generally fashioned like the American state general sales taxes. The former would be a direct tax; the latter two would be indirect taxes collected by vendors on transactions.

What can be said about the options? A personal consumption tax, because it is administered on a direct basis, could be tailored to the individual circumstances of the taxpaying unit—size of unit, special circumstances of the unit, level of consumption of the unit, etc.—all could be taken into account in determining the tax bill. Hence, circumstances that influence tax-bearing capacity could be given allowance, personal exemptions could be allowed, and statutory rates could even be graduated. Much of the tax could, in fact, operate in the same fashion as the current income tax. To those favoring radical restructuring, this is a problem, not a virtue; for others, it affords some possibility of easier transition. And such a tax would not directly impact the spending from savings that have already been taxed under the existing individual income tax. An aggressive personal consumption tax collected in this manner would break new ground: such an approach has never been attempted by an industrialized democracy. However, if there is a desire to personalize the tax, to apply graduated rates, to retain personal deductions and exemptions, to continue to use the tax system as a means for delivering income support programs like the Earned Income Tax Credit, and so on, then this direct format is necessary. Transaction-based taxes, like the retail sales or value-added taxes, cannot easily be personalized to take account of characteristics of the particular taxpayer; the same rate applies when any purchaser appears at the cash register. To attempt to vary rates by taxpayer would usually involve excess collection expense.

The retail sales tax and the value-added tax, in their ideal forms, are tax twins.[19] Each produces a uniform tax on household consumption expenditure, so they are economically equivalent. They are both indirect taxes collected by vendors on individual transactions, rather than collected directly from purchasers. They differ in that the retail sales tax is intended to be applied once in the flow of commerce from producer to distributor to vendor to household consumer, at the sale from vendor to household consumer to the total value of the product, while the value-added tax is intended to apply to each transaction in that flow on the value added by the seller. For any product, the sum of added values equals the total value at retail. Operationally the two taxes differ in how they exclude businesses from bearing the burden of the tax and hence prevent tax pyramiding. The retail sales tax manages this through suspension certificates: a business purchaser provides the certificate to a vendor and the certificate suspends collection of the tax. The value-added tax accomplishes the task by making businesses both tax payers on their purchases and tax collectors on their sales. They use the tax they have collected to reimburse the tax they have

18. The flat tax proposals of the Hall–Rabushka variety would be in this category [Robert Hall and Alvin Rabushka, *The Flat Tax*, rev. ed. (Stanford, CA: Hoover Institute, 1995)].

19. John L. Mikesell, "Changing the Federal Tax Philosophy: A National Value-Added Tax or Retail Sales Tax?", *Public Budgeting & Finance* 18, no. 2 (1998): 53–68.

paid, then remit the remainder to the government. When both systems are operating in textbook fashion, the taxes are identically applied to final household consumption.

The problem is that neither retail sales tax nor value-added tax operates perfectly in terms of excluding business purchases—but the value-added tax in practice provides more complete exclusion of business purchases than does the retail sales tax, thereby providing less discrimination against capital investment and economic development, and also provides more inclusive coverage of household consumption because it is more likely to include purchases of services in the taxable base.

Few tax scholars believe that a retail sales tax is administrable at statutory rates much above 10 percent—and to provide significant relief of the federal income taxes, let alone replace them entirely, would require a rate well above that critical level. European experience shows the much greater viability of value-added taxes in yielding a major share of total national revenue. As Daniel Mitchell of the Heritage Foundation put it, the value-added tax is "a perniciously effective way of raising revenues," "a relatively nondestructive way to raise tax revenue" that does not penalize saving and investment.[20] The tax is bad in the view of those favoring small and limited government because it is too good at yielding revenue without collateral damage to the economy or society. Furthermore, there is no compliance burden for the typical taxpayer—both taxes place the collection cost on the vendor, not the customer, so there is a veneer of simplicity for the taxpayer. Compliance issues fall at the feet of the vendor, so they are unseen by the customer and the tax looks simple to the typical taxpayer, regardless of the considerable compliance efforts that must be undertaken by the vendor.

Will fundamental tax restructuring emerge from the continuing efforts to restructure the federal income tax? It is impossible to predict, but the process is at least raising interesting alternatives.

Simplification

Tax simplification is a perennial in tax policy and is a standard evaluation criterion in studies of tax systems. There is, however, a practical problem. Tax simplicity is an excellent applause line in political campaigns, but the support declines when an effort is made to put simplification into practice. The provisions that create complexity have been inserted in the tax system on purpose in order to improve perceived equity or reduce perceived inequity, to encourage economic activities that are regarded as desirable, to accommodate certain economic circumstances, or to close some provision that appeared to inappropriately reduce tax liability of some economic entities. The people who put those provisions in the code know their intentions and intend that the provisions remain. In many instances, taxpayers support simplification that ends preferences available to others but not simplification that would end preferences that they receive. They are perfectly happy to continue dealing with the complexity that reduces their own tax

---

20. Daniel Mitchell, "What's VAT?" *National Review* March 1, 2005 [Online: *http://www.nationalreview.com/nrof_comment/mitchell200503010824.asp*].

liability. Nevertheless, simplification is a perpetual component of discussions of tax structure and administration, in spite of the extreme difficulty of the cause. It is an objective with great appeal that fades when it is necessary to get to the details.

Simplification often requires a fundamental restructuring of tax policy. The Tax Reform Act of 1986, by ending some deductions and other preferences and reducing the number of tax rate brackets and their level, did provide simplification, but only as part of an overall restructuring package—and complicating features began to return to the federal income tax almost immediately. There is a demand for complexity (i) because tax preferences are the source of much tax complexity (for example, the several provisions for encouraging saving for retirement) and those benefiting from the preferences are perfectly willing to keep the existing ones and add new ones and (ii) because complicated provisions have been added to prevent certain tax avoidance strategies. Nina Olson, the National Taxpayer Advocate, outlined in testimony to the President's Advisory Panel on Federal Tax Reform the major areas of complexity in the federal individual income tax to include the earned income tax credit, the alternate minimum tax, the many preferences for saving for retirement, the several credits, deductions, and exclusions for providing preferences for education expenditure, the "kiddie tax" to prevent high-income individuals from putting assets in the name of minor children to have income taxed at lower rates, family status provisions regarding dependents, filing status, and child tax credits, and rules regarding mortgage interest deductions.[21] Each of these complications represents a response to one or the other of those demands. Because of these basic demands for complexity, simplification is always difficult. To remove any of these complexities would either end a preference of value to somebody or open an avoidance approach.[22]

One pressing tax simplification challenges for American government finance emerges from the special problem that electronic commerce has created for the equitable and effective collection of state retail sales taxes. The problem is created because of the commerce clause of the United States Constitution. Under that clause, states are not permitted to place undue burden on interstate commerce and, according to the landmark U.S. Supreme Court case *Quill Corp. v. North Dakota* (91-0194), 504 U.S. 298 (1992), to

---

21. Nina E. Olson, "Complexity, Compliance, and Communication: Why Should Taxpayers Comply in a Complex and Changing Tax Environment?" Presentation to the President's Advisory Panel on Federal Tax Reform, March 3, 2005 [Online: *http://www.taxreformpanel.gov/meetings/docs/oslson_03032005.ppt*].

22. Another compliance simplification strategy would be a return-free system in which the tax agency prepares the tax return based on third-party data it receives (withholding, interest, dividends, etc.) and submits this preliminary return to the taxpayer to accept, modify, or replace with his or her own calculations. [Department of the Treasury, *Report to the Congress on Return-Free Tax Systems: Tax Simplification is a Prerequisite* (Washington, DC: Department of Treasury, 2003).] The approach relieves the taxpayer of most effort and makes income tax administration more like that of the real property tax. The California ReadyReturn pilot program for 2004 demonstrated the feasibility of such a program, although it only works for the least complex returns and hence is no substitute for more fundamental simplification. It will be expanded in 2005. An earlier Michigan experiment was a failure (fewer than 150 taxpayers took the option). The Treasury study also concluded that more fundamental simplification of the tax structure would be required for the United States to move to such a system.

require out-of-state (remote) vendors to register as sales tax collectors in a state would represent undue burden on them if that vendor has no physical presence within a state. This standard produces a compliance dichotomy between remote and in-state vendors. If a vendor selling by telemarketing, catalog, home shopping channel, or Internet website has no physical presence within a state, that vendor cannot be required to register to collect tax for the state. Purchasers may be required to pay a compensating use tax on the items after they have arrived, but collecting such a transaction-based tax directly from purchasers is almost impossible. Hence, these transactions are in practice outside the coverage of the sales tax, thus presenting issues of protecting both the state tax base and retailers in the state from this tax-free competition.[23]

Congress could remedy the problem. If Congress judges that placing a registration requirement on such vendors would not place an undue burden on them, it may permit the registration. This makes it absolutely incumbent on states to develop a system of sales and compensating use taxes which are simple enough in compliance that requiring vendors to register even if they do not have physical presence in a state would not be burdensome and which are simple enough that those registered vendors can comply with the provisions of all state sales taxes without it being an undue burdensome task. Since March 2000, a group of states has been involved in the Streamlined Sales Tax Project, an historic effort at tax simplification designed to eliminate—at least in the eyes of Congress—any undue burden that requiring remote vendors to register and collect sales and use tax might otherwise create. The simplification agreement, ratified by participating states in November 2002, involves uniform tax returns, state-provided rates and boundaries for local taxes, state-certified software or certified third-party providers of compliance service, state administration of local sales taxes, streamlined exemption procedures, liberalization of good faith protection in acceptance of resale certificates, and unification of definitions and other compliance regulations. It does not prescribe what the sales tax base will be in the states, however, so there would remain variation in the base across states.

The participating states hope that Congress will respond to this compliance simplification by changing the physical presence standard for requiring registration.[24] By January 2005, the following states had revised their sales taxes to make them in apparent conformity with the streamlined system: Arkansas, Florida, Indiana, Iowa, Kansas, Kentucky, Maryland (triggered when Congress changes the registration standard), Michigan, Minnesota, Missouri, Nebraska, Nevada, New Jersey, North Carolina, North Dakota, Ohio, Oklahoma, South Dakota, Tennessee, Utah, and Vermont. This certainly represents

---

23. The problem is not new, although its significance is greater because of the development of purchases made through the Internet. For an investigation of its problems in regard to catalog sales, see Keith Snavely, "State Taxation of Internet Sales: Enforcement Problems and Prospects," *Public Budgeting & Finance* 10, no. 2 (1990): 60–71.

24. There is some possibility that simplification could induce more voluntary registrants: Gary C. Cornia, David L. Sjoquist, and Lawrence C. Walters, "Sales and Use Tax Simplification and Voluntary Compliance," *Public Budgeting & Finance* 24, no. 1 (2004): 1–28.

the greatest accomplishment in state fiscal coordination in American history. Whether it achieves its ultimate objective remains to be seen. That lies in the hands of Congress.

Base Broadening

Base broadening is a perennial hope of tax policy, whether the tax system is that of the federal, state, or local government. The logic of base broadening is simple: high tax rates create economic distortions and inequities according to which taxpayers are able to escape payment of the tax. A given tax yield can be achieved with a lower tax rate if the tax base is broad than if the base is narrow. Better economic consequences are associated with a lower tax rate, so base broadening is sound tax policy so long as the broadening is consistent with the fundamental logic of the tax. In other words, to include previously exempt purchases of clothing in the sales tax base represents sound base broadening but to include business purchases of production inputs represents inappropriate base broadening. The former permits a lower sales tax rate while continues the philosophy of uniform and transparent taxation of household consumption; the latter, by embedding the tax paid on business purchases into operating cost, causes the effective tax borne by the household to be greater than advertised and distorts the way in which businesses conduct their operations. Base broadening within the principles of fundamental tax policy, however, is desirable for equity and efficiency reasons.[25]

Base broadening successes in recent years have been sporadic at best. The Tax Reform Act of 1986, as previously noted, broadened the base of the federal individual income tax by eliminating or narrowing a number of deductions (notably interest paid and state and local taxes) and narrowing some income exclusions (e.g., municipal bond interest) and that permitted both a reduction in the number of statutory tax brackets and the level of the marginal rates. However, as the years have passed, deduction categories have gradually returned, the number of brackets has increased, and the top marginal rates have risen. But, overall, some elements of that reform continue in place—the structure has not returned entirely to its prereform status. In this case, the incremental nature of tax policy has been a help: once the big change occurred, it is just as difficult to create mass changes in the policy as it was to get the 1986 changes approved.

Base broadening successes have been even rarer at the state level. Income taxes typically follow their federal counterpart, so as the federal base moves, so goes the state base. But an extra problem emerges with state corporate income taxes. In a quest for encouraging state economic development, states have been shifting from the traditional three factor (payroll, property, and sales) formula for apportioning corporate operating profit among states to either double-weighted sales or sales alone formulas. This reduces the state corporate profits tax burdens of firms with in-state manufacturing facilities (where property and payroll are housed) and encourages economic activity in the state. It

---

25. Tax expenditure budgets should provide a guide for base broadening. Unfortunately, many such documents promise more than they deliver. See John L. Mikesell, "Tax Expenditure Budgets, Budget Policy, and Tax Policy: Confusion in the States," *Public Budgeting & Finance* 22, no. 4 (2002): 34–51.

narrows the base and, unless the economic stimulation brings sufficient new tax base into the state, it will require higher burdens elsewhere in the state revenue portfolio to maintain state services.[26]

The other major state tax, the general sales tax, shows even less success in terms of base broadening. In fact, the trend is generally backward. Table 7 reports the implicit general sales tax base relative to personal income in each sales tax state for 1980, 1985, 1990, 1995, 2000, and 2003. By comparing the tax base to the size of the state economy, it is possible to gauge the relative coverage of each sales tax and the trend is toward lower shares. The national median has fallen from 63.2 percent of personal income in 1980 to 43.4 percent in 2003, a decline of 20 percentage points. Less potential base is included with each passing year, causing either higher taxes to be extracted from other tax bases, higher rates applied to the dwindling sales tax bases, or lower government expenditures. How has this happened? First, states have narrowed the statutory base of the sales tax by adding exemptions for food, medicine, clothing, and other household purchase items. In 1982, 18 states fully taxed food purchased for at home consumption, 40 fully taxed clothing purchases, and 42 fully taxed prescription medicine purchases. By mid-2005, 13 fully tax food, 37 taxed clothing, and none fully taxed prescription medicine.[27] Other narrowing has happened with utilities, motor fuel, and in miscellaneous purchase areas, including the spread of tax-free holiday periods in which certain classes of merchandise otherwise taxable are made exempt for limited periods. Second, states steadfastly refuse to add household purchases of services to the sales tax base, even as increasing shares of total consumption spending go to the purchase of services. And third, states experience continuing and expanding leakage to purchases from remote vendors via catalog, Internet, and telemarketing sales, categories of transactions for which the vendor cannot be required to register as sales tax collector, so the base is lost. Together these forces have brought the dramatic base narrowing portrayed in the table. While states can do little to deal with the remote vendor commerce problem, the wounds for failure to tax service consumption and from expanding the scope of exemptions are self-inflicted.[28]

---

26. Cornia and colleagues identify the decline in state corporate income tax reliance to be the result of shifting of business form to pass-through entities, changes in apportionment factors, economic development preferences granted corporations, and changing industrial structures. Gary Cornia, Kelly D. Edmiston, David L. Sjoquist, and Sally Wallace, "The Disappearing State Corporate Income Tax," *National Tax Journal* LVIII (2005): 115–138.

27. John F. Due and John L. Mikesell, *Sales Taxation, State and Local Structure and Administration* (Baltimore: Johns Hopkins University Press, 1983), 66–70; and Commerce Clearing House, *CCH Internet Tax Network* [Online: by subscription].

28. Not all the observed base narrowing is detrimental to sound tax policy. To the extent that the state is removing business purchases from the sales tax base, the tax is moving closer toward its ideal form as a uniform tax on household consumption expenditure. But these changes are modest in comparison with the consumption category exemptions. The pyramiding that taxation of business purchases creates causes the effective tax rate to be considerably higher than the statutory rate because consumption items get taxed multiple times in the production distribution chain. This pyramiding, combined with purchases made by tourists, causes the observed base in Hawaii to be larger than state personal income in Table 7.

TABLE 7
Breadth of State Sales Tax Base: Implicit Base as Percentage of State Personal Income: 1980, 1985, 1990, 1995, 2000, and 2003

	1980	1985	1990	1995	2000	2003
Alabama	56.3	52.2	47.8	43.8	45.2	40.0
Arizona	97.2	73.9	68.3	60.5	52.4	51.1
Arkansas	81.8	74.1	67.6	64.4	65.0	57.5
California	61.7	52.2	48.1	38.8	39.4	34.7
Colorado	70.8	49.2	47.2	45.7	48.2	40.5
Connecticut	36.4	38.1	38.2	37.9	44.2	34.0
Florida	74.4	59.1	61.1	54.4	60.1	48.5
Georgia	79.4	73.9	63.6	56.3	54.0	46.3
Hawaii	139.4	117.9	121.4	106.9	111.9	109.8
Idaho	66.7	57.6	55.1	52.4	52.3	47.6
Illinois	53.8	39.2	34.0	32.8	28.1	24.8
Indiana	52.3	50.1	49.0	45.2	46.1	39.3
Iowa	65.7	54.5	53.6	49.2	46.9	40.4
Kansas	63.8	57.4	49.5	50.2	49.9	43.7
Kentucky	54.1	50.1	50.3	45.5	46.7	43.5
Louisiana	80.9	61.1	55.8	54.2	58.0	59.2
Maine	55.5	54.8	51.3	43.4	52.4	45.6
Maryland	43.6	42.4	38.8	36.2	37.3	33.6
Massachusetts	29.1	32.6	29.8	29.2	32.5	29.0
Michigan	49.3	53.8	49.3	42.8	45.9	41.6
Minnesota	51.3	46.1	46.1	48.6	49.0	43.3
Mississippi	89.4	67.1	59.0	53.7	58.3	52.1
Missouri	63.1	55.0	53.5	47.8	45.7	40.0
Nebraska	67.2	49.1	50.7	44.2	45.4	48.3
Nevada	82.6	62.9	65.2	59.3	53.2	48.1
New Jersey	33.0	30.5	29.8	29.0	31.7	28.3
New Mexico	148.9	113.5	92.8	85.5	84.8	62.3
New York	44.3	40.1	39.7	33.0	33.5	30.3
North Carolina	55.8	57.0	59.2	45.7	42.1	37.4
North Dakota	76.4	59.1	52.5	55.9	53.0	46.5
Ohio	38.7	42.8	40.2	37.9	41.0	39.5
Oklahoma	75.4	60.3	52.0	42.1	41.9	35.7
Pennsylvania	33.1	33.2	33.9	32.5	34.3	31.8
Rhode Island	35.6	36.5	37.0	27.6	30.6	34.0
South Carolina	67.0	61.4	60.9	52.4	54.1	47.5
South Dakota	75.8	66.7	69.7	62.7	59.9	54.1
Tennessee	67.9	62.8	58.7	50.7	52.8	46.5
Texas	63.2	60.9	54.4	49.3	50.8	42.9
Utah	82.5	73.1	62.6	61.5	60.4	53.3
Vermont	47.5	45.2	44.3	44.7	45.4	33.3

TABLE 7 (Continued)

	1980	1985	1990	1995	2000	2003
Virginia	49.8	47.0	40.6	41.7	42.4	25.5
Washington	72.3	53.3	61.1	53.4	52.9	45.2
West Virginia	52.4	37.8	49.3	47.2	47.4	43.0
Wisconsin	53.3	48.5	49.6	45.1	49.2	44.3
Wyoming	121.8	95.4	78.8	52.4	72.8	64.6
National median	63.2	54.5	51.3	47.2	48.2	43.3

Source: U.S. Census Bureau, Governments Division, author's calculations.

CONCLUSION

Tax policy and administration present a challenge because most citizens understand at least at some level that taxes they individually pay have no impact on the government services they receive. If others pay enough, then the services will be there. Hence, narrow self-interest will present a considerable barrier to changing tax policy and the incremental nature of tax structures will mean that structural change will likely be gradual at best. These truths will shape every program of tax restructuring, whether it involves the sort of tax base to be employed, tax simplification, base broadening, or other changes and explains in large measure why these topics are persistent and perennial.

Basic tax structures in the United States have changed little over the past quarter century, particularly in comparison with the shift away from property taxation that marked the decade before. The federal system may face restructuring in the near future, but there has been little change in reliance patterns over the period, although levels have declined. Will the federal government restructure away from the individual income tax by significantly expanding the preferences for saving that already make the tax something of an income/consumption hybrid tax, but preserve the nature of the tax as one based on individual filing and preserve the easy link between federal and state income taxes? Will the federal government shift more toward a consumption base by adopting a transaction-based tax like a value added or retail sales tax? Or will the federal government stay with the basic income tax policy while making some changes toward simplification, even in the face of the demand for continued tax preference? What happens in regard to these changes matters for federal revenue policy, but they also matter for state and local governments. Some of these revisions could make some state and local taxes more difficult to collect, could move into taxes bases that have historically been the sole province of state and local government, and could make state and local taxes more expensive for the individual taxpayer. In an important sense, the future of revenue structure will depend on what happens with the federal system, and not just because the federal system is a major component of the total. State and local tax systems continue to rely on sales and individual income and property taxes, respectively. Direct charges for government services—the market solution to government finance—continue to be mostly a state and local phenomenon and have shown no great expansion. Corporate income taxes at all levels of government continue their gradual disappearance. And income taxation—individual, payroll, and corporate—continues as the dominant base for taxation in the United States, even as the rest of the world pursues balance between income and consumption as the basis for distributing the cost of government. The next great policy discussions will involve those of rebalancing revenue policy and the outcome is an open question, although it will be resolved well before the end of the next 25 years.

Chapter 6

The Evolution of the State and Local Government Municipal Debt Market over the Past Quarter Century[*]

W. BARTLEY HILDRETH and C. KURT ZORN

Much has happened in the municipal bond market during the past 25 years. This chapter provides a retrospective of some of the significant developments in the market during that period of time. These developments include passage of the Tax Reform Act of 1986, innovations in the market in response to changing economic and social conditions, and the regulation, increase in disclosure requirements, and proliferatioin of credit enhancements that renewed the efficacy of municipal securities for American state and local governments.

INTRODUCTION

The occasion of *Public Budgeting & Finance's* 25th anniversary provides an opportunity to reflect on how the municipal bond market in America has changed over the past 25 years.[1] It is striking how different the municipal bond market is today compared with the 1981 market. In the following pages, it is our intent to highlight some of the more important changes and events in the market during this time period.

The past quarter century indeed has been characterized by a lot of changes in the municipal bond market. As activity has increased dramatically, with outstanding debt

W. Bartley Hildreth, Regents Distinguished Professor of Public Finance, Hugo Wall School of Urban and Public Affairs, and W. Frank Barton School of Business, 1845 N. Fairmount Street, Wichita State University, Wichita, KS 67260-0155. He can be reached at *bart.hildreth@wichita.edu*.

C. Kurt Zorn, Professor and Associate Dean for Academic and Fiscal Affairs, School of Public and Environmental Affairs, 1315 East 10th Street, Suite 300, Indiana University, Bloomington, IN 47405-1701. He can be reached at *zorn@indiana.edu*.

[*]This chapter was originally published in *Public Budgeting & Finance*, Vol. 25, Silver Anniversary Edition (2005): 127–153.

1. The "market" for municipal securities issued by state and local governments in America is more accurately referred to in the plural form ("markets") because of investor segmentation, state tax law variations, pricing inefficiency in the secondary market, and other characteristics.

growing from approximately $400 billion in 1980 to over $2 trillion at the beginning of 2005,[2] the tax-exempt state and local bond market has been subjected to a major change in tax law that had a profound impact, has become increasingly creative in response to changing economic and fiscal conditions, and has weathered some crises and near crises. The result is a market that is much different from the one in existence in the early 1980s.

It is impossible for one article to adequately cover all the changes that have occurred in the market during the past 25 years. As a result, this article will serve as a retrospective of some of the major developments in the municipal bond market during this period of time. First, the Tax Reform Act of 1986 (TRA'86), which had a significant impact on the market, is discussed. Second, some of the innovations that have occurred in the market in response to changing economic and fiscal conditions are discussed. Third, the discussion turns to the crises or near crises experienced by participants in the market along with the way the market has responded through the increased use of credit enhancements, increased regulation, and disclosure requirements.

EVOLUTION IN TAX LAW

The watershed event in the market for municipal securities was TRA'86.[3] Its enactment significantly changed the way debt obligations of state and local governments were treated and its effects are still being felt today. Before its passage virtually all interest on state and local government debt was exempt from federal taxation. Once enacted, only particular types of debt were eligible for this federal subsidy and only certain investors could avail themselves of this tax break.

In the years leading up to the TRA'86, the total volume of new tax-exempt issues was growing robustly. In 1985 the volume of issues reached almost $229 billion dollars, a more than 72 percent increase from the previous year and an increase of more than 210 percent over the volume in 1980. Admittedly some of this increase can be attributed to activity in anticipation of the occurrence of tax reform. Not surprisingly new borrowing volume fell by almost 25 percent to $172.6 billion in 1986 and fell another 27 percent in 1987 to $125.5 billion. In 1988 the market began to rebound with the volume of new issues growing 12.3 percent to slightly less than $150 billion. Growth continued at a relatively modest pace for the next three years. It was not until 1991 that the volume of new issues returned to levels close to 1985, with totally new issues amounting to $217.7 billion.[4]

TRA'86 has been credited with transforming the once placid environment for municipal securities into a frenetic and arcane market.[5] The Act prompted a sizable re-

---

2. Source: *http://www.federalreserve.gov/releases/Z1/Current/z1r-4.pdf*.

3. Rosalyn Y. Carter and W. Bartley Hildreth, "The Evolving Regulatory Environment of State and Local Tax-Exempt Securities," *Public Budgeting and Financial Management* 4, no. 3 (1992): 491–527.

4. American Banker/Thomson Financial, *The Bond Buyer Yearbook* (New York: The Bond Buyer, assorted years).

5. John E. Peterson, "The Municipal Bond Market in a Changing Economy," *Public Budgeting & Finance* 8, no. 4 (1988): 22–34.

duction in the exempt nongovernmental bond area, what are commonly referred to as private purpose or private activity bonds, changes in arbitrage rules affecting municipal debt, and whether bonds are "bank eligible." These changes affected both the issuers of tax-exempt debt and the investors in this debt.

Effect on Issuers

The most pronounced effect of TRA'86 was on the issuers of private activity bonds. Private activity bonds are securities where the proceeds are utilized for a project or a purpose that is used by or benefits a private entity.[6] Concern had been mounting about the volume of tax-exempt bonds that were being issued for private activities. By one account, the volume of private activity bonds in 1981 was $25 billion, which accounted for 48 percent of the municipal bond market.[7] The result was a narrowing of the interest rate differential between taxable and tax-exempt issues, which raised the borrowing costs of state and local governments and the cost to the Federal Treasury.

The assault on private activity bonds was three pronged. First, tighter definitions were placed on what constituted a private activity bond. Second, limitations were imposed on the purpose for which bond proceeds could be used. Third, state-by-state volume caps on the issuance of these bonds were imposed.

Tax-exempt bonds were divided into two basic categories—essential function government activities and private activities. The latter category—private activity bonds—was created in response to the dramatic growth in the use of industrial development bonds, economic development bonds, housing bonds, and other specialty bonds for what were considered tangential government purposes.[8] Generally, two tests were used and continue to be used to determine whether a bond is considered a private activity bond. The private use test affirms that if more than 10 percent of the bond proceeds are used in any private trade or business, the bond is categorized as a private activity bond. In a similar vein, the security interest test states that if more than 10 percent of the debt service on the bonds is secured by or payable from property being used for private business purposes, it is considered to be for private use.[9] Bonds that fail to satisfy both of these tests are considered governmental use bonds and qualify for regular tax-exempt status.

---

6. Penelope Lemov, "The Municipal Bond Market after Tax Reform," in *Capital Projects: New Strategies for Planning, Management, and Finance*, ed. John Matzer Jr. (Washington, DC: International City Management Association, 1989), 135–147.

7. Joint Tax Committee, "Blue Book Explanation of TEFRA Changes Affecting Tax-Exempt Obligations," *Municipal Finance Journal* 4, no. 1 (1983): 56–91.

8. For a broader view of this issue, see Dennis Zimmerman, *The Private Use of Tax-Exempt Bonds* (Washington, DC: The Urban Institute Press, 1990).

9. D. William Graham, Paul L. Shinn, and John E. Petersen, "State Revolving Funds under Tax Reform," CIFA Monograph No. 2 (Washington, DC: The Council of Infrastructure Financing Authority, June 1989).

Not all types of private activities qualify for the tax-exempt private activity bond moniker. The activities must fall into well-defined categories including exempt facilities (such as government-owned airports, mass-commuting facilities, water and water treatment facilities, etc.), certain types of housing, certain types of economic and redevelopment activities, and certain types of nonprofit activities.[10]

Another change that affected issuers was restrictions placed on arbitrage earnings. Before, tax reform state and local borrowers were able to reduce their borrowing costs by taking advantage of the difference between the interest rates commanded by the tax-exempt bonds they sold and the interest rate they could realize by investing some or all of the proceeds in other investments. Often they were able to cover some or all of their operating and administrative expenses through arbitrage.[11]

Because this use of arbitrage earnings by state and local government entities was considered a misuse of the tax exemption, TRA'86 placed strict limitations on the borrowing of funds in the tax-exempt market and their reinvestment in the taxable market. Instead of allowing three years for unlimited arbitrage earnings that was the custom before reform, TRA'86 shortened the period to six months. In addition, issuers are required to keep track of all their investable proceeds and report these to the Internal Revenue Service.[11] Essentially, there is a limit of 10 percent of bond proceeds that can be invested in higher yielding securities and these proceeds have to be part of a reasonably required debt service fund. Any earnings in excess of those allowed have to be rebated to the U.S. Treasury in order for the bond to retain its tax-exempt status.[12]

Finally, TRA'86 constrained issuers by limiting the number of advance refundings that can occur for any bond issued after January 1, 1986 to one. In addition, the defeasance of the bond must occur at the first call date; refundings are not allowed at later call dates.[12] Clearly this provision limits the flexibility of issuers, implicitly raising the potential cost of borrowing to state and local governments.

Effects on Investors

Historically, institutional investors, specifically commercial banks and property and casualty insurance companies, had been big players in the market for tax-exempt bonds with individual investors assuming a smaller role. In the aftermath of TRA'86, individual investors, including mutual funds and unit trusts, adopted a more prominent role in the market. This shift in the relative importance of investors was because of a number of changes contained in the act that affected the desirability of holding municipal bonds as part of one's portfolio.

---

10. This list is not intended to be exhaustive. For more details, see Alan Walter Steiss, "New Financing Instruments for State and Local Capital Facilities," *Public Budgeting & Finance* 18, no. 3 (1998): 24–41.

11. Peterson, 22–34. Subsequent arbitrage regulations in 1993 by the Internal Revenue Service narrowed and clarified these provisions.

12. William H. May, "The Impact of Negative Arbitrage on the Advance Refunding of Tax-Exempt Municipal Debt," *Municipal Finance Journal* 20, no. 1 (1999): 68–84.

FIGURE 1

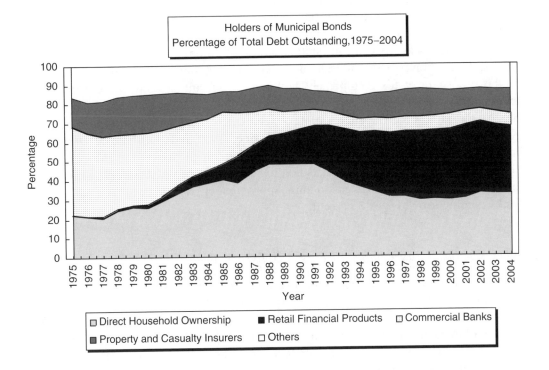

Holders of Municipal Bonds
Percentage of Total Debt Outstanding, 1975–2004

Legend: ☐ Direct Household Ownership ■ Retail Financial Products ☐ Commercial Banks ■ Property and Casualty Insurers ☐ Others

First, the tax advantages associated with holding tax-exempt securities were altered. On the supply side, municipal bonds were no longer treated as a homogeneous commodity. The type of security, the nature of the investor, when the bond was acquired, and other considerations resulted in differential tax treatment after passage of the act. In addition, TRA'86 lowered the marginal federal income tax rate, basically flattening the rate structure. The top marginal tax rate for individuals dropped from 50 to 28 percent and individual income now was subject to the alternative minimum tax (AMT). Corporations saw their marginal tax rates decrease from 46 to 34 percent.

Second, TRA'86 eliminated the deductibility of interest expenses incurred by banks on funds they use to purchase tax-exempt bonds. Under the old rules, commercial banks were allowed to deduct 80 percent of the interest expense associated with acquiring tax-exempt securities. This deduction was eliminated for bonds issued after August 7, 1986, with the exception of "purchases of governmental purpose or 501(c) (3) bonds from issuers of less than $10 million in new debt each year."[13] As can be seen in Figure 1 the tax law change with regard to bank deductibility has contributed to an eroding share for

---

13. Ronald W. Forbes and Paul A. Leonard, "Bank Qualified Tax-Exempt Securities: A Test of Market Segmentation and Commercial Bank Demand," *Municipal Finance Journal* 15, no. 1 (1994): 18–31.

commercial bank investors in the entire municipal bond market.[14] In terms of annual long-term municipal issues only, since 1986, bank-qualified municipal bonds have comprised an average of 6.7 percent of those issues, ranging from as much as 8.4 percent in 1998 to as little as 4.1 percent in 2003.[15]

Clearly, there was a significant shift in holdings among investors initiated by TRA '86.[16] Individual investors'—households, money market mutual funds, and mutual funds combined—share of tax-exempt debt had been increasing steadily since 1980 and its share increased dramatically in the years immediately following the enactment of TRA '86. At the same time the shares of tax-exempt debt held by commercial banks and insurance companies were steadily declining since 1980 and the share of commercial bank holdings decreased significantly in the aftermath of tax reform. More recently, things have stabilized with individuals holding about 64 or 65 percent of the tax-exempt securities, insurance companies holding approximately 13 percent, and commercial banks holding around 7 or 8 percent.

Other Significant Tax Reform Affecting Tax-Exempt Bonds

In 1982, Congress mandated that municipal bonds had to be issued in registered form in order to retain their tax-exempt status. In 1988 the U.S. Supreme Court ruled that Congress can eliminate the tax-exempt securities market because there is no constitutional requirement for tax exemption, despite arguments that this is a violation of the Tenth Amendment and the concept of federalism, as well as a violation of the intergovernmental tax immunity principle essence.[17] This case provides a foundation as Congress revisits fundamental federal tax reform and the potential that reform has for eliminating tax-exempt municipal bonds.[18] Subsequent legislation has targeted municipal securities in different ways, but none have been as significant as TRA '86.

INNOVATIVE DEBT INSTRUMENTS BORNE OUT OF NECESSITY

In the late 1970s and early 1980s state and local governments were faced with mounting capital needs and fewer degrees of freedom to deal with these needs because of high interest rates, inflation and a slowing economy, reduction in federal aid as a result of concern over mounting federal budget deficits, and tax and expenditure limitations on

---

14. Federal Reserve Flow of Funds, Tables L.2111.

15. American Banker/Thomson Financial, assorted years.

16. Matthew R. Marlin, "Did Tax Reform Kill Segmentation in the Municipal Bond Market?", *Public Administration Review* 54, no. 4 (1994): 387–390.

17. *South Carolina versus Baker, 48 U.S. 505.*

18. W. Bartley Hildreth, "Fundamental Federal Tax Reform and the States," *Book of the States 2005* (Lexington, KY: Council of State Governments, 2005).

state and local governments. Crises tend to spawn innovation and this certainly has been the case with capital financing.

Over the past 25 years, issuers have shown a steady preference for customizing their solution to a specific financing need rather than relying solely on a long-term, fixed-coupon general obligation (GO) bond. Revenue bonds predominate, not GO bonds.[19] Creative ways to avoid debt limits and procedural hurdles have propelled the growth of lease financing, including Certificates of Participation (COPs), and the increased use of tax increment financing (TIF), bond banks, and revolving loan funds. Issuers provide investors with protection against the credit risk of dedicated revenue streams by purchasing bond insurance or letter of credit (LOC) facilities. Issuers are prone to advance refund outstanding debt well ahead of the call date, even if it is done to gain the bare minimum interest rate savings on new debt, but exhausts the one-time option provided under federal tax laws.[20] Some issuers appeal to sophisticated investors (especially institutional and bank purchasers) by structuring debt obligations in ways that give investors added flexibility and risk. The continuing search for lower interest rates have propelled issuers to use reset securities, or floating rate debt, instead of fixed-rate coupons.[21] Infrequently, large and recognizable issuers have borrowed in foreign markets, especially in periods when the cost of borrowing here is high.[22] Interest rate exposure is mitigated by a variety of swap and other derivative products. All of these provisions introduce liability risks that must be managed, leading some to argue that simpler instruments might benefit both investors and issuers.[23]

Some Innovations in Debt Instruments

A scan of the literature indicates there have been many innovations in the way debt instruments are structured and used, including, but not limited to, variable-rate obligations, derivative securities, interest rate swaps, tax-exempt inverse floaters, puts, warrants, residual interest bonds, and zero coupon bonds.[24] Market professionals continue

---

19. Elaine B. Sharp, "The Politics and Economics of the New City Debt," *American Political Science Review* 80, no. 4 (1986): 1271–1288.

20. Wei David Zhang and Jinliang Li, "The Value of the Advance Refunding Option and the Refunding Efficiency of Tax-Exempt Municipal Bonds," *Municipal Finance Journal* 25, no. 1 (2004): 17–31.

21. Arthur E. Schloss, "Coping in a High Interest Rate Environment," *Public Budgeting & Finance* 2, no. 1 (1982): 9–18; and Joanne S. Feld, "Variable Rate Demand Obligations for Issuers of Water and Sewer Debt: An Analytic Framework," *Municipal Finance Journal* 22, no. 2 (2001): 14–34.

22. James R. Ramsey and Merl Hackbart, "Municipal Debt Issues in Foreign Markets: Managing Currency and Interest Rate Risk," *Public Budgeting & Finance* 11, no. 4 (1991): 33–48; and "Municipal Bond Sales in Foreign Markets: Experience and Results," *Public Budgeting & Finance* 16, no. 3 (1996): 3–12.

23. Jun Peng, "Managing the Risk of Variable-Rate Debt in the Public Sector," *Municipal Finance Journal* 23, no. 4 (2003): 1–16; and Lawrence Harris and Michael S. Piwowar, "Municipal Bond Liquidity" (American Finance Association 2005 Philadelphia Meetings, February 13, 2004) *http://ssrn.com/abstract=503062.*

24. John Petersen, "Creative Capital Financing in the State and Local Sector," *Public Budgeting & Finance* 2, no. 4 (1982): 73–89; and Steiss, 24–41.

to show their creative ability to design instruments around almost any impediment. This section uses tax-exempt reset securities and interest rate swaps to illustrate the ways issuers can design securities to appeal to certain investor segments and respond to changing market conditions.

Reset securities come in the two basic forms of variable-rate demand bonds (VRDBs) and auction rate securities (ARS). Variable-rate securities have a nominal long-term maturity, as well as a coupon that is adjusted frequently (usually weekly) to reflect market conditions. On the reset date, each investor faces a choice to either continue holding the securities at the new rate or put the bonds back to the issuer at par. Issuers use a remarketing agent to manage this process, including setting the rate to match supply and demand. This procedure gives investors more liquidity than under a fixed-rate security. Issuers, in turn, can borrow at lower rates but at the risk of having debt service increase to accommodate higher reset rates. Variable-rate securities require a stand-by bond purchase agreement from a commercial bank in the form of an LOC facility to ensure adequate liquidity.

VRDBs are held primarily by money market fund portfolios because these securities qualify under the federal regulatory rule that mandates the maturity and quality standards for money market funds. Money market funds must maintain a $1 net asset value, so their holdings must have high liquidity and stable values. Variable-rate securities offer weekly put options permitting the investor to liquidate its position with strong credit support offered by LOC and other provisions.

Recently, issuers have turned to ARS. Unlike VRDBs, ARS are long-term, variable-rate bonds tied to short-term interest rates.[25] ARS are priced and traded as short-term debt obligations. They are priced in a Dutch auction process, where securities are sold at the highest price at which sufficient bids are received to sell all the securities offered. In other words, the competitive bidding process determines rates on each auction date (held every 7, 28, or 35 days, as specified). The U.S. Treasury has used this process in selling coupon-bearing securities since 1976 and discount securities (T-bills and Treasury Notes) even longer.

Owners of ARS have the option to hold an existing position regardless of the new rate, bid to hold an existing position at a specified rate, or request to sell an existing position regardless of the interest rate set at the auction. Current and potential investors submit their bids, through a broker/dealer, to an auction agent. The winning bid rate is the rate at which the auction "clears"—defined as the lowest possible interest rate that equals the cumulative total of securities demanded (buyers) to the amount auctioned (sellers). All accepted bids receive the same interest rate. Generally, the securities are sold at or above the established clearing price and they trade at par. ARS have a variety of reset dates available, ranging from daily to quarterly. ARS have par values of $25,000, $50,000, or

---

25. California Debt and Investment Advisory Commission, *Issue Brief: Auction Rate Securities* (August 2004).

$100,000 per bond, and the minimum issue size is large ($25 million). The primary investors are corporate cash managers and high net-worth individuals, not tax-exempt money market funds (because of the lack of tender option).

Unlike VRDBs, ARS do not have the "put" feature and therefore do not require the third-party LOC facility. As bank liquidity facilities have become more expensive, the auction market provides an attractive low-cost and flexible way to obtain variable-rate debt. Because of this lack of a credit facility, most ARS are credit enhanced by municipal bond insurance.

Issuers can convert ARS into variable-rate or fixed-rate instruments. To limit risk, issues can enter into interest rate hedges including swaps, caps, or collars. The most common approach is to fix all or part of the variable-rate exposure through a "floating to fixed" interest rate swap. An advantage of fixing all of the exposure is that it results in a net fixed-rate payment obligation by the issuer. This makes debt service planning easier. Issuers can redeem the bonds anytime, without prepayment premium.

An interest rate swap is a derivative that alters the cash flows of a debt obligation. An issuer's exposure to increasing interest rates arising from outstanding reset securities may be hedged through a swap. Accordingly, the reset securities' cash requirements plus the effect of the swap should make the variable debt synthetically behave as fixed-rate debt. For example, a government may issue 3 percent variable-rate debt with terms that permit the debt's interest rate to range up to 7 percent. Working with a broker/dealer as counterparty, a swap may be constructed that is the mirror image of the potential variable coupon payments. Continuing with the example, a swap may vary from 7 to 3 percent, the opposite cash flows of the variable-rate debt. A synthetic fixed-rate debt is attractive when the cost of the variable-rate debt and swap is less than a conventional fixed-rate debt. Given these risks, state and local governments must have a swap management plan. Such a plan might include evidence that governing officials understand the advantages and disadvantages of planned actions, that staff know how to manage the complex contracts and cash flow scenarios, that procedures and internal controls are in place to mitigate the risks, and that there are clear exit strategies.

Various derivative products have been developed to meet the wide variety of financing needs of state and local government issuers. These types of debt issues are extremely complex and challenge even the most sophisticated issuers to manage their financial liability risks. State governments have responded with prescriptive rules while the government finance profession has adopted recommended practices.[26]

---

26. For recommended practices, see the Government Finance Officers Association (*www.gfoa.org*). In 2003, the Government Accounting Standards Board issued a technical bulletin (No. 2003-1), which requires state and local government borrowers to understand and disclose the objectives, terms, fair value, risks, and other material facts relating to all derivative instruments to which the borrower has entered into.

Innovative Ways to Access the Market

Confronted with mounting capital needs and shrinking resources for capital improvements, state and local governments renewed their search for innovative ways to access the capital markets. Particularly noteworthy are TIFs, revolving loan funds, leasing, and bond banks.

TIF

TIF is a financing vehicle that dates back to the mid-1940s when California enacted its Community Redevelopment Act. As early as 1980, 28 states had enabling legislation for TIFs, by 1982 nine additional states had adopted this financing tool, and by 1997, 48 states had the ability to use TIF.[27] Interest in TIF really began to intensify with the passage of the Tax Reform Act of 1986 when all economic development bonds were categorized as private activity bonds and were subjected to state-specific volume caps.

TIF bonds are attractive to localities because most of the interest earned on these bonds is exempt from federal income taxation. Generally, to qualify "as a TIF bond entitled to tax exemption, 95 percent or more of the net proceeds must be used for redevelopment purposes in a designated blighted area. Among some of the other requirements, the bond issue must be accompanied by a redevelopment plan, and the debt service must be primarily secured by general taxes imposed by a general purpose government or incremental taxes attributable to the improvement being financed."[28]

Generally, a local government entity forms a development authority that maps a special tax increment district that includes, in many cases, blighted or deteriorating properties. The intent is to invest in infrastructure improvements in the district and use a portion of the taxes that are generated as a result to finance the improvements. More specifically, when the district is created, the property tax base is frozen and any taxes generated by the increase in property value that occurs after the district is formed (commonly referred to as the tax increment) are pledged to pay for the infrastructure improvements.[29] The rationale is that the increased property value is because of enhanced economic activity directly resulting from the investments in infrastructure. An innovative variation is when property values decline rapidly because of environmental

27. Jack R. Huddleston, "Local Financial Dimensions of Tax Increment Financing: A Cost-Revenue Analysis," *Public Budgeting & Finance* 2, no. 1 (1982): 40–49, and Craig L. Johnson, "Tax Increment Debt Finance: An Analysis of the Mainstreaming of a Fringe Sector," *Public Budgeting & Finance* 19, no. 1 (1999): 47–67.

28. Johnson, 52.

29. Property taxes are not the only revenue source that may be used in a TIF. See W. Bartley Hildreth, and John Wong, "The Theme of Public Finance in the Amusement Park Industry," *Proceedings of the 95th Annual Conference on Taxation 2002* (Washington, DC: National Tax Association, 2003): 409–415.

contamination and a city freezes the value at the reduced level and considers the restored property value as the increment upon which to finance the cleanup.[30]

Proponents point out that TIF provides another vehicle for local governments to use to finance much needed capital improvements. It allows access to credit markets without pledging the jurisdiction's full faith and credit, without being constrained by constitutional debt limits, and without a referendum. Also, it provides a "shot in the arm" for blighted areas with a declining tax base. Those subscribing to the pure attribution theory argue that in the absence of TIF no development would occur. If developers were forced to bear the costs of infrastructure improvements and other development, they would not choose to make the investment.[31]

Opponents point out a number of difficulties associated with TIF. Sponsor governments, the ones that have a say in the design of the district and the projects within, make the development expenditures and collect TIF revenues. Contributor governments, on the other hand, do not directly participate in any of the decision making concerning the district, but must contribute a portion of their tax base to finance the district's projects.[32] Often the contributor governments complain that the sponsor governments gain at their expense, because successful development will result in increased service demands for the contributor governments without a requisite increase in the tax base wing to the lost increment.

TIFs detractors argue that this financing initiative results in a zero-sum outcome. Development that may have occurred elsewhere in the jurisdiction is lured to the increment district because of lower overall costs developers face owing to the public investment. Pure capture theory suggests that development would have occurred without the subsidy the increment provided to developers. Therefore, there is no net gain to the community.[33] Concerns have been voiced that successful development may have an ill effect on existing businesses and residents, pricing them out of the market and forcing relocation.[34] Opponents also point out there is a lack of voter participation in the decision making; TIFs involve a complex and costly approval process, at times TIF districts have included areas that are not blighted, and on occasion districts are drawn to include more than the area targeted for redevelopment in order to ensure financial viability.[35] Finally, TIFs involve a passive revenue stream that is based on the increment

30. Mark A. Glaser, Chris Cherches, and Jack Brown, "Rx for the Ills of Superfund: Cost Effective Local Solutions, Appropriate Financing, and EPA Responsiveness," *Municipal Finance Journal* 18, no. 3 (1997): 67–83.

31. Kenneth A. Kriz, "The Effect of Tax Increment Finance on Local Government Financial Condition," *Municipal Finance Journal* 22, no. 1 (2001): 41–64.

32. Jack R. Huddleston, "Local Financial Dimensions of Tax Increment Financing: A Cost-Revenue Analysis," *Public Budgeting & Finance* 2, no. 1 (1982): 40–49.

33. Kriz, 41–64.

34. Don Davis, "Tax Increment Financing," *Public Budgeting & Finance* 9, no. 1 (1989): 63–73.

35. Joyce Y. Man. "Introduction," in *Tax Increment Financing and Economic Development: Uses, Structures, and Impacts*, eds. Craig L. Johnson and Joyce Y. Man (Albany: State University of New York Press, 2001), 1–11.

of value in excess of the frozen base. If subsequent action by the state alters the base or the calculation of the increment, the ability to repay bond investors may be threatened.[36]

Evidence concerning whether TIFs are successful tools for capital investment is mixed. Rosentraub and Man demonstrated that TIF stimulated property values.[37] Another study determined that in order for a TIF to be successful, a large initial development is required to provide a sufficient flow of revenue throughout the life of the project.[38] Finally, Kriz concludes that TIFs most likely are a net financial loss to local governments. He states that "TIF may be best thought of as a large financial investment by local governments that may have a small chance of financial reward."[39]

Revolving Loan Funds

Revolving loan funds serve as another alternative to the more traditional tax and borrowing approaches to financing capital and infrastructure improvements. This financing vehicle leverages funds by capitalizing a loan fund administered by a state entity, usually through grants or appropriations, and providing below market interest rate loans to local government entities, sometimes referred to as qualified entities. As a result, qualified entities receive a subsidy to help finance their capital expenditures while replenishing the loan fund so that additional loans can be made to finance the capital expenditures of other local government bodies. Many consider revolving loan funds to be a specialized form of bond bank.[40]

The revolving loan fund's profile as an alternative means of financing capital expenditures was heightened by passage of The Water Quality Act of 1987. This amendment of the Clean Water Act phased out Environmental Protection Agency (EPA) grants for wastewater treatment construction, replacing them with the State Revolving Loan Fund (SRF) program. This program, administered by the EPA, provided capitalization grants for state-administered SRF funds with the proviso that states provide matching funds of at least 20 percent. Because the SRF funds are administered by the states, there is variation among states on how they provide matching funds, the amount they choose to match, and the way they choose to leverage the SRF funds.[41]

Generally, three types of SRF programs are offered by states. The direct loan program lends funds directly to qualified entities and, as per federal regulations, the

---

36. Johnson, 47–67.

37. Joyce Y. Man and Mark S. Rosentraub, "Tax Increment Financing: Municipal Adoption and Effects on Property Value Growth," *Public Finance Review* 26, no. 6 (1998): 523–547.

38. Davis, 63–73.

39. Kriz, 63.

40. Daniel R. Irvin, "State Municipal Bond Banks," CIFA Monograph No. 5 (Washington, DC: The Council of Infrastructure Financing Authority, March 1993); and Graham D. William, Paul L. Shinn, and John E. Petersen, "State Revolving Funds Under Tax Reform," CIFA Monograph No. 2 (Washington, DC: The Council of Infrastructure Financing Authority, June 1989).

41. Randall G. Holcombe, "Revolving Fund Finance: The Case of Wastewater Treatment," *Public Budgeting & Finance* 12, no. 3 (1992): 50–65.

qualified entities repay the principal. States have the option to charge interest on the loan with the amount of the subsidy being provided to the qualified entities equal to the difference between the prevailing market interest rate the qualified entity would face if it borrowed funds on its own and the rate of interest the SRF program charges on its loans.

A second approach is the matching loan program. Capitalization funds provided by the EPA are matched with proceeds from a revenue bond issued by the state. Funds are then loaned to qualified entities and loan repayments from the qualified entities are used to pay the debt service of the revenue bond issue. Again, qualified entities are required to repay the loan principal, but it is up to individual states to decide what rate of interest, if any, to charge on its SRF loans.

Leveraged loan programs constitute the third type of state SRF program. Under this approach SRF funds are not lent to qualified entities. Instead the state entity issues revenue bonds whose proceeds are lent to local government units. SRF funds serve as a reserve fund for the revenue bond issue and the interest generated from the investment of these SRF funds is used to subsidize the interest rates charged to qualified entities. This approach to the use of the SRF funds maximizes the amount of loanable fund capacity available, especially in the early days of the fund's existence, and generally improves the credit worthiness of the revenue bond issue because of its backing by SRF funds.[42]

By 1995 the EPA had provided over $11 billion in capitalization grants and there were over $18.9 billion total funds available in state SRF programs.[43] By fiscal year 2000 the EPA had provided over $20 billion in capitalization grants to states and states had contributed approximately $10 billion to their SRF programs. About $3.3 billion came from state appropriations with the remainder coming from leverage loans.[44] By 2001 all 50 states and Puerto Rico had SRF programs that had been in existence for more than 10 years. Over the life of the program over $30 billion in assistance had been provided through issuance of over 9,500 low interest loans, with annual assistance during the 1996–2001 period averaging about $3.2 billion per year. Finally, the program does a good job leveraging every federal dollar spent in the SRF, generating about 73 cents in additional expenditures from state contributions and interest earnings.[45]

Leasing

A third approach that has been used to provide another vehicle to finance capital and infrastructure expenditures is municipal leasing. These are complicated legal and con-

---

42. Laurence H. Wadler, "The Impact of Lending Velocity on Revolving Fund Performance," *Municipal Finance Journal* 16, no. 1 (1995): 32–62.

43. The Ohio Water Development Authority, "State Revolving Loan Fund Survey," CIFA Monograph No. 8 (Washington, DC: The Council of Infrastructure Financing Authority, May 1996).

44. United States General Accounting Office, *Water Infrastructure: Information on State Financial Assistance*, GAO-02-134 (Washington, DC: Government Printing Office, November 2001).

45. United States Environmental Protection Agency, Office of Water, *Financing America's Clean Water Since 1987: A Report of Progress and Innovation*, EPA-832-R-00-011 (May 2001).

tractual arrangements that allow local governments access to capital markets without the constraints of voter approval, constitutional debt limits, and other requirements associated with regular debt issuance in the municipal market.[46]

There are many different types of lease arrangements, but lease purchase arrangements seem to be the most popular among local governments, although hard data on leasing practices are difficult to collect.[47] Lease purchase agreements involve the government entity consenting to make installment payments based on the market value of the asset. When the lease terminates, the entity gains title to the asset thereby allowing the government unit to own the property without using debt finance. This right to ownership is what exempts the interest payments made by the governmental unit to the lessor from federal taxation. The list of assets that have been acquired through this financing vehicle include, among other things, buildings, vehicles, computers, and equipment.

Sometimes lease purchase agreements are underwritten and then sold to institutional and individual investors, generally as COPs. COPs allow an investor to own a portion of the lease, resulting in a lease agreement that has the appearance of a bond issue. The credit analysis performed on COPs is similar to that performed on other fixed income securities. Of primary importance is the lessee government unit's general credit worthiness followed by the ease with which the lessor can repossess property from the lessee if payments are not forthcoming, any credit enhancement backing the lease, and the nonappropriation clause.[48]

Proponents of leasing point out that this financing approach allows equipment costs and capital costs to be spread out over the useful life of the asset, much like debt financing, without accessing the municipal debt market. It can fill the gap between pay as you go and pay as you use (debt financing) when the life of the asset is not long enough to justify the costs associated with issuing bonds. In addition, it allows local government entities to benefit from federal tax deductions despite the fact that these entities are not subject to federal income taxes. In the case of a lease purchase, the interest paid by the lessee (the government unit) is tax-exempt income for the lessor. As a result, the lessor can offer the lessee more favorable lease terms, saving the governmental entity money.[49] COPs are structured much like regular debt, yet government entities can treat the annual lease payments as an operating expense rather that debt service, thus avoiding the re-

46. Congress is not hesitant to stop "abusive" municipal lease structures, such as in the American Jobs Creation Act of 2004, which ended the use of lease-in–lease-out transactions.

47. A. John Vogt and Lisa A. Cole, "An Introduction to Municipal Leasing," *Municipal Finance Journal* 4, no. 3 (1983): 231–238; Congressional Budget Office, "Trends in Municipal Leases," *Municipal Finance Journal* 4, no. 3 (1983): 239–249; Lisa A. Cole and Robert W. Jennings, "Master Equipment Leases: Form, Function, and Flexibility," *Municipal Finance Journal* 14, no. 2 (1993): 76–82.

48. C. Richard Baker , "Accounting and Credit Analysis of Leases with Governmental Units," *Municipal Finance Journal* 16, no. 4 (1996): 63–77.

49. Congressional Budget Office, 239–249.

striction associated with debt issuance. And the lessee can stop lease payments if it so desires.

The ability of the lessee to stop payments is because of the nonappropriation clause contained in lease agreements, which helps distinguish lease arrangements from regular debt arrangements. The nonappropriation clause states that the lessee can elect not to appropriate funds necessary to make annual lease payments. The existence of such a clause forces the lessee government to walk a tightrope of sorts, arguing that the lease payments are annual operating expenditures and not debt service on long-term obligations, while reassuring both the lessor and investors in COPs that annual lease payments will be forthcoming as outlined in the lease agreement.

General wisdom holds that COPs associated with lease arrangements involving essential services are more insulated from possible nonappropriation of funds and therefore are safer investments. The reasoning is that government entities will be reluctant to suspend lease payments for these assets in difficult financial times because of the essential nature of the services—such as services provided for public safety or for the health and welfare of the community. One study concludes that in tough financial times it is likely the opposite will occur. Because the leases involve essential functions, government entities may choose to renege on these payment agreements first, knowing that the lessor will be less willing to repossess equipment from or evict the delinquent government entity.[50] In fact, a 1998 industry study on municipal lease nonappropriation and defaults reported a low default rate, and although the lessee's fiscal condition was the most frequent reason for nonappropriation, the number of events was low relative to the market.[51]

Bond Banks

Bond banks have been around since the first one was established in Vermont in 1970. They are championed as a way to promote economic development and provide another tool to finance the rehabilitation and development of infrastructure.[52]

There is some disagreement about what exactly constitutes a bond bank. The traditional definition involves a state-sponsored entity that assists the government in the financing of local infrastructure projects by providing more affordable and practicable access to capital markets. The state entity may or may not choose to provide either direct or indirect subsidies through credit enhancements to the local governments. Regardless, the ultimate goal is to provide a relatively low-cost financing option to local govern-

---

50. Craig L. Johnson and John Mikesell, "Certificates of Participation and Capital Markets: Lessons from Brevard County and Richmond Unified School District," *Public Budgeting & Finance* 14, no. 3 (1994): 41–54.

51. Association for Governmental Leasing & Finance, "AGL&F Nonappropriation and Default Survey" (November 1998), available: *http://www.aglf.org/downloads/Default_Survey.pdf.*

52. C. Kurt Zorn and Shah Towfighi, "Not All Bond Banks Are Created Equal," *Public Budgeting & Finance* 6, no. 3 (1986): 57–69.

ments. A more generous definition characterizes a bond bank as an entity—private, nonprofit, and governmental—that sells its own securities and then lends the proceeds to local governmental bodies.[53] Depending on how one chooses to define a bond bank, it has been reported that there are between 10 and 27 bond banks operating in up to 25 different states.[54]

Not surprisingly, there are different mechanisms used by bond banks to achieve their objective of providing local governments affordable access to capital markets. Some banks rely on a long-term bond pool where the state entity issues bonds and then uses the proceeds to purchase debt obligations of qualified entities. The security behind the state entity's bonds is the debt service payments by the qualified entities plus, perhaps, a state credit enhancement. Qualified entities benefit from the interest cost savings associated with the pooled risk and economies of scale associated with the state bond issue rather than entering the capital market with their own debt obligations.

Other programs provided by bond banks include cash flow financing, equipment lease financing, and revolving loan programs. Cash flow financing involves the issuance of short-term securities by the state entity that provides for interim financing to qualified entities so they can smooth out traditionally lumpy revenue streams to match expenditures. Lease financing generally involves the state entity assisting qualified entities in placing loans for equipment with banks. These may involve pooled placements or individual placements. The bond bank's involvement helps standardize the process and documentation, resulting in increased interest among banks to bid on the loans and lower interest costs. Finally, revolving loan funds involve an initial capitalization of the fund and then below market interest rate loans to qualified entities.[55]

In a 1995 survey of 17 bond banks, 16 had long-term bond programs (Virginia had only SRF and other loan programs). Three states engaged in cash flow financing, four in equipment lease financing, nine in SRF financing, and five states had other programs. Indiana was the only state that had programs in all five categories—long-term bond, cash flow, equipment leasing, SRF, and other. Michigan and North Dakota had programs in all but the "other" category; three states had programs in three categories; an additional three had programs in two categories; and seven states had only a long-term bond program.[56]

53. Government Finance Group Inc., "An Analysis of State Bond Banks," CIFA Monograph No. 9 (Washington, DC: The Council of Infrastructure Financing Authority, February 1997).

54. Irvin and Mark D. Robbins and Daehwan Kim, "Do State Bond Banks Have Cost Advantages for Municipal Bond Issuance?", *Public Budgeting & Finance* 23, no. 3 (2003): 92–108.

55. Government Finance Group Inc.

56. The 17 states included in the survey were Alaska, Colorado, Indiana, Kentucky, Maine, Maryland, Michigan, Mississippi, Nevada, New Hampshire, New Mexico, North Dakota, Oregon, Texas, Vermont, Virginia, and West Virginia. The definition of bond bank used was a more traditional definition that did not include any stand-alone SRF programs, although some of the bond banks did have SRF programs as part of their portfolio. Government Finance Group Inc. (February 1997).

There are four types of credit enhancements offered by state bond banks. The moral obligation reserve fund involves funding a reserve equal to one year's debt service on the bonds issued by the state entity. If the reserve fund is insufficient because of the failure of one or more qualified entities to pay its debt service to the bond bank, there usually is a pledge to replenish the debt reserve fund through a state appropriation. A second enhancement, state aid intercept, involves the diversion to the state bond bank of state aid owed to the qualified entity if the entity defaults on its obligations. Some bond banks receive annual appropriations from the state that serve as banking for bonds they issue. Finally, it is possible for a state to guarantee the debt of a bond bank through a pledge of its full faith and credit.

In the same survey mentioned above, it was determined that five states used both the moral obligation reserve and state aid intercept enhancements, four states used moral obligation alone, two used full faith and credit, three used state aid intercept alone, one state used both state appropriation and moral obligation reserve, one state used moral obligation reserve and full faith and credit, and one state used aid intercept and other enhancements.[57]

Most observers agree that bond banks have achieved their stated goals. They provide smaller governmental units affordable access to regional and national capital markets. They overcome constraints on access faced by these units of government, such as relatively high legal and administrative costs per dollar of debt, lack of information about small issuers among underwriters and investors, and the lack of a bond rating.[58]

CRISES IN THE MARKET AND THE RESPONSE

As the 1980s opened, the cause célèbre of the public financial management community were Proposition 13 in California and urban problems mixed with fiscal mismanagement in New York City and Cleveland. In response to New York City's debt repayment moratorium in 1975, a state control board gained review and oversight responsibilities over city contracts and budgets while a special debt financing authority (the Municipal Assistance Corporation) helped restructure existing debt and provide the city with continuing access to the capital markets.[59] Cleveland followed in 1978 by defaulting on GO notes—the first GO default since the Great Depression era. This event prompted Ohio to pass general legislation in 1979 creating a control board mechanism similar to New

57. Government Finance Group Inc.

58. Robbins and Kim, 92–108; Paul Solano, "An Appraisal of the Interest Cost Savings of State Bond Banks," *Municipal Finance Journal* 25, no. 4 (2005): 13–48.

59. While the preapproval provisions of the emergency control board terminated in 1986, the board continues to review the city's financial plans (*www.fcb.state.ny.us*). MAC expires when its bonds mature.

York's to oversee the city's recovery from fiscal emergency, but Cleveland was just one of seven cities assigned a control board in the early years of this legislation.[60]

New York City's highly publicized fiscal unraveling highlighted a growing recognition that impairment of the repayment obligation to investors could extend the impact beyond city limits to investors nationwide. At the same time, "improper and unethical trading and selling practices" in the municipal securities industry led policy makers to conclude that there was a need for increased investor protection.[61] In 1975, Congress amended the securities laws to require municipal securities dealers to be registered with the Securities and Exchange Commission (SEC). Congress established the Municipal Securities Rulemaking Board (MSRB) as the self-regulatory organization with primary rulemaking responsibility for municipal securities dealers, but gave the SEC final approval authority. While giving the MSRB authority to regulate municipal securities dealers, Congress added an explicit provision known as the Tower Amendment that prohibited the SEC or the MSRB from requiring "any issuer of municipal securities, directly or indirectly . . . to file with the [SEC or MSRB] . . . prior to the sale of such securities by the issuer any application, report, or document in connection with the issuance, sale, or distribution of such securities."[62] There were no such restrictions on the SEC for protecting municipal securities investors from fraud committed by issuers, their officials, and the various parties advising on a public market transaction.

Although the Tower Amendment prevented the MSRB from requiring municipal issuers to file disclosure documents prior to sale, there remained an unease in the marketplace about the provision of information to bond investors by the issuers of municipal securities. By the end of the 1970s, the currently named Government Finance Officers Association responded to this reasonable concern by publishing a set of voluntary market disclosure guidelines for state and local governments.[63]

In the ensuing 25 years, several events further framed the evolution of state and local debt management. In 1982, the Washington Public Power Supply System defaulted on $2.25 billion worth of revenue bonds. A state court permitted affected local governments to abrogate take-or-pay contracts that had been the security for construction of several nuclear power facilities, ruling in essence that those local governments did not have the

---

60. Indeed, it was the Cleveland default and the issues it raised for municipal bonds that led the first author to accept his first academic position at nearby Kent State University and to attend for several years the meetings of the Cleveland control board to learn about the causes and solutions to fiscal emergencies. Case studies of the Ohio experience are contained in *Bankruptcies, Defaults, and Other Local Government Financial Emergencies* (Washington, DC: U.S. Advisory Commission on Intergovernmental Relations, 1985).

61. Municipal Securities Rulemaking Board, *Manual* (October 1, 1995), 201.

62. Securities Exchange Act of 1934, as amended, section 15B(d).

63. *Guidelines for Use by State and Local Governments in the Preparation of Yearly Information Statements and Other Current Information* (1978) and *Disclosure Guidelines for State and Local Governments* (1979), both by the then-named Municipal Finance Officers Association, Chicago.

legal authority to enter into the contracts in the first place.[64] What prompted these jurisdictions to seek legal relief was a change in circumstances brought on by unrealistic original energy demand estimates, extended project delays, escalating project costs in a high interest rate environment, and growing political pressures to maintain low power rates.

Nationally, the WPPSS bankruptcy intensified concerns about the adequacy of municipal bond disclosures. Issuers and other market leaders responded by publishing a revision of the voluntary disclosure guidelines.[65] In August 1989, the SEC responded more forcibly by adopting Rule 15c2-12, which required municipal securities broker/dealers to obtain market offering circulars, termed "official statements," from issuers before agreeing to purchase the bonds.[66]

Aside from WPPSS, there were local government bankruptcies, too.[67] The San Jose School District in California sought bankruptcy protection in 1983, due, in part, to Proposition 13 tax limits, but, more pointedly, to void a labor arbitration award. Although the city declared itself insolvent, it paid all debt service on schedule. In 1991, the Richmond Unified School District in California sought bankruptcy protection from financial problems that included a default on an $8.5 million lease transaction configured as COPs.[68] Although California passed bailout legislation allowing the district to withdraw its bankruptcy petition, a state court ruled that the bond disclosure document contained a nonappropriation clause that clearly stated the debt would be paid only when there was sufficient money to do so. These COPs remained unpaid until a court settlement resolved the matter.[69]

Across the country, Bridgeport, Connecticut, tried but failed to declare bankruptcy in 1991. The state countered, in part, with the assertion that the city first had to get the state's approval, and that had not occurred. (A subsequent change in federal bankruptcy law now requires specific state authorization before a municipality can file for bankruptcy.) However, the reason the court rejected Bridgeport's bankruptcy petition was because of the fact that the city actually was not insolvent. It had been paying its debts and had sufficient cash to pay them in the immediate future.[70]

---

64. L. R. Jones, "The WPPSS Default: Trouble in the Municipal Bond Market," *Public Budgeting & Finance* 4, no. 4 (1984): 60–77.

65. *Disclosure Guidelines for State and Local Government Securities* (GFOA, 1988). See "Symposium on 15-Year Anniversary of the *Disclosure Guidelines*," *Municipal Finance Journal* 12, no. 4 (1991): 1–22.

66. U.S. Securities and Exchange Commission, *Municipal Securities Disclosure*, Release No. 34-26985 (July 10, 1989).

67. James Spiotto, "Municipal Bankruptcy," *Municipal Finance Journal* 14, no. 1 (1993): 1–38.

68. Craig L. Johnson and John L. Mikesell, "The Richmond Unified School District Default: COPS, Bankruptcy, Default and State Intervention," in *Case Studies in Public Budgeting and Financial Management*, eds. Aman Khan and W. Bartley Hildreth (Dubuque, IA: Kendall/Hunt Publishing Company, 1994), 525–540.

69. Dale Recinella, "The Lesson of Brevard County," *Municipal Finance Journal* 13, no. 3 (1992): 16–27; Johnson and Mikesell, 41–54.

70. Carol W. Lewis, "The Bond Market and Bankruptcy: A Civic Perspective," *Municipal Finance Journal* 17, no. 2 (1996): 51–80.

In 1993, Brevard County's (Florida) public flirtation with exercising its nonappropriation right on a COPs transaction caused market-wide scorn, threatening to harm COPs transactions everywhere.[71] This experience highlighted the municipal securities industry view that the standard nonappropriation clause is an accommodation to circumvent a legal definition of debt, not the granting of a legal loophole for issuers to get out of a multiyear payment obligation merely because of a lack of willingness to pay during difficult times.

Issuers were quickly learning that they had an obligation to the market both at the time of original issuance and throughout the life of their debt instruments. If there was any doubt, a heightened municipal securities enforcement effort by the SEC drove home the point. With his appointment in July 1993, SEC Chairman Arthur Levitt Jr. brought an intensive focus on promoting investor protection, coupled with a particular interest in state and local finance as the only son of the long-serving elected New York State Comptroller.[72] Soon, Chairman Levitt created the SEC's Office of Municipal Securities to coordinate activities in reforming the municipal debt markets in conjunction with the enforcement efforts of the Commission.[73] This office initiated an extensive program to educate municipal market participants—including issuer officials, underwriters, bond lawyers, financial advisers, and others—in their securities law responsibilities.[74] Working in parallel fashion, the Internal Revenue Service started a comprehensive enforcement program in 1993, based, in part, on a 1993 report from the General Accounting Office that criticized IRS monitoring of tax-exempt securities.[75]

In late 1993, the SEC's Office of Market Regulation issued an extensive report on the "integrity and fairness of the municipal securities market," that concluded, in part, that "voluntary efforts to increase disclosure in the municipal securities market, while constructive, have not resulted in complete and comprehensive disclosure of the financial condition of issuers of municipal securities."[76] Short of Congress repealing the Tower Amendment, the only avenue open to the Commission was to approach the topic through broker/dealer regulations. Accordingly, in March 1994, the SEC issued a state-

---

71. W. Bartley Hildreth, ed., "Symposium: Certificates of Participation in Brevard County: A Local Political Issue and Its Implications for the National Municipal Market," *Municipal Finance Journal* 15, no. 1 (1994): 50–74.

72. "SEC Biography: Chairman Arthur Levitt" (1993–2001), *http://www.sec.gov/about/commissioner/ levitt.htm*; and Brett D. Fromson, "The Quiet Crusader at the SEC," *Washington Post*, September 28, 1997, *http://www.washingtonpost.com/wp-srv/business/longterm/ethics/levitt.htm*.

73. SEC Press Release, *http://www.sec.gov/news/press/2000-139.txt*.

74. Paul S. Maco and George L. Shepard, "Let There Be Light: The SEC's New Regulations for the Municipal Securities Market," *Public Budgeting & Finance* 16, no. 2 (1996): 133–140; Paul S. Maco, "Points for Municipal Issuers to Keep in Mind during Good Times," *Municipal Finance Journal* 21, no. 2 (2000): 43–54.

75. General Accounting Office, *Improvements for More Effective Tax-Exempt Bond Oversight*, GAO/ GGD-93-014 (May 10, 1993).

76. U.S. Securities and Exchange Commission, *Staff Report on the Municipal Securities Market* (September 1993).

ment on continuing disclosure responsibilities as a prelude to the adoption of related amendments to Rule 15c2-12 in November 1994.[77] The Rule, as a whole, establishes certain initial and continuing disclosure requirements. An initial issuer of municipal securities must prepare an official statement meeting certain content requirements before a broker/dealer may recommend securities to potential investors. Moreover, the issuer must agree in writing with the broker/dealer (through an "undertaking" agreement) that the issuer will file certain materials while the securities are outstanding. In particular, the issuer must agree to provide an annual report, audited financial statements, material event notices, and a notice stating any failure to file the other reports. Rule 15c2-12 requires the submission of disclosure documents to each of the Nationally Recognized Securities Information Repositories (NRMSIRs) and applicable State Information Depositories (SIDS).[78]

Orange County, California, filed for bankruptcy in December 1994 on the basis of a portfolio loss of $1.5 billion in its pooled investment fund. Local officials in Orange County, as well as certain other governmental participants in the investment pool, adopted budgets largely dependent upon interest earnings and approved municipal bonds that helped enlarge the investment pool, yet failed to oversee the investment function and issued misleading market disclosures.[79] Subsequent SEC enforcement action declared that elected and appointed officials have a personal obligation to investigate the nature of the jurisdiction's market disclosures before approving them.[80] Orange County's indifference to bond market responsibilities emboldened the SEC as it sought to protect municipal securities investors.

Local problems still emerged. Fiscal mismanagement led to respective state takeovers of several prominent cities, including Miami (Florida) in 1996,[81] and Pittsburgh

---

77. U.S. Securities and Exchange Commission, *Statement of the Commission Regarding Disclosure Obligations of Municipal Securities Issuers and Others*, SEC Release No. 33-7049, 34-33741 (March 9, 1994); U.S. Securities and Exchange Commission, *Municipal Securities Disclosure*, SEC Release 34-34961 (November 10, 1994).

78. Because of inconsistent handling at the various NRMSIRs of the hardcopy documents received from issuers, in September 2004, the SEC authorized issuers of municipal securities and others who make continuing disclosure filings to use a single Internet-based electronic filing system to satisfy their continuing disclosure obligations. Although referred to as the Central Post Office, the official name is DisclosureUSA (located at www.DisclosureUSA.org). This central mechanism is voluntary, but provides a viable alternative to dealing directly with each individual NRMSIR (and, if applicable, the SID). The Central Post Office, then, transmits the electronic documents to the NRMSIRs and SIDs.

79. See the two symposiums on Orange County in the *Municipal Finance Journal* 16, no. 2 (Summer 1995): 1–89; and 17, no. 2 (Summer 1996): 1–94; and Merton H. Miller and David J. Ross, "The Orange County Bankruptcy and Its Aftermath: Some New Evidence," *The Journal of Derivatives* 4, no. 4 (1997): 51–60.

80. U.S. Securities and Exchange Commission, *Report of Investigation in the Matter of Orange, California as it Relates to the Conduct of the Members of the Board of Supervisors* (January 24, 1996).

81. Milan J. Dluhy and Howard A. Frank, "Miami: Teetering on the Precipice of Disaster," *Municipal Finance Journal* 18, no. 1 (1997): 1–17.

(Pennsylvania) and Buffalo (New York) in 2003. The Miami situation, in particular, led the SEC to issue a landmark order against the city to cease and desist from committing any future violations of federal securities laws because of the city's dismissive attitude toward the value of disclosure and its accuracy.[82]

In Boston, the "Big Dig" construction project (formally the Massachusetts Central Artery/Ted Williams Tunnel Project) by the Massachusetts Turnpike Authority (MTA) led the SEC to conclude, in a settled action in 2003, that the delay in disclosing cost increases exceeding $1 billion in several 1999 bond transactions violated federal securities laws. The SEC raised important issues of disclosure of uncertain and ambiguous facts in a context in which the MTA asserted that it did not want to disclose emerging cost increases that had not been fully quantified or confirmed because disclosure could lead to a "self-fulfilling" prophecy.[83] Currently, San Diego faces a serious fiscal problem, including potential SEC enforcement inquiries, caused by its handling of pension obligations and subsequent questionable disclosures in the municipal debt markets.[84]

In terms of sheer magnitude, however, nothing compares with the turn to heavy debt financing by California in the last few years to deal with its aborted electric industry restructuring, and the precipitous decline in state finances because of the dot-com bubble. In this and a few other notable occasions (e.g., Louisiana in 1988 and Connecticut in 1991) states have borrowed money to cover operating deficits, the same problem that led New York City to its ignoble fiscal situation in 1975.

Despite this list of troubled issuers of municipal securities during the past two to three decades, the fact is that both municipal securities defaults and governmental bankruptcies are rare. Municipal securities not only have a generally low rate of default, but general governments, and GO debt, in particular, have the lowest default rates of all with the last big wave of GO defaults occurring during the Great Depression.[85] However, municipal securities backed by dedicated revenues display a more frequent default pattern, especially those issued for healthcare and industrial development purposes. In addition, land-secured bonds have been a notable problem.[86]

Bankruptcy involves the entire jurisdiction or organization, not just a debt obligation, and can involve many different creditors. Therefore, Congress sets the rules. In the face of municipal fiscal problems in New York City and Cleveland in the late 1970s, Congress responded by incorporating into the comprehensive U.S. Bankruptcy Code of 1979 a

---

82. SEC, *In the Matter of the City of Miami, FL*, Release No. 8213 and No. 47552 (March 21, 2003).
83. SEC, *In the Matter of The Massachusetts Turnpike Authority and James J. Kerasiotes*, Release No. 8260 (July 31, 2003).
84. See symposium, *Municipal Finance Journal* 25, no. 3 (Fall 2004): 1–146.
85. Natalie R. Cohen, "Municipal Default Patterns: An Historical Study," *Public Budgeting & Finance* 9, no. 4 (1989): 55–65; and Colleen Woodell, William Montrone and Brooks Brady, "U.S. Municipal Rating Transitions and Defaults, 1986–2003," *Municipal Finance Journal* 24, no. 4 (2004): 49–77.
86. Robert W. Doty, "Disclosure Responsibilities and Substance in Tax-Exempt Land-Based Financings," *Municipal Finance Journal* 16, no. 4 (1996): 1–30; and Matt Fong, "Report of the California Interagency Municipal Securities Task Force," *Municipal Finance Journal* 19, no. 4 (1999): 75–98.

modified municipal bankruptcy law that was codified as Chapter 9.[87] Unlike personal and business bankruptcies, municipal bankruptcy is an entirely voluntary action; creditors cannot force a municipality into bankruptcy. After Bridgeport's filing for bankruptcy over the objection of the state of Connecticut, Congress revised the law in 1994 to require specific state approval before a municipality can file for bankruptcy. From 1990 to 2002, there have been 135 Chapter 9 filings, with the bulk of the filings from land-secured special districts, not general governments, in California, Colorado, Nebraska, and Texas.[88]

Credit Enhancements as a Response

In response to the increased concern for and attention paid to the potential for default, state and local governments have turned to credit enhancements such as bond insurance and LOC to provide added protection for investors in municipal securities.[89] The most common form of credit enhancement is bond insurance, which is an unconditional pledge by a private insurance company to make principal and interest payments to bond investors. Bond insurers evaluate the creditworthiness of state and local governments and charge an appropriate premium based on their reviews. Independent bond rating agencies subject bond insurers to a stringent depression scenario stress test before awarding the insurer the coveted triple-A credit rating which the bond insurer "rents" (in exchange for a premium) to the insured. A higher credit rating translates into a lower interest cost of borrowing for the debt issue. Bond insurance is viewed as a way to simplify an otherwise complicated security arrangement, making it easier for investors to understand and evaluate the risks involved. Since its introduction in 1971, the market turned to municipal bond insurance following New York City's debt moratorium in 1975 and the WPPSS default in 1983, with bond insurance quickly representing over 25 percent of the new issuance market.[90] As shown in Figure 2, about one-half of all new issues are insured.[91]

---

87. Bennett J. Murphy, "Understanding Municipal Bankruptcy," *Municipal Finance Journal* 16, no. 3 (1995): 47–61.

88. Administrative Office of the U.S. Courts, *http://www.uscourts.gov/bnkrpctystats/statistics.htm#cal endar*. See also Natalie Cohen, "Understanding Municipal Bankruptcy," *Municipal Finance Journal* 16, no. 3 (1995): 62–69; James E. Spiotto, "Municipal Finance and Chapter 9 Bankruptcy," *Municipal Finance Journal* 17, no. 1 (1996): 1–28.

89. See John E. Peterson, "The Municipal Bond Market in a Changing Economy," *Public Budgeting & Finance* 8, no. 4 (1988): 22–34; Jonathan B. Justice and Stewart Simon, "Municipal Bond Insurance: Trends and Prospects," *Public Budgeting & Finance* 22, no. 4 (2002): 114–137; Jun Peng, "Do Investors Look beyond Insured Triple-A Rating? An Analysis of Standard & Poor's Underlying Ratings," *Public Budgeting & Finance* 22, no. 3 (2002): 115–131; and Dwight V. Denison, "An Empirical Examination of the Determinants of Insured Municipal Bond Issues," *Public Budgeting & Finance* 23, no. 1 (2003): 96–114.

90. For the history, see the first bond insurer—the American Municipal Bond Assurance Company (Ambac): *http://www.ambac.com/about.html*. Interestingly, municipal bond insurance is not covered in the index or the glossary of the influential book of that period: Lennox L. Moak, *Municipal Bonds: Planning, Sale, and Administration* (Chicago: Municipal Finance Officers Association, 1982).

91. *The Bond Buyer*, "A Decade of Municipal Bond Finance," various issues.

FIGURE 2

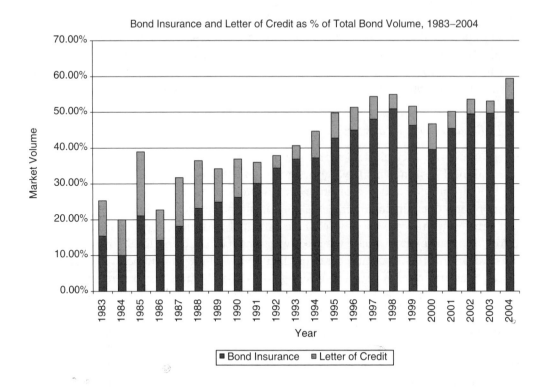

Bond Insurance and Letter of Credit as % of Total Bond Volume, 1983–2004

Another form of credit enhancement is LOC. These are financial instruments that substitute the credit risk of the provider of the LOC, usually a bank, for that of the weaker debt issuer. Basically, an LOC is an unconditional pledge of the bank's credit to make principal and interest payments of a specified amount on an issuer's debt for a specified time period, which may be shorter than the term of the bonds. Because the issue's rating is based on the bank's pledge to pay, issuers utilizing LOC are able to obtain more favorable interest rates than they would otherwise. LOCs are less prevalent than bond insurance as shown in Figure 2, with less than 6 percent in recent years, primarily a function of the changes in bank credits and the availability of other alternatives.[92]

Policy and Management as a Response

Regardless of the debt structures used, a hallmark of infrastructure financing in the United States is its decentralized, market-based approach, especially with the withering of intergovernmental grants. There is no federal oversight of state or local bond

92. *The Bond Buyer*, "A Decade of Municipal Bond Finance," various issues.

transactions, either before or after the transaction, save for that very rare occasion where the Internal Revenue Service determines that the bond does not qualify for tax-exempt status. Moreover, very few states impose any comprehensive oversight over local debt creation and repayment. Instead, state and local governments must subject themselves to the demanding requirements of the capital markets, and the penetrating analysts at independent credit rating firms.

Credit rating firms consider the management of a state and local government issuer one of four key assessment areas, along with its financial, debt and economic profiles. These four areas provide a convenient, but not definitive, way of characterizing related debt-related research. First, economic and demographic analyses illuminate ways to assess the wealth base that serves as the collateral for long-term bonds.[93] Second, research has also chronicled the changing financial condition of state and local governments and discussed new accounting standards that seek to improve the external reporting of financial results.[94] In regard to the third element, debt itself, studies have analyzed its level and affordability.[95]

Management, as the fourth part of credit analysis, involves a range of policies and practices that defy easy measurement.[96] Yet, it is the actions of policy makers that result in the decision to borrow and the methods and practices utilized.[97] Accordingly, this is a lively area of research in government finance. For example, alternative ways of structuring debt yield unexpected results.[98] The efficiency of selling bonds competitively instead of by negotiation continues to generate debate with an increasingly sophisticated slicing of the data.[99] Using the Internet to conduct an auction for selling debt expands this discussion.[100] A wide range of research focuses on issuer choices regarding the use of financial advisers

93. For example, economic diversification and expansion are key factors, see Anthony L. Loviscek and Frederick D. Crowley, "What Is in a Municipal Bond Rating?", *The Financial Review* 25, no. 1 (1990): 25–53.

94. This research is summarized elsewhere in this symposium.

95. Jack Rabin (ed.), "Public Debt: A Symposium," *Public Administration Review* 53, no. 1 (1993): 8–58; W. Bartley Hildreth and Gerald J. Miller, "Debt and the Local Economy: Problems in Benchmarking Local Government Debt Affordability," *Public Budgeting & Finance* 22, no. 4 (2002): 99–113.

96. See Salwa Ammar, William Duncombe, Bernard Jump, and Ronald Wright (eds.), "A Symposium on Evaluating Financial Management of Large Cities: An Application of Fuzzy Rule-Based Systems," *Public Budgeting & Finance* 21, no. 4 (2001): 44–110.

97. Mark Robbins, "Symposium Introduction: Municipal Bond Issuance: Can Research Help?", *Municipal Finance Journal* 21, no. 3 (2000): vi–ix.

98. Mark D. Robbins, Bill Simonsen, and Bernard Jump Jr., "Maturity Structure and Borrowing Costs: The Implications of Level Debt Service," *Municipal Finance Journal* 21, no. 3 (2000): 40–64.

99. Kenneth A. Kriz, "Comparative Costs of Negotiated Versus Competitive Bond Sales: New Evidence from State General Obligation Bonds," *Quarterly Review of Economics and Finance* 43, no. 2 (2003): 191–211; William Simonsen and William P. Kittredge, "Competitive Versus Negotiated Municipal Bond Sales: Why Issuers Choose One Method over the Other," *Municipal Finance Journal* 19, no. 2 (1998): 1–29.

100. Mark D. Robbins, Bill Simonsen, and Christine Rocco, "Municipal Bond Auctions and Borrowing Costs," *Municipal Finance Journal* 25, no. 1 (2004): 1–16.

and other financial certification agents.[101] Regardless of the manner of sale, municipal bond bid valuation research since the mid-1970s indicates that issuers should calculate the cost of capital using time value of money principles—specifically the "true interest cost" (TIC) factor instead of the "net interest cost" (NIC) calculation—while recent work suggests the need for a broader all-in cost of capital measure.[102] Studies also focus on the effectiveness of soft (e.g., management policies) and hard (e.g., constitutional) constraints on debt creation.[103]

CONCLUSION

In the United States, state and local governments' use of the capital markets to finance needed infrastructure and other public requirements has fostered economic growth and development, and a higher quality of life.[104] This historic perspective is no less relevant for the period covered by this paper.

Over the past 30 years, there have been five national recessions, with the last one ending the longest economic expansion in over 100 years.[105] While the early 1980s were marked with tax-exempt coupons in the double digits, most recently the rates have been

---

101. Mark D. Robbins and Bill Simonsen, "Financial Advisor Independence and the Choice of Municipal Bond Sale Type," *Municipal Finance Journal* 24, no. 1 (2003): 37–57; Kenneth A. Kriz, "Do Municipal Bond Underwriting Choices Have Implications for Other Financial Certification Decisions?" *Municipal Finance Journal* 21, no. 3 (2000): 1–23; and Craig L. Johnson, "State Government Credit Quality: Down, but Not Out!" *Public Administration Review* 59, no. 3 (1999): 243–249.

102. Michael H. Hopewill and George G. Kaufman, "Costs to Municipalities of Selling Bonds by NIC," *National Tax Journal* 27, no. 4 (1974): 531–542; George G. Kaufman, "The 'Oregon' Bond Project: Review and Evaluation," *Municipal Finance Journal* 1, no. 3 (1980): 192–198; Harold Bierman Jr., "The Valuation of Municipal Bond Bids: Four Solutions," *Municipal Finance Journal* 6 (1985): 263–268; Robert W. Zinn, "Applying the Bierman Technique: Municipal Bond Bid Valuation," *Municipal Finance Journal* 13 (1992): 51–60; Bill Simonsen, Mark D. Robbins, and Bernard Jump Jr., "Is TIC Always the Most Appropriate Cost of Capital Measure?", *Municipal Finance Journal* 22, no. 2 (2001): 1–13.

103. Rhonda Riherd Trautman, "The Impact of State Debt Management on Debt Activity," *Public Budgeting & Finance* 15, no. 2 (1995): 33–51; Bill Simonsen, Mark D. Robbins, and Bill Kittredge, "Do Debt Politices Make a Difference in Finance Officers' Perceptions of the Importance of Debt Management Factors?", *Public Budgeting & Finance* 21, no. 1 (2001): 88–105; Mark D. Robbins and Casey Dungan, "Debt Diligence: How States Manage the Borrowing Function," *Public Budgeting & Finance* 21, no. 2 (2001): 88–105; Beverly S. Bunch, "The Effect of Constitutional Debt Limits on Stage Governments' Use of Public Authorities," *Public Choice* 68 (1991): 57–69; James M. Poterba, "Capital Budgets, Borrowing Rules, and State Capital Spending," *Journal of Public Economics* 56 (1995): 165–187.

104. For an early indication, see David. M Cutler and Grant Miller, "Water, Water, Everywhere: Municipal Finance and Water Supply in American Cities," NBER Working Paper No. W11096 (January 2005), *http://ssrn.com/abstract=657621*; and Bruce Seely, "The Saga of American Infrastructure: A Republic Bound Together," *The Wilson Quarterly* 17, no. 1 (1993): 18–39.

105. Recessions of 1973–1975, 1980, 1981–1982, 1990–1991, and 2001. National Bureau of Economic Research, "US Business Cycle Expansions and Contractions," *http://www.nber.org/cycles.html*.

in historically low single digits. At the same time, citizen demand for services has outstripped the willingness of citizens to pay.

In the face of a constrained public budget environment, public officials and their finance managers have to be creative to achieve desired fiscal goals.[106] Fostering this behavior is a public finance community comprised of bond lawyers, investment bankers, financial advisers, credit rating firms, credit guarantors, and other experts. Investors have not wilted in the face of this onslaught of debt paper, nor with the prospect of having to trade municipal bonds in an inefficient secondary market.[107] In fact, institutional investors have created new products that generate demand for certain types of debt instruments, such as reset securities. A more aggressive regulatory scheme has emerged, albeit targeted at municipal securities dealers as a backdoor way to regulate issuers. Increased accountability, both internal and external to the government, has wedded with enhanced professionalism among the finance staff, to guide the capital market appetite of these governments. A new generation of scholars has addressed municipal bond questions with finance theory and sophisticated statistical methods.

More troubling is the prospect that Congress may use fundamental federal tax reform to end the tax exemption for municipal securities. If this happens, we only have to look at our northern neighbor to see the impact. In Canada, provincial and municipal governments have to borrow in an exclusively taxable market, in direct competition with its national government and private business. The result is that provincial and municipal governments pay up to one full percentage point (100 basis points) higher interest rates that the Canadian Treasury. For already strapped budgets among U.S. state and local governments, an increase in the cost of capital of this magnitude would be problematic.

Capital markets can be demanding masters as debt accumulation carries an obligation to repay. Over the past 25 years, for the most part, state and local governments have improved their capital market behavior. Learning has been steady, but with significant events propelling the march of progress. Efforts need to be intensified to wring out the inefficiencies in the municipal securities market and in issuers' debt acquisition practices. The past quarter century suggests that this decentralized approach to infrastructure financing works exceedingly well.

---

106. W. Bartley Hildreth, *State and Local Government Debt Issuance and Management Service* (Austin, TX: Sheshunoff Information Services Inc. 2004, updated yearly).

107. See, for example, Chris Downing and Frank Zhang, "Trading Activity and Price Volatility in the Municipal Bond Market," *Journal of Finance* 59, no. 2 (2004): 899–931; and the Web site: *www.municipal bonds.com.*

Chapter 7

The Discourse of Governmental Accounting and Auditing*

An overview is presented of the discourse during the past 25 years about governmental accounting and auditing. To discuss the nature of discourse, 975 abstracts were reviewed from applied and scholarly publications. To gain insight into the discourse, these abstracts are classified in various ways. And to foster future research, works with a high potential for informing future research are identified from this discourse of the past.

The purpose of this article is to serve as an introduction to the discourse about governmental accounting and auditing in the United States over the past 25 years and to identify works from the past 25 years that may be useful in shaping future discourse and in informing future research.

The observation of Professor R. M. Mikesell about governmental accounting is as true today as when it was written in 1956 in an early textbook.

> Even when developed to the ultimate stage of perfection, governmental accounting cannot become a guaranty of good government. At best, it can never be more than a valuable tool for promotion of sound financial management. It does not offer a panacea for all the ills that beset representative government; nor will it fully overcome the influence of disinterested, uninformed citizens. It cannot be substituted for honesty and moral integrity on the part of public officials; it cannot eliminate the demands of selfish interests, whether in the form of individual citizens, corporations, or the pressure groups which always abound to influence government at al levels.[1]

Although government accounting is not a guarantee, it is an important tool which may operate to benefit the public interest. As an important tool of sound financial management, it merits a thoughtful public discourse and serious academic research.

Jean Harris is Associate Professor of Accounting, School of Business Administration, Capital College, The Pennsylvania State University, 777 West Harrisburg Pike, Middletown, Pennsylvania 17057-4898. She can be reached at *jeh6@psu.edu*.

*This chapter was originally published in *Public Budgeting & Finance*, Vol. 25, Silver Anniversary Edition (2005): 154–179.

1. R. M. Mikesell, *Governmental Accounting, Revised Edition* (Homewood, IL: Richard D. Irwin, 1956), 10.

The accounting models, the professional jargon, and the technical complexities may discourage many from studying, from researching and from trying to improve governmental accounting and auditing. Despite the challenges, governmental accounting and auditing are of fundamental importance. Although not sufficient to establish public accountability, they are tools that are necessary in modern nation-states to establish public accountability.

This is an overview of the discourse in governmental accounting and auditing during the past 25 years. Looking at the history of discourse over two and one-half decades may be instructive. It shows issues that received attention, and it shows issues that may merit attention in the future.

To prepare this overview, abstracts of 763 articles were reviewed from a leading applied publication and abstracts of 212 articles were reviewed from various scholarly publications. As this review began, a series of steps were taken to gain insight into the discourse about governmental accounting and auditing. First, entries in the *Accounting & Tax Index* (formerly the *Accountants' Index*) under government accounting and under government auditing were reviewed for the past 25 years. Second, a table was developed to show publication outlets for indexed entries for the year 2000 and subsequent years. Third, abstracts about governmental accounting and/or auditing were collected from four sources: (1) *The Journal of Government Financial Management* and its predecessor *The Government Accountants Journal* (GFM/GAJ), (2) *Research in Governmental and Non-Profit Accounting* (RIGNA), (3) *Public Budgeting & Finance* (PB&F), and (4) a selection of other scholarly journals. This collection of 975 abstracts by no means represents the entire discourse about governmental accounting and auditing over the past 25 years, but it seems sufficient to provide a representative view of major themes in the applied and scholarly discourse. This review does not extend to a literature that might be described as the regulatory discourse. This literature would include research, publications, and preliminary drafts of standards issued by the various boards that establish accounting standards and auditing standards as well as comment letters provided to these boards by entities that prepare financial statements and other interested parties.

The 975 abstracts were classified in various ways and resources to inform future research were identified. Accounting for governmental entities outside of the United States, accounting for nongovernmental nonprofit entities, and discussions of general financial management including budgeting are beyond the scope of this review. However, because of the close connection of auditing to accounting, this article extends to the discourse about the auditing of governmental entities. As it proceeds, this overview is organized into five sections. These are as follows: (1) key happenings, (2) publication outlets, (3) applied discourse, (4) scholarly discourse, and (5) research.

KEY HAPPENINGS

The foundational changes that have occurred in governmental accounting and auditing over the past 25 years are revealed by considering the realities of governmental accounting and auditing 25 years ago. In 1980, there was no Governmental Accounting Standards Board (GASB); there was no Federal Accounting Standards Advisory Board (FASAB), and there was no Single Audit Act. The U.S. government did not publish audited financial statements, state/local government did not report on a government-wide basis, and the primary reporting of state and local governments was not the accrual basis of accounting. Of course, there were accounting and auditing standards prior to 1980, but many aspects of the currently accepted framework for accounting and auditing had not been implemented in 1980.

Spending by state and local governments accounts for roughly 11 percent of total GDP in the United States. And, spending by the federal government accounts for roughly 7 percent of GDP in the United States. However, government accounting has been a neglected subdiscipline for decades. It does not account for 18 percent of the discourse about accounting or 18 percent of the research pertaining to accounting. It is unlikely that any candidate for political office ever achieved election by promising to institute better accounting and auditing practices. Advances in governmental accounting and auditing seem to depend on dedicated accounting professionals who persist in advocating change, on crises that motivate stakeholders to demand change, and on public servants who are willing to invest their time and public resources to support change. When these three forces coalesce, change seems to be able to surface. Interestingly, the past 25 years have been a particularly rich time in the development of governmental accounting and auditing. Table 1 shows key happenings in chronological order.

PUBLICATION OUTLETS

An examination of the entries indexed in the *Accounting & Tax Index* (formerly the *Accountants' Index*) for articles about governmental accounting shows some possible publication outlets for refereed and nonrefereed publications. However, it appears that the premier scholarly journals in accounting and in public administration tend to neglect the publication of articles about governmental accounting. This neglect may reflect the small size of the pool of academic researchers with an interest in governmental accounting, the number of submissions, the research designs of submissions, and the relatively small audience for work about governmental accounting and auditing.

It is most encouraging that the scholarly research biennial, RIGNA, which is the only academic journal that is dedicated exclusive to governmental and nonprofit accounting and reporting, has resumed publication after a dormancy of five years. Table 2, shows the number of articles published by refereed and nonrefereed journals in the past five years. The articles appearing in accounting journals tend to be authored by persons whose primary disciplinary background is accounting rather than public administration or a related discipline. Collaborative research by accounting researchers with persons having backgrounds in other disciplines is not common. While this result is understandable, it is regrettable because governmental accounting and auditing has impor-

TABLE 1
Key Happenings

Date	Event
	Preparatory events, immediately pre-1980
1978	Inspector General Act of 1978 enacted
1979	OMB issued Circular A-102, Attachment P, audit requirements initiating single audits
	Events, 1980 and post-1980
1980	NCGA an agency of the MFOA and the standard-setting predecessor to GASB published a revised accounting manual GAAFR to define governmental Generally Accepted Accounting Principles (GAAP)
1980	Financial Integrity Act of 1980 enacted
1980	Cost Accounting Standards Board dissolved by Congress
1982	Federal Managers' Financial Integrity Act of 1982 enacted
1984	GASB established
1984	Single Audit Act of 1984 enacted
1984	Revised *Title 2, Accounting Principles and Standards of the GAO's Policies and Procedures Manual for Guidance of Federal Agencies issued requiring audited financial statements*
1986	Under Rule 203 of the AICPA, the GASB was designated as the primary body to establish Generally Accepted Accounting Principles (GAAP) for governmental entities
1990	FASAB established
1990	Chief Financial Officers Act enacted
1993	Government Performance and Results Act of 1993 enacted
1993	Cost Accounting Standards Board reestablished in OMB
1994	Government Management Reform Act of 1994 enacted
1996	Financial Management Improvement Act of 1996 enacted
1998	Audited, government-wide financial statements issued for U.S. Government
1999	GASB Statement No. 34 issued providing for dual reporting model
2000	Association of Government Accountants celebrated its 50th anniversary
2000	Under Rule 203 of the American Institute of CPAs (AICPA), the FASAB was designated as the primary body to establish GAAP for the federal government

OMB, Office of Management and Budget; NCGA, National Council on Governmental Accounting; MFOA, Municipal Finance Officers Association; GAAFR, Governmental Accounting, Auditing and Financial Reporting; GASB, Governmental Accountings Standards Board; AICPA, American Institute of CPAs; FASAB, Federal Accounting Standards Advisory Board.

TABLE 2
Publication Outlets
Entries as Indexed under Government, Accounting and Government, Auditing in the *Accounting and Tax Index*, formerly the *Accountants' Index*

	Total	2000	2001	2002	2003
Nonrefereed publications with two or more articles since 2000					
Accounting Today	16	2	4	5	5
American City & County	3	1		2	
Armed Forces Comptroller	4	4			
Asset	4	1	3		
California CPA	3	1	1	1	
CPA Letter	12	2	3	6	1
Government Finance Review	31	1	11	14	5
International Journal of Auditing	2				2
Leaders' Edge	10	4	2	2	2
Pennsylvania CPA Journal	2	1	1		
Practical Accountant	5		1	1	3
Public Manager	5		4	1	
All Others	18	3	5	6	4
Total	115	20	35	38	22
Refereed publications with two or more articles since 2000					
CPA Journal	10	3	1	4	2
Journal of Accountancy	14	7	2	1	4
Journal of Accounting and Public Policy	2			1	1
Journal of Government Financial Management and	47		18	26	3
its predecessor *Government Accountants Journal*	27	27			
Internal auditor	5	1		2	2
Issues in Accounting Education	5	3	1	1	
Municipal Finance Journal	13	4	4	3	2
Public Budgeting & Finance	8	2	5	1	
All Others	3	2	1		
Total	134	49	32	39	14

The classification of a journal as refereed or nonrefereed was taken from *Cabell's Directory of Publishing Opportunities in Accounting* and *Cabell's Directory of Publishing Opportunities in Economics and Finance*. Also, information for submitting manuscripts may be obtained from these directories or from the journal.

tance for many stakeholders beyond the disciplinary boundaries of accounting and auditing. Thus, the prerequisite requirement of technical knowledge seems to limit the discourse by frequently isolating debate within disciplinary jargon. Some gifted writers are able to break away from the confines of jargon and to bring the discourse of debate to a general audience. It is not possible to recognize all such writers, but two who merit

The Evolution of Public Finance and Budgeting

mention are Robert Anthony of Harvard University and Martin Ives, a past member of GASB.[2]

APPLIED DISCOURSE—ISSUES AND APPROACHES

Applied discourse describes writings that are intended primarily for persons working as administrators, managers, accountants, auditors, finance professionals, or others. Although scholarly research methods may be used and the publication may be written by scholars, the intended audience is not primarily an audience of scholars. There are many sources of applied discourse. Some of the major sources are *The CPA Journal, Government Finance Review, Journal of Accountancy*, and *Journal of GFM*. For this article, abstracts were reviewed from articles published during the last 25 years in the *Journal of GFM*, inaugurated in 2001 and its predecessor the *GAJ*, inaugurated in 1976.

The *Journal of Financial Management*, a publication of the Association of Government Accountants (AGA), is devoted almost exclusively to governmental topics, publishes articles that pertain to state/local accounting and to federal accounting, and has a history of related publications that began in 1952. Few topics of significant interest in governmental accounting would escape being discussed in this journal. For purposes of this article, topics that prevailed in the discourse over a period of time are most noteworthy. Table 3 shows a list of topics, the number of articles about each topic and whether the article had a state/local orientation, a federal orientation or a general orientation. This classification is presented to establish the diversity of articles considered. Table 4, a companion table, shows the frequency of topic over a 25-year time frame.

The applied literature tends to be a literature of description and of advocacy. Thus, it often (1) describes a present state or activity or (2) advocates a change in a present state with a proposal for a new kind of activity. This sort of applied literature is extremely valuable. It provides useful information to many stakeholders, and it serves as a basis for research. For the researcher, description of the present state raises the general question, Why? Why is the present state as it is? What sort of theory offers an explanation? Numerous specific questions arise from adoption of a change. Advocates for change often provide guidance for subsequently evaluating the change by setting forth a description of future benefits. After implementation, researchers may then look to the projected benefits in evaluating the change. Because of the breath and of the depth of changes over the last 25 years in governmental accounting, this is an important time for participants and for scholars to document the stories of changes, the motivations, the impacts, the beneficiaries, etc. In an article of this length, it is possible only to identify the dominant topics in major areas such as state/local accounting, federal accounting, and auditing.

---

2. Robert N. Anthony, "Games Government Accountants Play," *Harvard Business Review* 63, no. 5 (1985): 161–170; Martin Ives, "The GASB: A Fresh Look at Governmental Accounting and Financial Reporting," *Journal of Accounting, Auditing & Finance* 8, no. 4 (1985): 253–268.

TABLE 3
Topics in Applied Discourse

Topic	No.	Focus		
		General	Federal	State/Local
Auditing				
Agency audits or specific audit procedures	33	13	17	3
General audit topics	32	16	4	12
Single Audit Act	31	31		
Auditing standards	18	18		
	114	78	21	15
State/local accounting				
State/local model	54			54
State/local issues/standards	29			29
State standard setting process	8			8
	91			91
Federal accounting				
Federal model	29		29	
Chief Financial Officer Act	18		18	
Inspectors General Act	15		15	
Other federal acts	13		13	
Federal issues/standards	6		6	
Federal standard setting process	6		6	
	87		87	
Behavioral control				
Performance measurement/auditing	37	14	7	16
Internal controls	20	3	16	1
Ethics	16	12	3	1
Fraud	11	6	4	1
	84	35	30	19
Education and regulation				
Curriculium for degree	31	28		3
Regulation of profession	16	14		2
Postdegree training	10	6	3	1
Certification/standards	9	6	2	1
	66	54	5	7
Total	442	167	143	132

Source: Journal of Government Financial Management/Government Accountants Journal (GFM/GAJ)
Various peripheral topics not classified by focus—miscellaneous topics (50), technology (48), international (39), systems (27), and nonprofits (13). Financial management topics not classified by focus—general discussions (46), specific means (39), cost control (30), and budgeting (29).

TABLE 4
Frequency of Topics in Applied Discourse

Topics	No.	Years				
		1980 1984	1985 1989	1990 1994	1995 1999	2000 2004
Auditing						
Agency audits or specific audit procedures	33	9	7	4	5	8
General audit topics	32	5	11	6	3	7
Single Audit Act	31	14	8	5	4	
Auditing standards	18	3	1	7	4	3
		31	27	22	16	18
State/local accounting						
State/local model	54	14	20	6	4	10
State/local issues/standards	29	5	6	9	6	3
State standard setting process	8	5	1	1		1
	91	24	27	16	10	14
Federal accounting						
Federal model	29	6	17	3	1	2
Chief Financial Officer Act	18	1		14	1	2
Inspectors General Act	15	1	2	5	7	
Other federal acts	13	6	2	3		2
Federal issues/standards	6		1	2	3	
Federal standard setting process	6	1	4	1		
	87	15	26	28	12	6
Behavioral control						
Performance measurement/auditing	37	7	6	9	7	8
Internal controls	20	11	5	1	2	1
Ethics	16	4	3	2	3	4
Fraud	11	4	3		4	
	84	26	17	12	16	13
Education and regulation						
Curriculium for degree	31	8	7	7	6	3
Regulation of profession	16	3	4	2	5	2
Postdegree training	10	4	3	2	1	
Certification/standards	9	2	4	1	1	1
	66	17	18	12	13	6
Total	442	113	115	90	67	57

Source: *Journal of Government Financial Management/Government Accountants Journal* (GFM/GAJ)
Various peripheral topics not classified by frequency—miscellaneous topics (50), technology (48), international (39), systems (27), and nonprofits (13). Financial management topics not classified by frequency—general discussions (46), specific means (39), cost control (30), and budgeting (29).

State/Local Accounting

Standard Setting. The rules for state/local accounting apply to all 50 states and roughly 88,000 other reporting entities. Some of the discourse in the early 1980s was a debate over the nature of the body that should set accounting standards. Prior to 1984, standards for state/local governments were established by the National Council on Governmental Accounting (NCGA) and several of its predecessor organizations that were affiliated with the Municipal Finance Officers Association (MFOA). By the early 1980s, the Financial Accounting Standards Board (FASB), which sets accounting standards in the private sector, had been formed and consideration was given to having FASB establish accounting standards for state/local governments. Issues in the debate involved the enforceability of accounting standards, the role of accounting in government, the need for diverse representation in the process, the utility of a full-time staff, and most importantly the distinctiveness of governments as reporting entities. The debate was not a prolonged part of accounting discourse. In 1984, The Financial Accounting Federation (FAF), which had established FASB, established a sister body to set standards for state/local governments, the GASB. Both boards are housed in the same building in Norwalk, Connecticut. Currently, the GASB has a full-time chairman, six other part-time members, and a professional staff. To date, the GASB has published 46 standards. These may be found on the website of the GASB (*www.gasb.org*) under "Publications."

State/Local Accounting Model. More than any other topic, the debate over the appropriate model of accounting for state/local reporting dominated applied accounting discourse of the past 25 years. In 1974, New York City faced a severe financial crisis, and the reality of bankruptcy threatened. The enormity of this event forced an examination of the reporting model used by state/local governments. Soon the debate, which had been limited largely to a small audience with a strong technical orientation, was of interest to a rapidly growing audience of stakeholders. This debate surfaced in the late 1970s. Then it continued to rage for 15 years, from the founding of the GASB in 1984 to the issuance in 1999 of *GASB Statement No. 34, Basic Financial Statements—and Management's Discussion and Analysis* (MD&A)—*for State and Local Governments.* An attempt to resolve the debate with an accounting standard that would have abandoned fund reporting on the modified accrual basis in favor of full-accrual reporting failed. Finally, a dual model of reporting was proposed and adopted. However, the debate continues with some viewing the dual model as an interim step in a shift to exclusive use of full-accrual accounting.

For nonaccountants, the debate over the accounting model is difficult to understand. This debate centers on whether a distinct "public sector" model of accounting is desirable for governments or whether a "private sector" model with some modifications is suitable for governments. Four basic issues are measurement focus, basis of accounting, accounting entity, and method of aggregation.

In traditional state/local accounting, measurement focused on financial resources, primarily on current receipts and current disbursement of the financial resource cash. In contrast, the private sector full-accrual model, measures the receipt and the use of total economic resources. It was argued that the broader focus on total economic resources should provide a better measure of financial stress than a narrower focus on financial resources. To a large extent, the basis of accounting derives from its measurement focus.

TABLE 5
Contrasting Models of Accounting

Issue	Traditional State/ Local Accounting	Private Sector Full-Accrual Accounting
Measurement focus	Financial resources—primarily cash and other current assets offset by current obligations	Economic resources—all assets offset by all claims, current and future, against those assets
Basis of accounting	Modified accrual for general fund (primary operations) and some other funds. Full accrual for funds with business-like activities.	Full accrual for all reporting
Accounting entity	Funds—multiple funds with multiple sets of financial statements	Reporting entity—one entity with one set of financial statements; reporting for two types of activities nonbusiness and business-like activities.
Method of aggregation	Combining data	Consolidating data

The basis of accounting defines when revenues are recognized and when expenses or expenditures are recognized. Traditional state/local accounting, for primary operations, used the modified accrual basis of accounting, which more closely resembles cash basis accounting than an accrual basis accounting. Using the modified accrual basis of accounting, the recognition of future obligations is delayed if current financial resources would not be consumed. In contrast, the private sector full-accrual model provided for the present recognition of current and future obligations that would consume a reporting entity's economic resources.

Traditional state/local accounting used a system of accounting called fund accounting with a complete set of financial statements being issued for each fund. Thus, one government (reporting entity) presented financial statements for many funds (accounting entities). Under the private sector, full-accrual model there would be one reporting entity and two accounting entities, one for nonbusiness activities and one for business activities. In traditional state/local accounting, data from the fund statements were aggregated in one combined statement. But for several reasons, the combined data lacked reliability. Under private sector accounting, the data are consolidated (not combined). The consolidating procedures eliminate data from being counted twice. Thus, consolidated data are more reliable than combined data.

Table 5 shows the key points in the debate over the model of accounting for state/local accounting. The discourse of the debate involved many other issues, such as the nature of reporting entity, accounting for fiduciary funds, accounting for nonexchange transactions, and accounting for noncompensated absences. However, the four issues shown in Table 5 were central to the discourse. Of these four issues, the central issue was measurement focus because basis of accounting derives from measurement focus.

TABLE 6
Dual Model of State/Local Accounting

	Fund-Level Reporting	Government-Wide Reporting
Measurement focus	Financial resources—excludes assets that will not be measurable and available in current period and obligations that will not be met in current period	Economic resources—measures all assets and all obligations, current and future
Basis of accounting	Modified accrual for general fund (primary operations) and some other funds. Full accrual for other business-like funds	Full accrual for all reporting
Accounting entity	Funds—multiple funds with multiple sets of financial statements	Reporting entity—one entity with one government-wide set of financial statements
Method of aggregation	Separate combining statements for governmental funds and for proprietary (business-like) funds	Consolidated data for nonbusiness activities and for business-like activities

One question to ask is why was this debate so prolonged? This is a question that merits research. The simple answer may be that different participants had conflicting preferences and interests. Some financial statement users wanted different information. For example, investors seem to prefer full-accrual reporting, while other stakeholders prefer modified accrual reporting. Also, cost was a consideration. Investors do not pay for the information they receive, and switching a basis of accounting can result in substantial costs to the reporting entity. Thus, in a way GASB, a nonelected body, had the power to impose substantial unfunded mandates on entities, a sort of quasi-indirect tax. Both direct costs and indirect costs loomed on the horizon. The financial costs of new systems would be direct financial outlay, but suddenly reporting large deficits as a result of the change in basis of accounting would create political costs. Some reporting entities saw benefits resulting from change while others saw costs. Some reporting entities were in a better position to bear the costs of a change than others were. Large auditing/consulting firms had a pool of talent with the technical expertise to participate in the debate, but these firms had the potential of reaping enormous amounts of consulting work from a change. To address the issues raised in this debate, GASB proposed a dual model that was subsequently adopted in *GASB Statement No. 34*. This model is illustrated in Table 6. The model is described as a dual model because it provided for two distinct reports at two levels, the fund level and the government-wide level.

With many modifications, the dual model approach retains the fund-level reporting of traditional state/local accounting while adding a government-wide set of financial statements based on full-accrual reporting. The two levels of reporting are connected by a reconciliation that would have meaning to only a master of accounting gymnastics. In some ways, *GASB Statement No. 34* is an experiment. Various possibilities loom for the

TABLE 7
Potential for Expanison of State/Local Model

Basis of Accounting	Modified Accrual for General Fund (Primary Operations) and Some Other Funds, Full Accrual for Other Funds	Full Accrual
Government-wide reporting	Potential for expansion with consolidation of funds reported on same basis of accounting	Required by *GASB Statement No. 34*
Fund-level reporting	Required by *GASB Statement No. 34*	Potential for expansion

GASB, Governmental Accountings Standards Board.

long-term future. The model may contract with fund-level reporting disappearing or by governmentwide reporting being abandoned. Alternatively, the model may expand with both forms of reporting moving up or down a level. Two cells in Table 7 show the potential for expansion.

Debate over a state/local reporting model centered on defenses of the status quo and on criticisms of the status quo. In building arguments for a change, many benefits were attributed to use of the accrual basis of accounting. These benefits included better assessment of fiscal position and of performance, better measurement of the costs of operations and of interperiod equity, and greater utility for allocating resources and for preparing financial plans. In the early 1980s, reporting entities were experimenting. Various studies examined financial statements to determine compliance with GAAP and to identify differences in the way financial statements were prepared. Users' needs were discussed; efforts were made to identify users and to gather input from users about the desirability and acceptability of standards and proposed standards. Being central to the core of measurement focus, capital reporting and the depreciation of capital assets were much debated. Several states began to develop financial management and accounting systems of a comprehensive nature.

By the late 1980s, the concept of interperiod equity was flourishing in the discourse. This is the concept that accounting should show if current year revenues are sufficient to pay for current year services. The debate was captured by the GSAB with the terms measurement focus and basis of accounting (MFBA). Exposure drafts (EDs) were proposed, revised, and revised again. Parties disagreed about the use of funds as accounting entities, the method and level of aggregation for the presentation of data, and accounting for fixed assets. An accounting standard was issued, but its implementation delayed. Agreement could not be reached about MFBA. Then in the mid-1990s, proposals for a dual model began to emerge. This proposal became the basis for *GASB Statement No. 34* that was issued in 1999 to define the new model for state/local reporting. The reporting of capital assets in account groups was eliminated and the reporting of depreciation, including depreciation for general infrastructure assets, was instituted. This statement also required the inclusion of MD&A in financial reports. After the adoption of *GASB Statement No. 34*, much of the discourse shifted to its implementations.

The struggle to define a new model for state/local reporting raises many questions. Among these questions are, Why have governments been so slow to move to reporting on an accrual basis of accounting? What groups were advantaged and disadvantaged by the delay? What forces were in operation to promote change? Does support for accounting standards tend to percolate bottom-up from stakeholders or do standards tend to be imposed top down? Who are the power players in standard setting and what are their agendas? The rich history of the emergence of the present model merits examination.

Other State/Local Issues. During the past 25 years, many issues have surfaced and receded from the discourse. These include accounting for encumbrances, for defeasance of debt, for risk financing including self-insurance, for investments including derivatives, for landfills, for tax revenues, and for nonexchange transactions. Every major issue, addressed by an accounting standard, will motivate discussion. But a few issues seem to endure in the discourse. These enduring topics are those about the nature of reporting entity, accounting, and disclosure for pensions, and accounting for leases. For governments, the reporting entity is not defined by ownership. Thus, creative arrangements with other governments and with nonprofits organizations turn entity into a nebulous notion. Aside from the accounting challenges, accounting and disclosures for pensions incorporate many political considerations. And, leases are a challenge because governments continue to find so many creative ways to use them.

Summary. In 1992, Martin Ives of the GASB, enumerated the significant developments in financial reporting by state/local governments. They are as follows:

(1) Emergence of a permanent structure to concentrate on accounting standards;
(2) The development of the requirement that accounting principles take precedence over legal provisions in financial reporting;
(3) The emergence of the integrated operating statement as a means of reporting on performance;
(4) The development of a reporting entity concept;
(5) The emergence of an accountability-based approach to financial accounting; and
(6) The recognition of the need of accrual accounting.[3]

This list of developments foreshadowed the adoption of the accrual basis of accounting for government-wide reporting and requirements for an integrated Statement of Activities about operations and integrated statement of net assets about financial condition.

Federal Accounting

Although federal accounting applies to one entity, the U.S. Government, it is the largest single reporting entity in the world and arguably the most complex reporting entity in the world. Possibly the most significant events in federal accounting during the past 25 years are the attention given to federal financial reporting and the attention given to federal financial management. For the first time in its history, the U.S. Government began to prepare and to publish audited annual financial statements. The goal of publishing

---

3. Martin Ives, "25 Years of State and Local Government Financial Reporting—An Accounting Standards Perspective," *Government Accountants Journal* 41, no. 38 (1992): 1–5.

financial statements for the U.S. government necessitated the establishment of a separate accounting standard setting body for purposes of federal accounting. This was a technical, legal, and diplomatic challenge. Thus, establishment of the FASAB ranks as another major accomplishment in federal accounting. To date, FASAB has published 28 accounting standards. These may be found on the website of the FASAB (*www.fasab.gov*) under "Listing of Documents."

At the federal level, use of the accrual basis of accounting, as the theoretical model for federal accounting, was readily accepted. The challenge was to find a way to establish a standard setting body. This body would need to adapt the broad principles of the accrual basis of accounting to the federal government by thoughtfully constructing accounting standards in areas where issues are technically complex and politically sensitive. It is probable, that the efforts and changes made to enable the U.S. Government to issue financial statements contributed to parallel efforts to establish controls, install financial systems, improve financial management and enable audits.

Federal Reporting. In the early 1980s, discourse reported the inadequacies of financial data. Then on November 14, 1984, after several years of work, the General Accounting Office (GAO), issued *Revised Title 2, Accounting Principles and Standards of the GAO's Policies and Procedures Manual for Guidance of Federal Agencies.* The *Revised Title 2* required executive branch agencies and departments on an annual basis to prepare summary-level financial statements, and it required the government as a whole to prepare Consolidated Financial Statements of the U.S. Government. Subsequent requirements for federal financial statements may be found in *OMB Bulletin No. 01–09, Form and Content of Agency Financial Statements (2001)* and *Statement of Federal Financial Accounting Concepts No. 2, Entity and Display (SFFAC No. 2).*

Fourteen years later, in 1998 the first audited government-wide financial statements were issued by the U.S. Government. When the enormity of this task is considered, it is a most significant accomplishment that the government could move forward as rapidly as it did to construct a standard general ledger and to sufficiently integrate the computer and information systems to support government-wide accounting. Improvements in financial reporting and in related disclosures are part of an ongoing process. However, financial statements have been issued for a sufficient number of years to support an analysis over time of the performance of agencies, departments and the government as a whole.

In the early 1980s, many of the financial reporting systems and supporting information systems were inadequate and old, sometimes decades old. They were not meeting the needs of stakeholders for information. Thus, the efforts made in the 1980s and 1990s represent a major remodeling of the financial infrastructure of the federal government. This remodeling may now lead to several questions. Has the attention given to accounting altered the operational decision making within government? What kinds of decisions are most affected by the availability of financial data? In what manner has decision making been altered? What sort of financial data are the most desired? And, by what stakeholders are financial data desired?

Federal Standard Setting. In May 1989, five years after the adoption of *Revised Title 2,* the GAO released a *Proposed Framework for Establishing Federal Government Accounting Standards.* Then about a year and one-half later in October 1990, the FASAB was established.

For legal reasons relating the separation of powers, the board is advisory. It was established by a memorandum of understanding signed by the secretary of treasury, the director of the Office of Management and Budget, and the comptroller general of the United States who heads the GAO, an audit agency of the legislative branch of government. In April 2000, the American Institute of CPAs (AICPA) recognized the authoritative status of the FASAB to establish generally accepted accounting principles (GAAP) for the federal government.

To date, the FASAB has published four conceptual statements and 28 accounting standards. The conceptual statements of FASAB address reporting objectives, issues of reporting entity and display, management discussion and analysis (MD&A), and the audience for consolidated financial statements. Standards address various issues which, as they came under consideration, surfaced in the discourse about accounting. One standard that attracted broad attention was the standard about accounting for capitalizing and depreciating capital assets.

Federal Financial Infrastructure. The 1980s and 1990s were two decades when Congress adopted a number of statutes that in combination would modify, expand, and improve the financial infrastructure of the federal government. Table 8 shows key federal acts. One question that merits examination is, after decades of neglect, why did Congress turn its interest to accounting and financial management? Were spending caps encouraging Congress to invest in a financial infrastructure to examine the operation of the government? Had states, by operating as laboratories, provided an example by modifying, improving, and expanding their financial infrastructures? Of the acts adopted by the federal government, those that are most prominent in the discourse of accounting and auditing are the Inspector General Act of 1978, the integrity acts of 1980 and 1982, The Single Audit Act 1984, and The CFO Act of 1990. Although relevant to building a financial infrastructure, The Inspector General Act of 1978 and The Single Audit Act of 1984 pertain directly to auditing and will be discussed as a part of that topic.

The integrity acts of 1980 and 1982 were motivated by an interest in curbing fraud and waste by instituting strong and effective internal controls. It is possible that as controls were examined on a broad basis across the agencies of government that weaknesses in the financial management infrastructure became apparent.

The Chief Financial Officers (CFO) Act was crafted as the centerpiece of reform in the federal financial management infrastructure. This act created an organizational structure for a unified leadership of financial management, required improvements in internal controls and in financial systems, and established a plan for the production of audited financial statements. It created the Office of Federal Financial Management (OFFM) within OMB and provided that the head of this office, a deputy director of OMB, would report directly to the director of OMB. It set forth the responsibilities of OMB and of affected agencies. Initially, it created CFO positions in 23 departments and agencies. Later the Government Management Reform Act of 1994 extended the requirements of the CFO Act to all major agencies. The agency CFOs are responsible for standardizing and centralizing financial reporting to support the production of audited financial statements and for submitting CFO annual reports that include performance measurement information. However, the CFO Act represented more than the creation of positions. It was an attempt to modify organizational culture and to alter the means of management by linking together budgeting, accounting and financial management.

Although annual audited financial statements were required and many accounting standards had been approved to provide guidance for financial reporting, compliance remained an

TABLE 8
Federal Financial Management Acts

Date	Act	Purpose
	Acts immediately prior to 1980	
1978	Inspector General Act of 1978	
1979	OMB Circular A-102 Attachment P, Audit Requirements	Required single audit every two years for state/local governments
	Acts 1980 and post-1980	
1980	Financial Integrity Act of 1980	Requires agency heads to certify adequacy of internal of controls
1982	Prompt Payment Act	Promotes prompt payment by U.S. Government to suppliers
1982	Federal Managers' Financial Integrity Act of 1982	Mandates evaluation of internal accounting and administrative controls
1984	Single Audit Act of 1984	Required single audits every year for state/local governments receiving federal monies in excess of a threshold amount.
1989	Credit Reform Act of 1989	Requires all cost of credit, including loan guarantees, be reflected in budget
1990	CFO Act	Establishes organizational leadership for financial reporting
1993	GPRA of 1993	Institutes a framework for performance measurement and reporting
1994	GMRA of 1994	Extends requirements of CFO Act to all major agencies
1996	FFMIA of 1996	Requires agency compliance with financial management systems requirements and federal accounting standards and the use of standard general ledger

CFO, Chief Financial Officers; GPRA, Government Performance and Results Act; GMRA, Government Management Reform Act; FFMIA, Financial Management Improvement Act.

issue. Statements were audited, but the audits could show noncompliance with reporting requirements. To motivate compliance, Congress adopted the Financial Management Improvement Act of 1996 which required agencies to report noncompliance and to establish plans to ensure timely compliance.

A peripheral topic in federal accounting does not pertain to the accounting of the federal government but to the accounting that the federal government will accept from companies with which it contracts. For cost plus contracts the determination of costs is an especially critical issue. In August 1970, Congress established the Cost Accounting Standards Board to promote consistent and uniform cost accounting by defense contractors. This Board, which was dissolved in 1980, was reestablished in 1993 within the OMB to issue policies about accounting practices of companies with which the federal government contracts.

Auditing

The most enduring discourse about auditing tends to pertain to one of three topics. Each of these topic begins with an advocacy—(1) advocacy for use of a single audit approach for the oversight of federal disbursements to state/local governments, (2) advocacy for the implementation of strong internal controls and the evaluation of internal controls as part of an audit, and (3) advocacy of performance auditing and development of a measurement infrastructure to support performance auditing. Each of these three topical areas of advocacy can be associated with one or more federal acts. Beyond the discourse in these three topical areas, one may find discussions of general interest topics such as discourse about auditor independence and liability, management of audits, oversight of audits including the use of audit committees, and ways to judge materiality. In addition to these general topics, numerous articles appear on a one-time basis to advocate various audit procedures or to report the experience of auditing within various organizations.

Audit Standards. Financial statements are prepared in accordance with accounting standards. For state/local governments accounting standards are promulgated primarily by the GASB. And, for the federal government, accounting standards are promulgated primarily by the FASAB. Audits are conducted in accordance with auditing standards. The AICPA establishes generally accepted auditing standards (GAAS) that apply to all CPAs in conducting audits of state and local governments. Additionally, the comptroller general, in the GAO, establishes auditing standards that apply to federal organizations and to organizations receiving federal funds. These standards are published in *government auditing standards* (the Yellow Book). They are commonly referred to as generally accepted government auditing standards (GAGAS). First published in 1972, they have been revised many times. As well as covering financial statement audits, these standards now extend to other attestations and to performance audits. A large body of discourse relates to these standards, proposals for modifying standards, explanations of adopted standards, discussion of ways to comply with standards, etc. A public body, the Public Companies Accounting Oversight Board (PCAOB) establishes auditing standard for auditors of publicly traded companies, SEC registrants.

Single Audit. Single-audit requirements were first initiated 1979 by OMB in *Circular A-102, Uniform Administrative Requirements for Grants-in-Aid to State and Local Governments, Attachment P, Audit Requirements.* Using this approach one audit is conducted of an entity, a state/local government, to assess the fairness of financial reporting about the expenditure of all federal funds received by the entity. For example, a state may satisfy its audit obligation arising from the receipt of federal funds with one audit rather than with a dozen grant-by-grant audits conducted by a dozen different federal agencies making disbursements to the state. Use of the single-audit approach was subsequently reviewed by Congress. Moving beyond advocacy, the initial discourse centered on the need for guidance and for ways to coordinate auditing. Problems were discussed and addressed. In 1983, Tennessee became the first state to release a statewide audit using the single-audit approach, and that same year single-audit legislation was introduced in Congress.

In 1984, Congress passed the Single Audit Act of 1984 which mandated annual audits of all states and major local governments. In 1985, administrative guidance was provided by *OMB Circular 128, Audits of State and Local Governments*. Adoption of single-audit requirements created a need for strong internal controls as well as demands for better accounting and auditing standards. The postadoption discourse of the late 1980s shows numerous issues arose and were resolved. In the early 1990s, discourse shifted to the utility of single-audit data for federal managers and to ways for reshaping reporting to maximize its utility. In particular, the use of the single-audit approach for Medicaid programs posed special problems. Also, in 1990, *OMB Circular A-133, Audits of Instructions of Higher Education and Other Nonprofit Institutions* extended the single-audit approach to universities and nonprofit organizations receiving federal funds thereby creating various new issues. In 1996, the Single Audit Act was amended, and in 1998, *Circular A-133* was revised. The discourse shows that with almost every change there is advocacy and then a subsequent need for guidance.

Internal Control. At the federal level the Inspector General Act of 1978 was marshaling an advocacy for internal controls. The inspector generals (IGs) had two primary responsibilities: (1) investigation to identify fraud, waste, and abuse and (2) audit. Without strong internal controls, the audit function would be impossible. At the federal level, strengthening internal control was a focus of the Financial Integrity Act of 1980 and of the Federal Managers' Financial Integrity Act of 1982. At the state/local level, the Single Audit Act of 1984 and it predecessor OMB Circular A-102 directed attention to internal controls. Audits conducted under the Single Audit Act had to include a separate opinion about the internal controls of the organizations receiving federal funds. Discourse tended to explain the role of IGs, discuss the management of the IG function, and to review the strengths and weaknesses of the office.

Performance Audits. Performance auditing goes by many names. Some of its names are auditing for efficiency, value-for-money auditing, auditing for results, operational auditing, and performances auditing. The central questions are whether or not an activity is operating efficiently and effectively. In the early 1980s, the discourse begins with advocacy, but soon the hard challenges surfaced, both accounting and political challenges. In financial auditing, accounting standards define a model about the way financial statement should be prepared. The auditor may then evaluate actual statements relative to the defined model. The absence of a commonly defined comparative model is a central challenge in performance auditing. Some means of comparison is essential, and data are essential for comparison. Interest in performance auditing increased as federal programs were shifted to the states and as state/local governments begin to contract out services. The organizations providing the resources needed more than assurance that monies were not being squandered, it needed assurance that the desired service was being delivered efficiently and effectively. The suppliers of resources asked, is it possible to manage activities in a ways that would improve service or cost less or both?

The discourse explained the concept of a performance audit, described the benefits of performance auditing, provided "how to" guidance, and introduced various methods such as data envelope analysis (DEA). One challenge was that measures of performance were essential. In 1984, GASB organized the service efforts and accomplishment (SEA) Experimentation Project Team to investigate and report about the different means used to measure performance at the state/local level. Several years later a series of SEA reports pertaining to different service areas was issued to describe prevailing practices with respect to the use and construction of performance indicators, such as measures of inputs, of outputs and of outcomes. At the federal level, Congress adopted the Government Performance and Results Act of 1993 (GPRA) to institute a framework for performance measurement and reporting.

Following the discourse of advocacy, guidance for implementation was discussed. Soon thereafter, the discourse shifted to the challenges of performance auditing. The skills of financial auditors were essential but not sufficient, cost accounting systems were woefully deficient, cooperation was difficult to secure when loss of resources loomed. The AGA asked, why in cases of scandal were the early warnings in performance audit findings ignored? Despite the challenges, the slow steady work of finding guidance and of addressing problems continued at the state/local and federal levels. By early 2000, the discourse was portraying performance auditing, not as an instrument of dramatic change, but as tool with potential utility.

Financial Management

Among financial managers the dominant discourse is about ways to improve financial management. Rather than being debated or discussed, the availability of accounting data and the conduct of audits are assumed. Thus, this discourse is on the edges of the focal topic of accounting and auditing. The most common connection is that accounting data is often used in seeking improvements, and the most common path to improvement is defined as cost/expenditure control. Various procedures, controls, comparisons, means of analysis, and systems for cost accounting are discussed. Overall, the discourse is one of advocacy for and description of managerial accounting in government. In another area, this discourse is directed to ways to allocate resources, and in particular to ways to cut spending for various programs.

In addition to cost control, one area of discourse pertained in general to an advocacy for improving financial management. Common topics were improving productivity, finding fraud, strengthening controllership, altering management structure, etc. In contrast to the generality of this discourse, another area of discourse pertained to description of specific mean of financial management in specific departments, agencies, or state/local governments. Popular topics included cash management, procurement, investing, communications, etc.

SCHOLARLY DISCOURSE—ISSUES AND METHODOLOGIES

Scholarly discourse takes place through the published writings of scholars in refereed journals. For this article, the abstracts of 212 articles were reviewed from three sources: (1) RIGNA, (2) PB&F, and (3) a selection of other scholarly journals. RIGNA is recognized as primarily an academic journal. Unfortunately, its publication as an annual has not

TABLE 9
Orientation of Scholarly Articles

Orientation	Total	RIGNA	PB&F	Other Scholarly Journals
Microorganization to organization	167	57	68	42
Macroorientation to market	42	33	2	7
Not classified	3	2	1	
Total	212	92	71	49

been steady from year to year. PB&F has both a scholarly and practitioner audience. It is classified here as a scholarly journal because most of the articles it has published about governmental accounting and auditing were written by academics in a scholarly manner. To expand the scholarly perspective, 49 other abstracts were identified and secured from other scholarly accounting or auditing journals. These other scholarly journals, followed by number of abstracts in parenthesis, include the following: *Abacus* (1), *The Accounting Historians Journal* (3), *Accounting Horizons* (7), *Accounting Organizations and Society* (3), *The Accounting Review* (2), *Accounting, Auditing & Accountability* (3), *Auditing* (1), *Critical Perspectives on Accounting* (14), *Financial Accountability, & Management* (3), *Journal of Accounting and Public Policy* (8), *Journal of Accounting, Auditing & Finance* (2), *Journal of Accounting Research* (1), and *Research in Accounting Regulation* (1). Many of these articles were identified from indexing in the *Accounting & Tax Index* (formerly the *Accountants' Index*). Additional searching, beyond articles indexed, was limited to accounting journals. This collection of abstracts by no means represents the entire scholarly discourse about governmental accounting over the past 25 years, but it seems sufficient to provide a representative view of major themes in the scholarly discourse. Abstracts of scholarly articles were classified in five ways. See Tables 9–13.

First, abstracts were classified as having a microorientation or a macroorientation. See Table 9. Micro was interpreted as being oriented to the study of one of more organizations. In contrast, macro was interpreted as being oriented to the study of a market in

TABLE 10
Focus of Scholarly Articles

Focus	Total	RIGNA	PB&F	Other Scholarly Journals
State/local	116	56	35	25
General	53	24	11	18
Federal	31	4	24	3
International	12	8	1	3
Total	212	92	71	49

TABLE 11
Nature of Research

Nature	Total	RIGNA	PB&F	Other Scholarly Jounals
Nonempirical	106	38	53	15
Empirical, quantitative	60	37	14	9
Empirical, qualitative	46	17	4	25
Total	212	92	71	49

which organizations participate. This review of abstracts showed two markets were of primary interest to academics: the market for municipal bonds and the market for audit services.

Second, abstracts were classified as having a state/local, general, federal, or international focus. See Table 10. Perhaps reflecting the vast number of entities to which state/local accounting standards apply, over one-half the scholarly abstracts pertained to state/local activities. Abstracts classified as having a general focus either were not written with reference to a specific level of government or pertained to both state/local governments and to the federal government. For example, articles about the Single Audit Act were classified as having a general focus because the act is a federal statute that defines the conduct of state/local audits. The federal classifications encompassed the accounting of the national government of the United States and a few other nations. Because the topic was beyond the scope of this review, abstracts about international accounting were not actively sought. Nevertheless, given the ways abstracts were identified and collected, some international abstracts surfaced. International may be a misnomer in that most of these abstracts describe papers that are about models and procedures for accounting in a given country. Thus, it may have been more apt to describe many of these abstracts as being about country-specific accounting.

Third, abstracts were classified based on the nature of research: nonempirical, empirical qualitative, and empirical quantitative. See Table 11. Nonempirical was used to describe papers that presented informed perspectives, discussions of issues, or arguments built on reason. Empirical was used when the abstract made reference to the use of evidence. The evidence was sometimes of a qualitative nature and tended not to be examined with quantitative analysis. And at other times, the evidence was quantitative and tended to be examined with statistical analysis. Surprisingly one-half the total number of scholarly abstracts were of a nonempirical nature. This result is somewhat distorted by the abstracts of articles published in PB&F. Perhaps because this journal is committed to serving both an applied and an academic audience, it tends to publish three sorts of nonempirical papers: (1) papers that present the informed perspectives of experienced officials, (2) papers that explain and discuss key points with reference to an issue, and (3) papers that build arguments of criticism or advocacy.

TABLE 12
Approaches to Research

Approach	Total	RIGNA	PB&F	Other Scholarly Journals
Discussion, argument, advocacy	68	26	31	11
Perspective	29	8	20	1
Market analysis, municipal bonds	16	11	1	4
Case study	12	2	4	6
Analysis of documents—financial statements or audit opinions	11	5	4	2
Application of organizational and/or institutional theory with example	11			11
Literature review, bibliography	11	8	1	2
Survey, operating practices	10	4	4	2
Survey, perceptions, opinions, preferences, and perspective	8	4	3	1
Content analysis	7	5	1	1
Data envelopment analysis	5	5		
Experiment	5	5		
History	5			5
Theory proposed	5	5		
Market analysis, auditing	4	2		2
Analysis, research model	2	2		
Analysis, operations	2		2	
Analysis, financial performance	1			1
Total	212	92	71	49

When abstracts from PB&F are excluded, classification of the remaining abstracts is 37 percent nonempirical, 33 percent quantitative, and 30 percent qualitative. Thus, the literature is open to conceptually based, nonempirical discussion. And although classification is not precise and in some instances may have been modified from reading an entire paper rather than an abstract, it is apparent that the scholarly discourse is about equally open to quantitative and qualitative works. And the scholarly discourse has not shifted in major ways. Rather, the division has been roughly steady over time.

Fourth, abstracts were classified based on approach with approach being interpreted as the sort of methodology used to guide the work. See Table 12. Almost one-half of the papers were structured as discussions, explanations, arguments, and informed perspective. Informed perspective is interpreted as a special class of discussion by a writer whose position, such as being top official with a government or standard setting board, provides a special perspective. Other methods that are common to the discourse are analysis of municipal bond markets, case studies, analysis of documents, illustrations of theory with

TABLE 13
Topics of Research

Topic	Total	RIGNA	PB&F	Other Scholarly Journals
Reporting	35	11	11	13
Auditing	17		11	6
Standard setting	14	3	6	5
Bond returns, prices, and regulations	13	9	2	2
Model for accounting	13		11	2
Performance measures, performance auditing	10	3	5	2
Various types of research	10	10		
CFO Act	9		9	
Fraud/internal control	9	2	5	2
Research method, variables, etc.	8	7		1
Financial management	6		6	
Profession	6	1	1	4
Efficiency	5	5		
Accounting, rhetoric	4			4
Audit fees	4	4		
Accounting choice	3	2		
Cost/managerial accounting	5		1	4
Accounting innovation	3	3		1
Credit risk, insurance	3		3	
Demand for audits, auditors	3	3		
Pension reporting	3	3		
Privatization	3	2		1
Audit quality	2	2		
Entity	2	2		
Interperiod equity	2	2		
National accounting, reporting	2	2		
Other topics*	18	16		2
Total	212	92	71	49

*Eighteen other topics with one article in each category: Analyst decision, Asset acquisition, Audit agencies, Audit research, Audit standards, Costs and performance control, Culture, Decision Usefulness of data, Financial condition, Fiscal stress, Assets, Governance, Lobbying, Public choice, Ratio management, Resource allocation to systems, Revenue recognition, Standards, and Theory.
CFO, Chief Financial Officers.

example, literature reviews, and surveys. The applications of theory tend to be grounded in sociology and to illustrate theories of organizational and/or institutional change with reference to the environment of accounting or the rhetoric of accounting. This line of research is especially popular in *Critical Perspectives on Accounting,* and it represents a valuable contribution to the discourse as a sort of sociology of accounting.

TABLE 14
Theoretical Streams

Approach	Total	RIGNA	PB&F	Other Scholarly Journals
Not classified	129	32	70	27
Organizational choice/institutional theory	25	8		17
Capital markets	16	11	1	4
Public choice	11	11		
Behavioral, behavior of individual	10	10		
Management science, DEA	8	8		
Contingency theory	5	4		1
Agency theory	4	4		
Other—contracting, harmonization, positive theory, public management	4	4		
Total	212	92	71	49

DEA, data envelopment analysis.

To a lesser extent, some of the other methods that sometimes are utilized in the discourse include content analyses, data envelopment analyses (DEA), experiments, histories of events, proposals of theory, and analyses of some aspect of the market for auditing services. As would be expected, the approaches found in the scholarly discourse are richer and are more varied than the approaches in the applied discourse. It should be noted that although valuable, comparative studies and longitudinal studies are rare. With the exception of bond market studies, archival data are seldom used. Also, collaborative projects that extend beyond two or three coauthors are rare. One notable exception is the collaboration that went into the SEA Experimentation Project, sponsored by the GASB that produced eight separate reports about the sort of performance measures used in different service areas by state/local governments as well as other performance measurement research sponsored by the GASB.

Fifth, abstracts were classified by topic. Whereas applied research tends to be about accounting models, standard setting for accounting, and matters proposed or adopted as standards, the scholarly discourse is much more varied topically than the applied discourse. Consistently across sources the most frequently addressed topics pertain to some aspect of reporting. Other common topics related to auditing, standard setting, municipal bond markets, the model for accounting, types of research, the CFO Act, fraud and/or internal controls, and examination of research methods. Although the scholar discourse spreads across many topics, with the occasional exception, it seems to be largely removed from regulatory debates about accounting standards. Also, thoughtful examination from a historical context of key happenings and their consequences seems to be neglected. Examples of such key happening would include the financial crisis that beset New York City, the adoption of the CFO Act, the establishment of the FASAB, the

TABLE 15
Discussion of Literature and of Research Questions

Year	Citation
1980	Elmer B. Staats, "Why Isn't Policy Research Used More by Decisionmakers?" *GAO Review* Winter 15 (1980): 21–28.
1985	Florence C. Sharp and Robert W. Ingram, "Measuring the Periodic Performance of Government: Policy and Research Issues," *Research in Governmental and Nonprofit Accounting* 1 (1985): 149–180.
1986	Leonard Eugene Berry and Wanda A. Wallace, "Governmental Auditing Research: An Analytic Framework, Assessment of Past Work, and Future Directions," *Research in Governmental and Nonprofit Accounting* 2 (1986): 89–118.
1987	Rajiv Banker and James M. Patton, "Analytical Agency Theory and Municipal Accounting; An Introduction and An Application," *Research in Governmental and Nonprofit Accounting* 3 (1987): 29–50.
1987	James L. Chan and Marc A. Rubin, "The Role of Information in a Democracy and in Government Operations: The Public Choice Methodology," *Research in Governmental and Nonprofit Accounting* 3 (1987): 3–28.
1987	Susan Herhold, Robert W. Parry, and James M. Patton, "Behavioral Research in Municipal Accounting," *Research in Governmental and Nonprofit Accounting* 3 (1987): 71–110.
1987	Robert W. Ingram, and Earl R. Wilson, "Governmental Capital Markets Research in Accounting: A Review," *Research in Governmental and Nonprofit Accounting* 3 (1987): 111–132.
1987	Wanda A. Wallace, "Agency Theory and Governmental and Nonprofit Sector Research," *Research in Governmental and Nonprofit Accounting* 3 (1987): 51–70.
1988	Irvine Lapsley, "Research in Public Sector Accounting: An Appraisal," *Accounting, Auditing & Accountability* 1, no. 1 (1988): 21–33.
1992	Nicholas G. Apostolou, Richard C. Brooks, and W. Bartley Hildreth, "Research and Trends in Governmental Accounting and Reporting," *International Journal of Public Administration* 15 (1992): 1121–1149.
1992	Rajiv D. Banker, William D. Cooper, and Gordon P. Potter, "A Perspective on Research in Governmental Accounting," *The Accounting Review* 67, no. 3 (1992): 496–510.
1992	Sharon L. Green, "Behavioral Research in Governmental and Nonprofit Accounting: An Assessment of the Past and Suggestions for the Future," *Research in Governmental and Nonprofit Accounting* 7 (1992): 53–78.
1996	James L. Chan, Rowan H. Jones, and Klaus G. Luder, "Modeling Governmental Accounting Innovations: An Assessment and Future Research Directions," *Research in Governmental and Nonprofit Accounting* 9 (1996): 1–20.
2000	Wanda A. Wallace, "GASB Statement No. 34: Research Opportunities," *Financial Accountability & Management* 16, no. 3 (2000): 179–199.
2004	Jacqueline L. Reck, Earl R. Wilson, David Gotlob, and Carol M. Lawrence, "Governmental Capital Markets Research in Accounting: A Review, Extension, and Directions for Future Research," *Research in Governmental and Nonprofit Accounting* 11 (2004): 1–34.

issuance of audited government-wide financial statement by the U.S. Government, and the struggle to reach a dual model of reporting for state/local reporting. Topically, the most impressive aspect of the scholarly discourse is the variety of topics addressed (see Table 13).

Finally, abstracts were classified as drawing on various theoretical streams of research. Many of the works did not draw on any stream of theoretical research. The nonclassified works often represented discussion and informed perspective. The most popular theoretical basis for grounding research included theories about organizational/institutional choice to explain various accounting choices, theories of capital markets to posit associations between behaviors of the municipal bond market with various accounting policies, the use of pubic choice theory to explain accounting choices, and behavioral theories to explain the actions of accountants and auditors. As one would expect those article tied to a theoretical stream tend to be oriented to fostering an understanding by reaching for an explanation (see Table 14).

RESEARCH OPPORTUNITIES

During the past 25 years a number of useful articles were published that may inform future research. Although the list is not complete, some of these articles are listed in Table 15 for the readers' reference. This is not intended as a comprehensive list, but it is a list that is representative of calls for research in the discourse over the past 25 years.

SUMMARY

This review shows that over the past 25 years governmental accounting and auditing have been areas of significant change. For those who wish to engage in the discourse there are a number of publication outlets that offer the opportunity for the exchange of ideas. From the applied perspective and the scholarly perspective, there is record of discourse that addresses a variety of topics and employs an array of methods. Sustaining this discourse will require the commitment of publishers, editors, reviewers, and authors. The discourses of accounting and of auditing merits contributions because accounting and auditing are essential aspects of sound financial management. And, the public is well served by the sound financial management of public monies. Effective accounting fosters accountability, and accountability for the public purse is essential for a government accountable to its people.

NOTE

The assistance of Mr. Brian D. Montalbano, Graduate Assistant, in the Capital College of The Pennsylvania State University, in preparing this article is freely and gratefully acknowledged.